When Christians Were Jews
(That Is, Now)

COWLEY PUBLICATIONS is a ministry of the brothers of the Society of Saint John the Evangelist, a monastic order in the Episcopal Church. Our mission is to provide books and resources for those seeking spiritual and theological formation. COWLEY PUBLICATIONS is committed to developing a new generation of writers and teachers who will encourage people to think and pray in new ways about spirituality, reconciliation, and the future.

When Christians Were Jews (That Is, Now)

Recovering the Lost Jewishness of Christianity with the Gospel of Mark

WAYNE-DANIEL BERARD

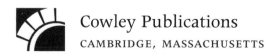

Cowley Publications
CAMBRIDGE, MASSACHUSETTS

Library of Congress Cataloging-in-Publication Data

Berard, Wayne-Daniel.
    When Christians were Jews (that is, now) : recovering the lost Jewishness of Christianity with the gospel of Mark / Wayne-Daniel Berard.
        p.   cm.
    Includes bibliographical references.
    ISBN-13: 978-1-56101-280-0   ISBN-10: 1-56101-280-7 (pbk. : alk. paper)
        1. Bible. N.T. Mark—Criticism, interpretation, etc. 2. Jesus Christ—Jewish interpretations. I. Title.
    BS2585.6.J44B47   2006
    226.3'06—dc22

                                                                    2006019338

Page 248 constitutes a continuation of this copyright page.

Cover design: Brad Norr Design
Cover art: Odilon Redon (1840–1916). The Sacred Heart. 1910. Pastel.
Photo: C. Jean. Fonds Orsay.
Photo credit: Réunion des Musées Nationaux / Art Resource, NY
Interior design: Wendy Holdman

This book was printed in the United States of America on acid-free paper.

Cowley Publications
4 Brattle Street
Cambridge, Massachusetts 02138
800-225-1534 • www.cowley.org

To Rabbi Alan Ullman,
teacher of Torah,
and to the Mansfield Inter-Faith Bible Study,
my co-authors

For Christine,
the presence of the Shekinah
in my life

"You worship what you do not know."

John 4:22

. . . light blue still slumbers
In the memory of dark blue night.

Yehuda Amichai[1]

Contents

Acknowledgments

THE DEEPEST GRATITUDE OF MY HEART IS EXTENDED TO ALL OF those who helped make this work a reality:

To Rabbi Alan Ullman, whose teaching is in each page of this book and whose friendship is in each page of my life.

To the members of the Inter-Faith Bible Study of Mansfield, Massachusetts: Cindy Blanchard, Christine Cassidy, Linda D'Agostino, Anne and Bill Daunt, Tim Fox, Craig Hoyle, Chris Kiley, Linda Kiley (with special thanks for her invaluable notes), Amy Ruda, Pauline Sibilia, and Jim Woods. Our two-year exploration together of Mark's Gospel essentially became this volume.

To the members of the Rank and Appointments Committee of Nichols College, Dudley, Massachusetts, particularly its Chair, Professor Louise Nordstrom, and Academic Dean Alan Reinhardt, for their gracious support of sabbatical leave to accomplish this work; likewise to President Debra Murphy, Professor Thomas Lelon, my Department Chair, Professor Jeffrey Halprin, and Andrea Becker for their encouragement and support.

To my students at Nichols, who in their responses and questions to this material have nurtured its growth and mine in ways unimagined.

To Brother John Doyle, CFX, for his enduring and invaluable friendship, and the opportunity to present many of the ideas contained here as a guest lecturer in his classes at Assumption College.

To Bill Milhomme for countless discussions on these topics over coffee or on walks, and for our brotherhood.

To the monks of Weston Priory, for providing a spiritual

home for a wandering Jesus Jew, and for their continuing witness to that Jesus' marginless God.

To Hanna Sherman, Daniel Sheff, Melissa Wenig, and Yoel
Gordon, who teach by their caring example the fullness,
depth, joy, and openness of Jewish life.

To Father Chris Renz, op for creating opportunities. To Roy
Carlisle for his invaluable encouragement, to Rob Hopcke for
his advocacy, friendship, and editing skills, and to Michael
Wilt and the Society of St. John the Evangelist for so fully
embracing the manuscript and its author.

To Judy Cassidy for her loving support, and for listening
to chapter upon chapter, read aloud for review.

To each of my children, the embodiment of God's infinite love, and to all the Berards, Abbeys, Abramowitzes, and
Abramses, for their unqualified support.

And most of all to my wife, the lovely Christine, who believes in me, loves me, and frees me always to be myself—in
my writing and in all things. *Matzati otah she'ahav nafshi.*

Return of the Repressed

I and Jerusalem are like a blind man and a cripple.
She sees for me
out to the Dead Sea, to the End of Days.
And I hoist her on my shoulders
and walk blind in my darkness underneath.

Yehuda Amichai[2]

THE GREAT CANADIAN NOVELIST AND ESSAYIST ROBERTSON
Davies once spoke of a certain type of criticism as being, in
reality, "an escape from direct experience of a work of art."[3]
The same may be said of some works that delve into matters
of spirituality or religion; whether they aspire to a scholarly
or popular audience (or to both), such works seem to separate
knowledge of the *things* of God from the seeking of an *experience* of that God. In other words, they treat their subject as an
end rather than a means. Such is not the intended case with
this book.

In essence, this is a book about lost identity. From ancient
fables of missing princes raised by kind peasants, through
Shakespeare's "twin switch" comedies, to the *Star Wars* films,
the subject of identities lost and found has proven irresistible,
if not archetypal. Yet, I would venture to say that the overwhelming majority of those who today identify themselves
as Christians have no idea that their own lives are engaged
in just such a fabled adventure, in exactly this kind of archetypal situation. And like all such tales, this one, too, is a family story.

The first acts of this drama could be set in the first century

CE, around the year 90. The city of Jerusalem has been destroyed twenty years earlier, and with it the great Temple, so central to Jewish identity, spirituality, and worship. The entire future of the Jewish people seems in doubt. In or around 90, a meeting of remaining Jewish rabbinical leaders is held in the town of Yavneh (Jamnia) on the coastal plain west of the ruined city. Among a multitude of pronouncements aimed at preserving and galvanizing the Jewish people is one declaring any Jews who believe that Jesus of Nazareth is the Messiah to be *minim*, "heretics." "May the *minim* perish!" Yavneh declares.[4]

At about the same time, 90 CE, the Gospel of John is coming into existence. It, too, is part of this family story; in fact, like all the gospels, it is a largely a story *about* that story. Those who believe that Yeshua—Jesus—is the Messiah are themselves mostly Jews. Still, John's Gospel very clearly portrays *oi Ioudaioi*—"the Jews" themselves—as enemies of Jesus, and worse: "You are of your father, the devil; your will is to do your father's desire. He was a murderer from the beginning" (John 8:44).

It is no good trying to determine which part of this divided family acted first; finger-pointing is always a circular activity in family breakdown. The bitterness of terms like "heretic" and "murderer," "devil," and "perish" speaks for itself. By the time such words are spoken aloud, a split is no longer about reasons; it is about dehumanization and hatred. The split becomes about itself.

Such a story should not surprise any of us who have been members of a family: bitterness arises over an issue, a family struggle ensues. Each side declares the other to no longer belong, or one group may "remove" itself from the family altogether, disowning it and villainizing its remaining members. It is the common story of fratricide, of civil war.

In later acts of this drama, the enmity between the two camps of the broken family grows so severe that the very fact that they are or ever have been family at all is consciously obliterated on both sides. One camp grows in number and power to the point that it completely dominates the other, even to the extent of attempting genocide against its members.

Finally, imagine a set of scenes in which the lost identity is finally, definitively revealed. As with the old stand-bys of stage and screen, the indisputable family birthmark or a reunion of separated twins, no doubt remains. Like it or not, the two groups of antagonists are family to each other. Specifically, Christians are members of the Jewish family. Although many of its members would rather learn that their last name is Vader, Christianity is indisputably a Jewish faith.

Parts of this plot-line may seem familiar; over the last several decades, Christian interest in "the Jewish Jesus" and in the "Jewish roots" of Christianity has grown exponentially. Still, that final act, particularly the scene in which the more powerful, privileged camp embraces its membership in its lost, despised family, has yet to be enacted.

Although there is growing acceptance in Christianity of its "Jewish roots," there has been little practical movement among Christians to re-understand themselves in Jewish terms, in their spirituality, in personal and communal reading and application of the scriptures, in homilies, in self-image. A nod is occasionally given to the roots, but few among the followers of Yeshua see the stem, leaves, and flower of their spiritual lives as in any way Jewish. I have a dear friend, a messianic Jew, who is fond of saying that "all Christians are messianic Jews with memory loss . . . they've forgotten they're Jewish."

This book is informed by the premise that, although the renewed interest in Jesus as a Jew and of Christianity's "foundation" in Judaism has been essential as a first step, it is only that, a first step. These are the beginnings of an essential process that must not be allowed to stall on the thin fuel of mere intellectual assent.

Jesus of Nazareth was a Jew with a Jewish mindset and Jewish worldview. Most, if not all, of his early followers were Jews, as were all the writers of Christian scripture save one, and tradition portrays him as a Jewish proselyte. St. Paul, in a much-vaunted phrase, calls on the followers of Jesus to put on the mind of Christ (1 Cor. 2:16). But this mind is a Jewish mind. Does it not follow that the more we "put it on," the more Jewish our own mind, our own heart should become?

And beyond this, we have the reality of Christian anti-Semitism still very much with us. Unlike a Shakespeare comedy, our realization of shared family will not, of itself, bring about a happy ending to the family split. James Carroll writes of recognizing "the Jewishness of Jesus, but not only his."[5] Rosemary Radford Ruether maintains that "the Christian anti-Jewish myth can never be held in check, much less overcome, until Christianity submits itself to that therapy of Jewish consciousness that allows the 'return of the repressed.' This means establishing a new education for a new consciousness."[6] But before one can submit to therapy, one needs to know viscerally, in one's gut, not just in the head, that one has a serious problem.

And Christianity's problem is in some ways one that therapists see often: We do not truly know who we are. Our image of ourselves has proven largely inaccurate. We are like adopted children who suddenly learn that our birth parents belonged to a despised race. What, if anything, does this mean for us? Such a child could push away his or her newfound knowledge, or intellectualize it as a fact, but one of little daily significance. This has largely been the case with the "Jewish Jesus" movement to date. Alternatively that child could refrain from answering the question before it's truly finished being asked. He or she could, with open mind and heart, explore, in this case, the Jewishness not only of Jesus but of themselves, and thus respond to a universal human need to know oneself, and more, to love oneself as one truly is.

By way of example of both need and response: I am often asked to speak to groups of Christians—teens in Sunday school, members of adult ed classes, retreatants—on the subject of the Jewish Jesus and the Jewishness of Christianity. I almost always begin in the same way, by asking those present to give a word that for them describes Jesus of Nazareth. The results are sincere, sometimes moving, and usually predictable; terms such as "Lord," "Messiah," "God," and "Son of God," mix with words like "Friend," "Love," "Companion," "Life." After thanking and commending the group, I then usually say, "There is one word that was conspicuous in its absence, although it wasn't one that I truly expected to hear. To you, Jesus is Lord and Love and Messiah, and that is certainly fine. The word that I didn't hear, however, was '*Jew.*'"

At that point the room falls into stunned silence.

It took some time for me to understand the nature of this silence. A major revelation occurred as I was teaching a college class entitled *Abraham's Issue: Religion in Today's Middle East.* I noticed that each time I would utter the word "Jew," many of my students would wince (none of them were Jewish). When finally I asked about this, my students told me that in their experience "Jew" was a dirty word, an insult; "Jewish people" was the more acceptable form. I decided to take that bull (pun intentional) by the horns and asked my students to list, with absolute candor, the first words that came into their heads when they heard the word "Jew."

The results were, I suppose, sadly predictable; the blackboard filled with words like "cheap," "money-grubbing," "clannish," "Christ-killer," "pushy," and "demanding." Not a single positive term was offered. Not one.

So for me to describe Jesus as a Jew struck, at a gut level, even the most intelligent in those Christian audiences as a slap. Still, I absolutely refused to shift to the phrase "Jewish people,"—as if we must state that Jews are human beings! Rather, with each group in that moment of pause, I would say, "Yes, Jesus was a Jew. Mary was a Jew, so was Joseph; his disciples and most of the early Christians were Jews. Jews . . . just like me." At that point, I would take my *kepah* from my pocket, place it on my head, and pray aloud, "*Baruch ata, Adonai, Elo-henu, Melech haOlam.* Blessed are you, Lord God, Master of the universe."

To be precise, I am half-Jewish, my birth-father having been Jewish and my birth-mother Portuguese.[7] I was an adopted child; my adoptive parents are both Roman Catholics, and I was raised as such (I even went on to spend five years in Franciscan seminary). The adoption had been of the type called "indirect"; no family on either side of the adoption knew anything about the other.

Much later, in adulthood, when I'd searched out my background and learned of all this, I was not sure what, if anything, it meant. I was half-Jewish, but had not been raised in Judaism. Did any of it mean anything?

It was at that time that I met Rabbi Alan Ullman, who had come to the college in which I teach to speak on the prophet Elijah. Alan is a dynamic young teacher who uses the Socratic method, overcoming the passivity even of a group of business students there only to earn the "cultural credits" required for graduation. After the session, I approached him with my story; he invited me to join others studying Torah with him. That invitation would change everything in my life.

At this writing, I am in my thirteenth year of study with Alan. His subject is not just "Torah as a spiritual path," but our studies have extended throughout the Jewish and Christian scriptures. Alan's knowledge of New Testament is vast and deep. In the course of that study, something along the same order began to happen in my spiritual life; it, too, began to broaden and to deepen in never-imagined ways.

The great spiritual writer Evelyn Underhill describes an experience of spiritual awakening as being akin to the situation of a hearing-impaired person at a classical music concert who suddenly regains his or her hearing. Previously the person may have heard some of the instruments, some of the strains of music: now the entire range of the orchestra, the full power of its music, pours in upon him or her.[8]

This was what it was like for me, as a lifelong Christian, to begin to experience the Torah, the other books of the Jewish scripture, and the gospels in Jewish terms. I had been a spiritually oriented person from childhood, long before I had ever heard of the phrase, even to the point of entering seminary at fourteen. Now it seemed that I had lived my life in a breathtaking castle, or perhaps a fortress, carved into the side of a mountain. That mountain gave shape and dimension to the edifice, which was one with its living rock. But I had barely even known the name of the mountain, let alone anything about its properties, its life. That mountain was Judaism, and the Christianity in which I had been raised was of the same stock; the mountain informed every part of its being, determined its very substance. I felt like exclaiming, as did Jacob, "God—the God of Israel—was in this place, and I, I did not know!" (Gen. 28:16).

Something further emerged for me in these studies as well. I realized that it was not only because of my being half-Jewish that these scriptures and the whole of Jewish life sang to me so, although that was clearly true. It was also because I was a Christian; it was my Christian upbringing, education, spirituality that rose and responded to Judaism as a muster to the soul. And I was not alone; any number of Alan's Christian students, from a variety of denominations, responded in the same way. It became crystal clear to each of us: all Christians were children who did not truly know their birth-parents, their substance, their being. Christianity had been indirectly adopted.

Soon I volunteered to lead a Torah study for Christians at my parish. Over its five-year existence, we have studied much of the Five Books, other parts of Tanakh (the Jewish Bible), Paul's Letter to the Romans, sections from the Gospels, and Mark in its entirety. The study has continued in my wife's and my home; its membership has included Protestants and Catholics, and, of course, one half-Jew! The one thing we all have in common is our growing understanding that we are all

Jews as well and that our following of the Jewish Jesus hinges on making this awareness a lived reality in our lives.

I worship in more than one context, Jewish and Christian. The reaction to a *kepah*, the small, knit yarmulke, in a Christian church can be interesting. Some, in an enthusiastic display of ecumenism, go out of their way to welcome their "guest." Others aren't quite so sure. On one occasion, on my way out of the pew toward the communion line, an usher whispered to me, "Do you know Jesus?" I responded, "Know him? I'm a blood relative." But that was just my bit of fun. That usher was every bit as Jewish as I am, without knowing it.

As I close my talks to church groups, endeavoring to help them see their own Jewishness, I often end with this statement: "You see, the question really isn't 'Why do I wear my yarmulke in church?' but rather, 'Why aren't you wearing yours?'"

When Christians Were Jews
(That Is, Now)

CHAPTER I

The Case to Date

The patches of no-man's land were like placid bays.
Longing floated overhead in the sky
like ships whose anchors stuck deep in us, and sweetly
ached.

Yehuda Amichai[9]

IF THE TIME HAS INDEED COME TO OFFER A SPIRITUALITY OF
the Jewishness of Christianity, it is important to acknowledge
its starting points, the Jewish Jesus movement as it exists today
for Christians.

It is equally important to note that this work has been carried out almost solely by academic scholars, chiefly historians
on the quest for the "historical Jesus." The job of such thinkers is not to provide a spirituality based on their findings, but
rather to search for the facts of the historical Jesus and to ex-
trapolate theories based on those facts. It is then up to others
to take their invaluable work and explore the implications it
may hold for the spiritual life.

Chief among these scholars is an ongoing group called the
Jesus Seminar, founded by Robert Funk, and including such
notable members as John Dominic Crossan and Marcus Borg.
The makeup of the Jesus Seminar is overwhelmingly Christian
with very few Jewish members.

The original goal of the Jesus Seminar was to determine as
best its members could the historical authenticity of Jesus'
sayings in the four canonical gospels as well as in the apocry-
phal Gospel of Thomas. Members of the group would write and
share papers making the case for or against the authenticity of

a particular saying; in the end the members would vote on their findings. The results were color-coded: red, pink, gray, and black. Sayings that received the majority of votes as most authentic were designated "black"; the least, "red."

The resulting picture of Jesus is one that may be described as minimalist. It would seem that there is very little one can say definitively about the historical Jesus—hardly a surprise for a figure from two thousand years ago. The members of the Seminar then went on to apply its method to propositions and beliefs concerning the life and work of Jesus. These ranged from "Jesus was born in Bethlehem" to "Mary conceived Jesus without sexual intercourse from a man." The Seminar also considered several versions of the same idea, e.g., "Mary conceived of Joseph" or "Mary conceived of some unknown man by rape or seduction," among other possibilities. In this phase of its work, the Seminar reversed it color code; red came to indicate "virtually certain" while black meant "improbable."[10] The results were controversial, to say the least; many, including some Seminar members themselves, found them offensive (the virgin birth, for example, was coded black).

Obviously, criticism of the work of the Jesus Seminar has been extremely strong. Putting aside attacks based primarily on outrage and defensiveness, much concern has been expressed regarding the possible ideological slant of the group. Charges that the group's work has not been objective but begins with a preconceived leftist ideology have been hard to refute, particularly when Robert Funk maintains that the goal of the Seminar is "to set Jesus free from the scriptural and creedal prison in which we have entombed him."[11]

More telling for our purposes, however, is the view, voiced by critics such as Craig Blomberg of the Denver Seminary that, "the Seminar's Jesus simply is not sufficiently Jewish to be historically credible."[12] And Blomberg is a Baptist! As already stated, there have been few Jewish members of the Jesus Seminar; the risk of a more Jewish viewpoint being consistently outvoted must be seen as a very real one.

Here we find illustrated one of the fundamental problems with the Jewish Jesus Movement to date. Of course, there is no doubt in anyone's mind that Jesus was a Jew, although how "marginal" a one remains a matter of debate. In seeking to understand this Jewish Jesus, however, and to interpret Gospels written for an audience then overwhelmingly Jewish, we must rely almost solely on scholars who are not Jews, but Christians, many of them clergy or ex-clergy. They may have a strong academic knowledge of the Jewish world of Jesus' day, but they are not students of the Torah or engaged in Jewish practice, and thus cannot enter into the heart and soul of Jewish life and spirituality in the same way a Jew can.

As scholars, of course, it is not their intent to offer a spirituality in the first place, but even if it were, their background and study would hardly ground them sufficiently in the Jewish experience to do so. Imagine the limitations of a white scholar, no matter how brilliant, writing on the black experience or of the strongest male feminist doing the same for women's issues? How seriously would anyone take the findings of a group called the Woman Seminar or the Black Seminar that contained almost no women or blacks?

A possible exception to this condition, a non-member of the Seminar and a scholar who represents a case unto himself, is Geza Vermes. His Jewish, though non-observant, family converted to Catholicism largely in an effort to afford their brilliant son educational opportunity simply unavailable to Jews in pre—World War II Hungary. Vermes went on to become a priest and scripture scholar, ultimately returning to the Judaism of his birth. His work, particularly the groundbreaking *Jesus the Jew* (1973) offers the insights of one who has thoroughly and wholeheartedly embraced and immersed himself in the Torah and in Jewish life, with the topical advantage of a Christian background. From that vantage point Vermes writes, "In many respects, the Hebrew Bible, the Apocrypha, the Pseudepigraphs, the Qumran writings and the enormous body of rabbinic literature, are better equipped to illumine the original significance of words and deeds recorded in the gospels."[13]

By extension I think it could be said that the spirituality of the gospels is much closer to that of modern Judaism, based upon and nourished by Torah, the rest of Tanakh and Talmud, than to modern Christianity. And yet, at heart, Vermes is an academic scholar; his concern is not a renewed Jewish spirituality for Christians.

Among Christian scholars, E. P. Sanders is widely considered to have the fullest understanding of the Jewish life of Jesus' day. Mark Allan Powell of Trinity Lutheran Seminary maintains that "few people alive today know as much about life, practice and religion of first-century Jews as E. P. Sanders."[14] Again, however, this is the academic knowledge of a Christian centering on scholarship; applying the life, practice, and religion of the Jewish Jesus to contemporary Christian life is not a matter that Sanders takes up.

There *are* Jewish scholars in the Jewish Jesus/Jewishness of Christianity field; notably these include David Daub, Chaim Cohn, and Alan Segal, among others. I think it is fair to say that much of the Jewish work on this subject has been in essence a defense of Judaism from the charges and attacks against it, charges that have characterized its relationship with Christianity. After all, only since 1965 has the Roman Catholic Church officially held that Jews are not responsible for the death of Christ. How thoroughly this declaration has filtered into the attitude of the rank and file toward Jews is a matter of debate. Each Good Friday, Catholic faithful still listen to the reading of St. John's Passion, with its accusatory references to "the Jews." A note does appear on the printed version in the pews, warning the congregation against the idea of corporate Jewish guilt; still, there has been no official Catholic move to use another Gospel's account of the passion on Good Friday.

For the more fundamentalist denominations that see each word of the Scripture as literally and unchangeably true, the blood of Christ must forever be upon the Jews and upon their children (Matt. 27:25).

When I speak to groups on the Jewishness of Jesus and of Christianity, I am often asked the question, "Why don't Jews simply accept Christ?" It is at best a naïve question and at worst incredibly arrogant. I often reply by asking the group for a show of hands: "In the wake of 9/11, how many here would be inclined to join Al Qaeda?" No hands go up. "How many feel that they might be more inclined to do so ten years from now? Thirty? Fifty?" Still no hands.

I then ask the group to imagine Al Qaeda stretched out across time, to visualize not one 9/11, but innumerable atrocities of that sort and worse perpetrated upon them by this group over the course of centuries. I further ask them to imagine that the attitude of Al Qaeda toward Americans becomes standard throughout the world, so much a part of the mindset of global culture that few blink an eye when a 9/11 happens, and punishment is almost never doled out to the perpetrators. How many Americans would ever join such an organization?

Little wonder that Jewish scholars have tended to shy away from anything concerning Jesus and Christianity. Much of the Jewish scholarship on the subject has understandably centered on countering Christian notions of Jewish culpability for Jesus' death. Chaim Cohn's book *The Trial and Death of Jesus*, Ellis Rivkin's *What Crucified Jesus?*, and Paul Winter's *On the Trial of Jesus* exemplify this type of effort. Other works, from Schalom Ben-Chorin's *Brother Jesus* to Alan Segal's *Rebecca's Children* have attempted to demonstrate the "family nature" of the split between Christians and Jews, and to emphasize the commonality of the two groups. However, Jewish scholars of Jesus can hardly be expected to offer a renewed Jewish spirituality for believing Christians.

Of all the modern scholars in this field, the one who comes closest to suggesting a spirituality based on his work is Marcus Borg. Borg, a Christian, is well known for his spiritual autobiography, *Meeting Jesus Again for the First Time*. A member of the Jesus Seminar, Borg has sought to "sketch a fairly full and historically defensible portrait of Jesus,"[15] for the purposes of discovering the sort of person Jesus was, a sort which Borg labels the "religious personality type." Borg, who has been heavily influenced by Buddhist thought and such writers as Carlos Casteneda, then compares Jesus to other spiritual figures and social leaders, both Jewish and Gentile. In his spiritual autobiography, Borg also describes a number of mystical experiences that drastically altered his views on Jesus and religion in general.

Borg's work has moved many to ask the same question that he has asked, "What type of person was Jesus?" and to ask it, not simply for the purpose of academic knowledge but as a possible catalyst to personal, spiritual awakening. Yet, in Borg's reliance on comparisons with other spiritual and social figures, Jesus' uniquely Jewish character can seem lessened or lost. Borg seems more interested in Jesus as an archetype than as an active, dynamic Jew. His is not so much the Jewish Jesus as Jesus the Type (Spirit Person, Healer, Sage, and Movement Initiator). Borg's work centers on finding the common denominator in Jesus and others of his "type" in world history, rather than asking the question, "What should Jesus' Jewishness mean for today's Christians?"

Taken as a whole, then, modern scholarship on the Jewishness of Jesus and of Christianity has performed an invaluable service. James Carroll writes that, "Having learned in parochial school that Jesus was racially not Jewish, I learned in graduate theological school that he was religiously not Jewish either."[16] The Jewish Jesus Movement has changed all that, one would hope, permanently.

Even those who find the work in the vein of the Jesus Seminar too radical should remember how firmly entrenched was the denial of the relevance, if not the very reality, of Jesus' Jewishness; it takes an outrageously strong force to clear such a block. Those who tend to "push the envelope" to the edges also open up a wider center for others.

The thinkers who have been described here and their col-
leagues have had the audacity to question a dearly held but
clearly inaccurate notion, that of an essentially non-Jewish
Jesus. Whether the Jesus they then espouse is primarily a
"Jewish Cynic peasant" (Crossan), an "eschatological prophet"
(Sanders), or a "Galilean Hassid" (Vermes), there can be little
doubt that Jesus cannot even begin to be understood apart
from his Jewishness. All who care about intellectual accuracy,
let alone the future of two of the world's great faiths, owe a
tremendous debt to these scholars.

Nevertheless, the role of such writers is entirely academic;
they do not attempt to propose a spirituality based on their
work, and, as acknowledged earlier, the body of their work
has suffered from an understandable sparseness of Jewish con-
tribution. As well informed as Christian scholars may be on the
subject, Judaism is still for them foreign territory, whereas for
those to whom the Gospels were first addressed, it was home.
That is a sizable barrier to overcome.

Still, the groundwork has been laid, and the once unthinkable topic is now a movement. That which was repressed may
have not yet returned, but the door to a new education—a
new, Jewish consciousness for Christians—is now open. Its
success could mean, in its own way, a type of Second Coming.

CHAPTER 2

The Burning Issue

The sun thought that Jerusalem was a sea
and set in her, a terrible mistake.
   Yehuda Amichai[17]

THE GOSPEL OF MARK IS WIDELY ACCEPTED TO BE THE FIRST
of the canonical gospels. Scholars are nearly unanimous in dating it at around 70 CE. This is also a pivotal year in Jewish history, the year of the destruction of Jerusalem by the Romans
and the burning of its Great Temple.

The first of two Jewish revolts against Roman rule began in
66 CE; most of our knowledge of it comes from a Latinized Jew
of the day named Josephus who wrote a contemporaneous
history of it. Josephus did not approve of the rebellion, which
he saw as doomed from a military point of view. His opinion
proved to be correct. The war proved a disaster for the Jewish
people; according to Josephus, 600,000 Jewish lives were lost;
one Jew of every three living in Judea was killed. No count
is offered for the wounded, disabled, the scattered, and the
homeless. Jerusalem was leveled. But, in another sense, the
dearest blow of all to Jewish life was the loss of the Temple.
Every people of the ancient world had its temples and offered
sacrifices to its gods. It was basically impossible to imagine religious life without these two elements. Modern observers of
contemporary Jewish life should not be misled by the fact that
today some Jewish houses of worship are called "temples";
this term has become almost synonymous with "synagogue."
For the Jews of Jesus' day, this was not so.

There was only one Temple, the Great Temple in Jerusalem.

Only there could the ritual sacrifices and offerings be carried out and the Torah's commands to do so be fulfilled. The term "synagogue" itself is of Greek origin, and means "a place of meeting." In Hebrew, such a place was called *beit k'nesset*, house of assembly; in the later Yiddish, a *shule* or house of study, reflecting the fact that study of the Torah and the other books of the Jewish scripture was a primary purpose. Communal prayer certainly was held there, but never sacrifices; these were reserved for the great Temple in Jerusalem. Hence we see in the Gospels Jesus and his followers going to the capital for the celebration of the great feasts of the Jewish calendar. In 70 CE, all this disappeared.

Stephen Wyler in his book *Settings of Silver* describes the situation in this way:

> There was no religion without sacrifice. The Jews had lost their temple once before, centuries earlier, but at that time the Jews were content to wait until they could rebuild. This time, considering the power of the Roman Empire and its determination not to allow the Temple to be rebuilt, the Jews would have to either disappear or develop a religion that did not depend on sacrifice.[18]

To determine what sort of religion Judaism should become, one burning question had to be addressed: Why did God allow the razing of the Temple in the first place? Why had the Jewish people been "punished" in this way?

This was not the sort of spiritual universe in which a cause for the destruction of the Temple could have been sought in military or geopolitical terms. The very home of God on earth had been destroyed, and, as they had at the time of the Babylonian destruction of Jerusalem and their subsequent exile, the Jews of 70 CE saw this question strictly in terms of religious guilt and divine punishment or abandonment. If Judaism were to survive, if the Jewish people were to regain

God's favor and avoid further punishment, it was paramount for them to discover "where they had gone wrong" in the first place.

James Carroll has written that "to read the New Testament apart from the context of the Roman war against the Jews—as it almost always is—amounts to reading *The Diary of a Young Girl* without reference to the Holocaust."[19] Likewise Mark's Gospel. Depending on how close to 70 one dates it, this Gospel was being created either during the siege of Jerusalem, a time when it had become clear that nothing short of a miracle would save the Temple, or after the fall and burning of the entire city. In either event, the question "How did we get into this mess?" was a religious one, occupying central stage in the life of any Jew, including those who believed in Jesus.

For in 70 the overwhelming majority of those who believed in Jesus were Jews who saw themselves as such. At the time of the creation of Mark there was no such thing as "Christianity" as we conceive of it today. There were Jews who believed that Jesus was the Messiah (just as there were Jews who believed in the Messiah-hood of others, including John the Baptist). There was also a minority of Gentiles who believed in Jesus, but many of these, as we see from the Acts of the Apostles, had been drawn from the ranks of Jewish proselytes, people with a strong interest in Judaism and who might frequent the synagogue in a Gentile town, but had not taken the step of formal conversion. Hence, the world to which Mark's Gospel is addressed is one in which "Christians" were Jews or largely of Jewish consciousness.

This being the case, the desperate questions facing the Judaism of their day were theirs as well; Jews who believed in Jesus regularly worshiped in the Temple and followed the Mosaic practices of sacrifice. They did not see themselves as a separate people or religion for whom the destruction of the Temple had no meaning.

In fact, as witnessed by Mark, the "Jesus Jews" had an

answer they wished to propose to the question of why God had permitted this catastrophe to happen. It was over this very question and the competing answers which emerged between 70 and 90 CE that the family split in Judaism occurred.

First, it is important to recognize the major factions within the family at the time of the first Roman War. These were the Sadducees, the Pharisees, the Zealots, the Essenes, and the Jesus Jews.

The Sadducees and Pharisees were members of opposing movements made up of educated and pious Jews, some from the priestly class. The approach of the Sadducees focused on the centrality of the Temple and its rituals; for them, cooperation with the Romans was essential to preserving the Temple. The Pharisees, too, loved and revered the Temple, but emphasized the role of Torah in Jewish life, promoting its study and the rigorous observance of its precepts.

The Essenes, on the other hand, found the Temple of their day to be somewhat suspect, as it had been built by King Herod the Great, a puppet of Rome and a non-Jew, who had only converted upon being selected to rule Judea by the emperor. The Essenes, who have been compared to later Christian monks, believed that it was almost impossible to lead a ritually pure, Torah-centered life in the Judea of their day. They had withdrawn into communities in the desert or into their own enclaves in cities, where they practiced an ascetical and mystical form of Judaism and awaited a cataclysmic judgment of Jewish society by God.

The Essenes enjoyed a certain amount of admiration in the Judea of Jesus for the sacrifices they were willing to undergo to achieve a "spiritually pure" life. Thus they were given the same type of respect that orthodox Jews or strict monastics are sometimes accorded by the rank and file of their respective faiths. Essenes even merited their own entrance into the city of Jerusalem, the still-extant Essene's Gate, the use of which would help maintain their separate way of life. Because of his time in the desert and the nature of his message, many scholars maintain that John the Baptist was at one time an Essene, and as such greatly influenced his cousin, Jesus.

Far from being withdrawn, the Zealots were a revolutionary movement composed of varying strains. Some seemed to have been almost purely secular in their advocacy of violent resistance to Roman occupation. Other groups within the Zealots saw such a revolution in religious terms, wishing to purge Judea of Gentile influence and to create a society based on strict observance of the Toraic law. This group assumed the leadership of the revolt of 66–70; that leadership fell into discord and splintered during the siege of Jerusalem, their followers turning upon each other.

The Jesus Jews, as has already been discussed, were Jews who believed that Jesus of Nazareth was the Messiah. Already somewhat suspect in the eyes of more traditional Jews for their liberal attitude toward the letter of the Law and their acceptance of Gentiles, the Jesus Jews, like the Essenes and others, were apocalyptic in their outlook, believing that God would use a catastrophic event or series of events to bring about a new spiritual kingdom.

The appeal of such a liberal group was clearly to the lower classes and those marginalized by the Jewish and Roman establishments. Its openness to the downtrodden, Jew and Gentile alike, coupled with its belief in an impending apocalypse in which their oppressors would be defeated, made the Jesus Movement a convenient scapegoat after the great fire of Rome (64 CE). The emperor Nero blamed Jesus Jews for the fire, claiming that it was started in an attempt to ignite that apocalypse. Jesus Jews were crucified, burned, or exiled from Rome; among these exiles was the author of the book of Revelation.

The fall of Jerusalem and devastation of the Temple left only two of these factions with any credible base. The Zealots who had led the debacle and the Sadducees whose spirituality centered on a now-leveled Temple were no longer viewed as providing mainstream solutions, although a group of Zealots would stage one more revolt in 133 CE. The Bar Kochba rebellion would end with the expulsion of Jews from Judea in 135 CE and the beginning of the Diaspora.

During the first Jewish War, the Romans also turned their fury upon the Essenes; their communities in Judea were wiped out, leaving behind the hidden Dead Sea Scrolls to which future scholars would dedicate so much attention.

The events of 70 CE left only the Pharisees and the Jesus Jews in a position to sort out the reason for God's "punishment" of the Jewish people and to attempt to chart a new course for a Temple-less Judaism. One major leader of the Pharisee movement, the Hillelist Yohanan ben Zakkai, somehow escaped from Zealot-controlled Jerusalem and negotiated an agreement with the Roman general Vespasian. He was given permission to regroup the Sanhedrin, the governing body of Judaism, in the town of Yavneh, for the purpose of restoring some order to a defeated Judea.

The Jesus Jews, for their part, had never been in favor of the revolution. They believed that the Messiah had already come and favored the non-violence Jesus had preached. Like the Essenes, the Jesus Jews would wait out the storm. Early in the revolution, the Jesus Jews of Jerusalem removed themselves to Pella in the Decapolis region west of Galilee proper under the control of the Roman governor of Syria.

The sharp disagreement of these two Jewish groups over the questions posed by the events of 70, and the bitterness of the family split that ensued, would become the defining themes of all four of the Gospels, but particularly that of Mark, which was being created at the very time of the Temple's destruction. It is, therefore, essential to keep in mind Mark's primary purpose as a propagandist for the Jesus Jews in this critical debate. (I use the term "propagandist" in its most positive sense, the sense in which it could be applied to Thomas Paine and Harriet Beecher Stowe.)

After 9/11, it seemed that every aspect of American life was now, in some way, about that event; it filled the American consciousness and preempted virtually all other concerns. Questions of cause, of blame, and of response dominated American life, from Main Street to Wall Street, from Pennsylvania Avenue to Harvard Yard. Imagine, then, the effect of something far more central than the Twin Towers being obliterated; imagine the defining center of a nation's life, the spot where it touched God, lying in ruins. One out of three of the nation's citizens is dead. It would have been almost impossible for Mark's Gospel to be about anything other than the destruction of the great Temple and the questions it thrust upon Jewish life.

For an exposition of Mark's answers to those questions as compared to those of the Pharisee movement, we turn to his treatment of Jesus' experience in that great Temple itself.

CHAPTER 3

Cleansing the Cleansing
of the Temple

Loneliness is always in the middle
protected and fortified. People were supposed
to feel secure in that, and they don't.
  Yehuda Amichai[20]

MOST SCHOLARS AGREE THAT THE TEMPLE WAS THE SITE IN
which Jesus' fate was decided; in response to his actions there
"the chief priests and the scribes . . . looked for a way to bring
about his death" (Mark 11:18). These words directly follow a
scene traditionally known as "The Cleansing of the Temple."
Mark describes it this way:

> So they came to Jerusalem, and he went into the temple
> and began to drive out those who bought and sold
> there. He upset the tables of the money-changers and
> the seats of the dealers in pigeons; and he would not
> allow anyone to carry goods through the temple court.
> Then he began to teach them, and said, "Does not the
> scripture say, 'My house shall be called a house of
> prayer for all nations?' But you have made it a robbers'
> cave." (Mark 11:15–17)

The traditional Christian interpretation of this scene advocates the view that the Temple had become corrupted by
commerce. Indeed, the term "moneychangers in the Temple"
has become a condemnatory catchphrase for those in religious

life overly involved with money. It hardly needs to be mentioned here how far this passage's interpretation has gone in helping to create and sustain the stereotype of the "money-grubbing Jew." Even in their own Temple, they were thieves! In response, we must remind ourselves that Mark's Gospel was addressed to an overwhelmingly Jewish audience who was mourning the destruction of their Temple. Mark would make no more headway with such an audience by denigrating the Temple, somehow suggesting that its destruction was a punishment it earned by its corruption, than would an American voice directly after 9/11 portraying to fellow Americans the World Trade Towers as symbols of capitalist crime, deserving of everything they got!

Neither must we forget the overwhelming questions on the mind of any Jew of that day: Why did God do this to us? How can we prevent further punishment? Where do we go from here?

It is a sad testimony to the depth and power of the split in the Jewish family that Christians are unable to read this passage with the Jewish eyes needed to truly see. If modern Jews are indeed closer to the spirit of Mark's original audience than modern Christians, the loss of that Jewish vision when approaching the New Testament is crippling, to say the least. Christian teaching has focused on what Jesus *did* in this scene, the overturning of tables, the expulsion of money-changers, but has virtually ignored what he *said*. And it is in those words that his inherent Jewishness and the intent of his actions in Mark's Gospel become clear.

Imagine the scene: after this horrific to-do, this whirl of anger and violence, all eyes are on Jesus, the people naturally expecting an explanation. When Jesus "begins to teach them," the words are not his own but are quotes from the Jewish scripture, specifically Isaiah 56:7 ("My house shall be called a house of prayer for all peoples") and Jeremiah 7:11 ("Do you consider this House, which bears My name, to be a den of thieves?").

Mark's Jesus clearly expects his hearers to recognize the references, and Mark has the same expectations of his own Jewish audience. Justifiably so, for the books of the Tanakh (Torah, *Nevi'im* or Prophets, and the remaining Writings or *Kethuvim*) were not only central in Jewish life, they were virtually its only literature. (The Talmud would be assembled in the second century in written form, but in Mark's time most of this important work was still in oral form.)

Most people in the ancient world could not read, but Jews of Jesus' day would hear the scriptures regularly at synagogue services, and study them with the help of the local synagogue leader. The Jewish scriptures, then, were the popular oral literature of their day for Jews; the psalms could be heard, not only in the Temple or synagogue, but being sung by people as they worked or played.

These two particular passages would have a special significance for the audience of Mark's Gospel: they both have to do with the Temple and originate with prophets who worked at times when the Temple also was threatened with destruction, Isaiah and Jeremiah.

The first, Isaiah, lived in the second half of the eighth century BCE, at a time when the kingdom of Judah had been invaded by Assyria, from whom it had decided to withhold tribute. The Assyrians were known as particularly vicious and overwhelmingly successful warriors; soon Judah had been laid to waste and the Assyrian army surrounded Jerusalem, besieging it.

The similarity between this situation and that of 70 BCE should be obvious to all who know the story of the Jewish people; certainly those in Mark's audience knew it. Indeed, in that similarity, the Jews of Mark's time must have found hope, for, in the end, Jerusalem did not fall to the Assyrians. A sickness of some sort broke out in the invaders' camp, so decimating their ranks that they had no choice but to withdraw. The Temple was saved from destruction by a seeming act of God; giving rise to the popular notion that Jerusalem and its Temple were invulnerable.

Modern scholarship often attributes Isaiah 40 through 55 to an unknown Jewish writer living toward the close of the Babylonian captivity; a figure usually called "Deutero-Isaiah." Those who favor a stricter handling of the scriptures subscribe to the notion that the original Isaiah, as a prophet, foresaw the ultimate destruction of the Temple, and the exile and return of the Jewish people. In either case, it can be fairly stated that Jews of Jesus' day had no notion of a Deutero-Isaiah, and would have considered the entire work to contain the prophecy of one man, an eighth-century prophet to the kings of the southern kingdom of Judah.

Isaiah served as prophet in the royal court, first to King Ahaz and then to his son and successor, Hezekiah. Ahaz largely ignored Isaiah's words; his son, however, listened more attentively and instituted spiritual reforms, although disregarding the prophet's warning against his Assyria policy. Still, apparently, enough of a spiritual change had occurred for God to save the Temple and the city. What exactly had Isaiah preached?

As Jesus quotes from part of that teaching; let us examine it in its context in Chapter 56:

Thus said the Lord:
Observe what is right and do what is just;
For soon My salvation shall come,
And my deliverance be revealed.

Happy is the man who does this,
The man who holds fast to it;
Who keeps the Sabbath and does not profane it,
And stays his hand from doing evil.

Let not the foreigner say,
Who has attached himself to the Lord,
"The Lord will keep me apart from his people";
And let not the eunuch say,
"I am a withered tree."

For thus said the Lord:
"As for the eunuchs who keep my Sabbaths,
Who have chosen what I desire,
And hold fast to my covenant—
I will give them, in My House,
And within My walls,
A monument and a name
Better than sons and daughters.
I will give them an everlasting name
Which shall not perish.
As for the foreigners
Who attach themselves to the Lord,
To minister to Him,
And to love the name of the Lord,
To be his servants—
All who keep the Sabbath and do not profane it,
And who hold fast to my covenant—
I will bring them to My sacred mount
And let them rejoice in My House of prayer.
Their burnt offerings and sacrifices
Shall be welcome on my Altar;
For my House shall be called
A House of prayer for all peoples."

In Isaiah's time as in Jesus', Gentiles were not allowed into the Temple proper, nor were those who were ritually unclean according to the Law of Moses or otherwise described by Torah as outcast. Isaiah singles out eunuchs, those who had been castrated, usually (in the popular imagination of the day) to minimize their threat as slaves or government servants. Torah insists that "No one whose testes are crushed or whose member is cut off shall be admitted into the congregation of the Lord" (Deut. 23:1).

Traditionally, Jews did not practice castration, as it directly prohibits the carrying out of the first command God utters to living things, "Go forth and multiply" (Gen. 1:28). But it was common practice in many Gentile cultures, including some that would later conquer Judah; Jewish tradition maintains that Jews such as Daniel, as well as Shadrach, Meshach, and Abednego (of fiery furnace fame) who were pressed into service to the Babylonian king, were probably first castrated. Isaiah seems to use the term to signify an *uber*-foreigner, one irrefutably outside the Jewish way.

People like those mentioned in Isaiah 56 were not the only ones discouraged from entering the Temple proper. Those who were marginal in their Judaism, those of mixed parentage, although not forbidden outright, would have similarly felt less than welcome there. The Temple was the most holy site in Judea, and if there was even a question about its possible defilement, many felt it was better to be safe than sorry. An outer portion, called the Court of the Gentiles, was as far as all such people were expected to go. Josephus describes the signs hung on the barrier between this court and in the inner Temple:

NO FOREIGNER IS TO GO BEYOND THE BALUSTRADE AND THE PLAZA OF THE TEMPLE ZONE. WHOEVER IS CAUGHT DOING SO WILL HAVE HIMSELF TO BLAME FOR HIS DEATH, WHICH WILL FOLLOW.[21]

Even Paul himself runs into trouble on this count. According to the later Acts of the Apostles, the leadership of the Jesus Movement was worried about the reaction of Jews to Paul's message of inclusion for the uncircumcised. They had in their midst four Jesus Jews who had apparently made a certain set of promises called *Nazirite* vows. *Nazirim* vowed for a set period to live a life of sacrifice, abstaining from wine and the cutting of the hair; they dedicated themselves solely to the spiritual life for the period of their vow. No one could doubt a *Nazir*'s devotion to Judaism.

The period of these vows was now over for these four in Acts, and they were about to go to the Temple to have their heads shaved as a sign of its successful completion. The leaders of the Jesus Movement suggested that Paul go with them to make the arrangements, thus displaying himself as a good Jew. Paul does so without incident.

But a few days later, while again visiting the Temple, Paul is accosted by some who accuse him loudly of being "that fellow" who preaches against the Torah and who had just brought Gentiles into the Temple! A mob tries to kill him, and Paul is only rescued by a group of Roman soldiers. So serious was the charge of defiling the Temple by bringing in Gentiles that Paul faced several hearings on the matter and, as he was a Roman citizen, had eventually to appeal to the emperor himself (Acts 21:27–36).

This may seem like a terribly foreign attitude to Christians, until we stop for a moment to consider: Have we never seen or heard of a person or class of people being made to feel unwelcome in a Christian church? If we know of someone's less-than-perfect background, have we ever thought to ourselves, "What is he or she doing here?" Do we seriously believe that such people cannot feel that attitude? Roman Catholicism still denies the sacraments to those who divorce and remarry; in some cases, just being divorced, regardless of who initiated the action, will result in a loss of office such as eucharistic minister or parish council member. How welcome would a person of color be made to feel in an all-white Christian congregation, and vice versa? Indeed, there was a time when some denominations provided separate sub-denominations altogether for minorities. Priests and ministers have been known to discourage people from attending because of their style of dress. Those who, for whatever reason, choose not to pledge in advance to the church budget may be made to feel "not part of the team."

Some Protestant denominations are divided along lines often labeled "low" and "high," "low" being closer to evangelicalism and "high" to Catholicism. The story is told of a low-church congregant who attended a service in a high church in another town. During the sermon, the person, deeply moved, would punctuate the pastor's remarks with cries of "Hallelujah!" and "Praise Jesus!" The very staid congregation did not appreciate this, and an usher approached the person. "May I help you?" he whispered. "I've found the Spirit!" replied the exultant worshiper. "That may be so," said the usher, "but you certainly didn't find it here. *Shhhh*."

According to the teachings of Isaiah, teachings that marked the saving of the Temple from destruction, such divisions should not exist. The Gentiles, even the eunuchs, who attach themselves to the Jewish God, who respect the covenant and the sabbath, should not be excluded from the temple, but rather would be treated in a way better "than sons and daughters."

The quote Jesus uses from the second source, the prophet Jeremiah, provides a much bleaker view. Jeremiah was born about 650 BCE, and during his lifetime, Judea also suffered from an invasion, on this occasion by the Babylonians who had defeated the Assyrians and were expanding their empire. This time, however, no miraculous illness struck the besieging army around Jerusalem. The city fell, the Temple was utterly destroyed in 586, and most of the Jewish people were carted off into exile in Babylon.

Jeremiah in his role as spokesperson for God had tried to warn the king and the people that a change of heart and practice was the only way to avert this disaster:

> The word which came to Jeremiah from the Lord: Stand at the gate of the House of the Lord, and there proclaim this word: Hear the word of the Lord, all you of Judah who enter these gates to worship the Lord!
> Thus said the Lord of Hosts, the God of Israel:
> "Mend your ways and your actions, and I will let you dwell in this place. Don't put your faith in illusions and

say, 'The Temple of the Lord, the Temple of the Lord, the Temple of the Lord are these [buildings].' No, if you really mend your ways and your actions, if you execute justice between one man and another; if you do not oppress the stranger, the orphan, and the widow; if you do not shed the blood of the innocent in this place, if you do not follow other gods, to your own hurt—then only will I let you dwell in this place, in the land which I gave to your fathers for all time. See, you are relying on illusions that are of no avail. Will you steal and murder and commit adultery and swear falsely, and sacrifice to Baal, and follow other gods who you have not known, and then come and stand before Me in this House which bears My Name and say, 'We are safe'?—(Safe) to do all these abhorrent things? Do you consider this House, which bears My Name, to be a den of thieves?" (Jer. 7:1–11)

Clearly, then, the two passages that Jesus quotes in explanation of his actions in Mark 11:15–19 refer to much the same set of situations. Jesus does not quote from any biblical passages condemning commerce in the Temple. The selling of animals and the changing of money went on for good reasons. Torah delineates sacrifices for different feasts and occasions in the spiritual life. People would come great distances—at major feasts from across the Empire and beyond—to pray in the great Temple in Jerusalem, and they could hardly be expected to haul the animals for the sacrifice with them. At the same time, Torah prescribes that the animals had to be without blemish and/or of a certain age. Selling the animals on site made the sacrifices possible at all for many Jews.

As for the money-changers, coins from all over the known world would come into the Temple. If you were to take a coin from your pocket today, you would probably find someone's likeness engraved upon it, Lincoln's or Jefferson's or

Washington's. The second commandment, however, forbids the making of graven images (Exod. 20:4). As almost all ancient coins featured such images, they had to be changed for coins that did not, before they could enter a Temple dedicated to the God who gave the commandments! It has often been suspected that the Temple did not deal fairly in the exchange, and that it made money on the deal. This may or may not have been true, but if this had been Jesus' issue, it would have made much more sense for him to quote one of the biblical injunctions against charging interest.

Thus, from a superficial point of view, it might seem that the words Jesus quotes are a mismatch to his deeds—or at the very least to the traditional Christian interpretation of them. Or could it be that that interpretation lacks the Jewishness needed to truly see Mark's true intentions in this scene?

Recall that Jesus and a group of his followers had just entered Jerusalem for the Passover celebration. We are not certain how many made up this group; Mark indicates that they are more than just Jesus and his inner circle: "Jesus was leading the way; and the disciples were filled with awe, while those who followed behind were afraid" (Mark 10:32). In the scene usually read on Palm Sunday, we find Jesus making a very big and splashy entrance; in Mark's Gospel he then goes directly to the Temple, and it can be safely assumed that a sizable crowd would have followed this celebrity there. As it is already late in the day, Jesus leaves the city for the night, returning to the Temple the next day. It is at this point that the "cleansing of the Temple" scene occurs.

Here it is important to recall the type of people Jesus tended to attract as his followers. First of all, many were Galileans like himself. Galilee, the northernmost outpost of ancient Israel, had always been considered spiritually suspect territory. It was a heavily mixed area, with Jews and a variety of Gentile people sharing the land. In 733 BCE the Assyrians destroyed the northern kingdom of Israel (the Jewish nation had split in two after Solomon's death). Most of the Israelites were taken into exile, never to be heard of again—the famous "Lost Tribes of Israel." The Assyrian practice was to replace troublesome people with others from different conquered territories, thus keeping their internal enemies always off guard. Such was the case with Galilee, which then became Gentile territory.[22] Indeed, Isaiah refers to it as "Galilee of the Nations" (Isa. 9:1).

After its conquest by Babylon and the exile of most of its inhabitants, the southern kingdom, called Judah, would not be politically free until the reign of the Maccabees beginning in 166 BCE. At that time only a few isolated Jewish villages remained in Galilee. The Maccabees king John Hyrcanus (134–104 BCE) conquered Galilee; he and his successors gave the inhabitants two options: convert to Judaism via circumcision or leave the territory. Many took the first option, but knowing that their conversion was less than voluntary, other Jews looked on Galileans as marginal Jews at best.

During the same period, the ruling Maccabees encouraged groups of Jews who had remained in Babylon and Persia to settle in Galilee.[23] These were called *natzorim* or offshoots. In contrast to the new "converts," the *natzorim* were more sophisticated, coming from the centers of empire, where there flourished Torah academies. Over the years of exile, they had had to make a strong, conscious effort to maintain their Jewishness and avoid assimilation. The Benedictine scholar Bargil Pixner makes a strong case that the town called Nazareth in Jesus' day, apparently abandoned from Assyrian through Hellenic times, had been resettled by *natzorim*, who lent it their name.

Hence the Galilee of Jesus' day was truly a study in contrast. The majority of Jews who lived there were of families that had been forced to convert within the previous century; their brand of Judaism was not at all as strict of that of its southern neighbors, who held them in a certain amount of contempt. Many Galileans probably had Gentile family just over

the border in non-Jewish territory, among those who had chosen to leave rather than convert. Additionally, some Gentiles
had gradually moved back into Galilee during the Roman period; the very mixed population of Galilee itself would make
it difficult to follow all the laws of ritual purity in daily life.

Along with this, there existed pockets of *natzorim*, who,
to borrow a phrase, would appear to be "more holy than the
pope!" Their families had been invited to Galilee exactly for
their strict faithfulness to Jewish life, and so faithful were
they, in fact, that they often criticized the Jews of Jerusalem
and of the Temple, as well as Herod, for not being strict
enough in their Judaism. Given this background, one can see
how the message of John the Baptist could be attributed to a
natzor background; the Qumran scrolls also imply a connection between the Essenes and the *natzorim*.

If Jesus did come from *natzor* stock, he would have been
extremely well versed in the Jewish scriptures and practice,
and probably able to read both Hebrew and Aramaic. We see
in his life story as told by Mark a strong affinity, not only
for great sinners such as prostitutes and traitorous collectors
of the Roman tax, but for Gentiles as well. He often enters
Gentile territory and performs healings there; in Mark there
are two scenes of multiplying loaves, once for Jews and once
for Gentiles.

If we examine Jesus' inner circle, we find an equally mixed
group. Among the apostles were Jews with Hebrew names
and Jews with Greek names (Philip, Andrew). Ever since the
conquest of the entire area by Alexander in the fourth century BCE, a great spiritual battle had been waged over how
"Hellenized" Jewish life should be, strict Jews insisting that
Greek culture needed to be rejected *in toto*. Jesus included
a member of the Zealot party among his twelve lieutenants
as well, a man who might not even have been Jewish at all,
"Simon the Canaanite" (Mark 3:18). One of the two Judahs
among the twelve may have belonged to an even more extreme
sect within the Zealots, the "Iscariots" or "Assassins."

More unsettling still would be the presence among Jesus' followers of those described as "sons of Alphaeus," James (the Less) and Levi (or Matthew, who gives his name to a gospel). The name "Alphaeus" is a Hellenized version of the Hebrew *Chalpai*—and *Chalpai* means "unknown." Here again we see how deeply an understanding of the gospels is damaged by our lack of Jewish eyes! To describe someone as "father unknown" is to indicate that his/her birth was "illegitimate."

Attitudes toward those conceived or born out of wedlock have historically been quite severe; the "stain of illegitimacy," the passing of the sin of adultery onto the offspring, was considered very real. In the book of Deuteronomy (directly after its rejection of the eunuchs!) come these words: "No one misbegotten shall be admitted into the congregation of the Lord, none of his descendants, even in the tenth generation, shall be admitted into the congregation of the Lord" (Deut. 23:3).

I can speak from personal experience of this "taint." As previously mentioned, I was an adopted child of (as I would later learn) mixed Jewish and Gentile parentage. My adopted parents were Roman Catholic, and I applied for acceptance to Franciscan minor seminary at age thirteen. When a very kind friar came to our home for the family interview, at one point, my father asked me to go upstairs to my room so that he and my mother could "speak to Father alone." Years later I learned the content of the conversation: my father had heard that children born out of wedlock could not become priests! The friar assured him that, although this had sometimes been the case in medieval Europe, all of that had changed.

Mark, writing for the Jewish audience of his day, is therefore communicating the fact that Jesus had "bastards" in his inner circle—people who definitionally would not be considered Jews and certainly would not have been welcome in the inner Temple. And there could be even more potentially shocking news in the Good News: there are two apostles named James listed in Mark's Gospel: James (called the Greater), the brother of John, whose father is named as Zebedee, and James son of Unknown (Mark 3:16–18). In another place, Mark lists the brothers of Jesus, naming "James and Joses, Judah and Simon" (Mark 6:3). After Jesus' death, a person designated "James, the brother of the Lord," is clearly part of the leadership circle of the early Jesus Jews (Gal. 1:19). If this James and James son of Alphaeus are the same man, it does not cast a very flattering light on Mary, their mother.

Mark's Gospel, chronologically the first of the canonical four, makes no mention of Jesus' birth at all, and, contrary to common practice, names no father in identifying him, not even Joseph. In the same passage in which the brothers are listed, incredulous residents of Nazareth are described as asking, "Is he not the carpenter, the son of Mary . . . ?" (Mark 6:3). In Jesus' day, Jews were identified by paternity, hence "Peter son of Jonah," or "James and John, the sons of Zebedee." So it is especially curious that the people of Jesus' own town do not refer to him as "Jesus bar (son of) Joseph."

In the Gospels of Matthew and in Luke, these two writers apparently believe there to be an issue here that needs clarifying. Although Mary is described in both these Gospels as being pregnant before marriage, "she found she was going to have a child by the Holy Spirit" (Matt. 1:18), which had "come upon" her (Luke 1:35). Mark, however, makes no mention of any of this; on the contrary, he makes a rather broad implication that Jesus himself was illegitimately conceived! As such, he would have come under the Torah injunction and, if his background were known, would not have been allowed beyond the Court of the Gentiles himself! Mark states that scribes came from Jerusalem to Galilee to observe and investigate Jesus; it is altogether possible that his (seemingly) questionable birth could have been found out by them (Mark 3:22).

So when regarded through its Jewish lens, this section of Mark yields an intriguing portrait of Jesus and the group of his followers who entered the Court of the Gentiles during that Passover season. Jesus is a Galilean, the region where many Jews are thought to barely qualify for the name. Although quite possibly of *natzir* stock, he leads a spiritual movement that seems to make no distinction between Jew and Gentile. It welcomes the worst of sinners, prostitutes, and traitors to Judea. There is someone within his inner circle to offend every taste—a Zealot, Hellenized Jews, traditional Jews, a Canaanite, an Assassin, a collaborator, even the illegitimate, a designation that he himself well may share. This motley group, apparently of some size, enters the outer Temple, where its leader begins what appears to be an incipient riot.

But why? Why does the Jesus of Mark's Gospel overturn the tables of the money-changers and drive out those who bought and sold? The combination of Jesus' quotes from Isaiah and Jeremiah, an understanding of his own background and that of his followers, and the recognition of the burning Jewish question of Mark's day, when taken together, should provide an answer.

Recall that by the time of Mark's Gospel the destruction of Jerusalem and the loss of the Temple had left only two movements in Judaism in a position to help decide the future of the religion and its people, the Pharisee movement and the Jesus Jews. That future had to be based on an understanding of the past, particularly the cause of God's actions (or withholding of action) with regard to the catastrophe of 70 CE. It was on this all-important, decisive question that the two movements differed and the Jewish family split apart.

Jews had to determine how to have a religion without a Temple or sacrifices. One thing remained, however, that the Romans could not destroy: Torah. The Pharisees, in comparison to the Sadducees, had been the more Torah-centered party to begin with. And so the remaining Pharisee leaders decided that Jewish life should be guided by close attention to Torah in all things, as had been their longtime practice.

As Wylen writes,

> The rabbis were surely as overcome with sorrow as
> anyone over the great tragedy that had befallen the

Jews. But for them, the destruction of the Temple was in many ways a benefit. It allowed them to promote the doctrines and practices of the Pharisees as a way of life for all Jews. The Pharisees had already developed a way of life that made the Temple unnecessary. They had been living "as if" they were Priests. They had observed the laws of priestly purity everywhere, extending the sanctity of the Temple precinct into the entire world. . . . Obedience to the *mitzvoth* (commands of Torah) established a connection between God and humankind and brought God's grace upon his people.[24]

Stated another way, the surviving rabbis of the Pharisee movement answered the question: "Why did God punish us in this way?" by saying, "It was our failure to keep the *mitzvoth* that brought this upon us." As the Babylonian exiles before them had done, the Pharisees understood the destruction of the Temple as a result of laxity in keeping the commands of the Torah. Accordingly, a renewed strictness was in order, one with the added benefit of binding the Jewish people together, of preserving their identity and helping to stem assimilation.

As Mark's "cleansing of the Temple" scene shows, the Jesus Jews saw things very differently. To them, Jewish life had been *too strict* with regards to the *mitzvoth*, not too lax; it had too closely followed the letter of Torah, but not its guiding spirit. The Judaism of 70 had created a spiritual class system in which far too many were considered outcast, just as had been the case in Isaiah's day and in Jeremiah's. Had not God, through these prophets, called for such people to be admitted fully to the Temple and to the fullness of Jewish life? For the Jesus Jews, this treatment of the marginal, the outcast, and the stranger had once again caused God to withdraw his protection from the Temple, as it had done in Jeremiah's day. A commitment to "mend ways and actions" with regard to such treatment might have prevented the fall of Jerusalem and the burning of the Temple, as it had in Isaiah's time.

The types of individuals who would be excluded or made to feel unwelcome at the Temple, the ones who would not proceed past the Court of the Gentiles, were exactly those who made up a significant part of Jesus' following. Their inclusion was his hallmark. When he and they arrived in the area where sacrificial animals were purchased, the fact that many, perhaps even he himself, could go no farther seems to have incensed Jesus. He lashes out at the immediate surroundings, at a place where human beings were relegated to the status of animals.

Jesus' statement of explanation, quoting two prophets concerned with the potential loss of their Temple, leaves little doubt: Mark is putting forth the argument of the Jesus Jews on the burning question of his day. It was not the selling of sacrificial animals or the changing of coins that sent Jesus into this rage, rather it was the attitude toward the foreigner and outcast on the part of those running the Temple. Jesus is clearly frustrated that, after all his efforts to change minds and hearts on this issue, so little progress has been made.

Mark takes this opportunity to make clear the position of the Jesus Jews: the future of Jewish life depends on welcoming those previously outcast. When asked to denote the most important *mitzvoth* of all, Jesus first quotes Deuteronomy 6:4–5, and then Leviticus 19:18: "You shall love the Lord your God with all your heart, all your mind, and all your soul," and "You shall love your neighbor as yourself" (Mark 12:30–31). Later Luke would add to this story the parable of the Good Samaritan, to reinforce the point that one's neighbor included the outcast, and even one's perceived enemy (Luke 10:29–37).

Unfortunately, those very *mitzvoth*, which combined came to be called the Great Command, were thoroughly ignored by those on both sides of the post-70 debate. The rabbis of Yavneh, in their zeal to preserve Jewish life, wished death upon heretics, Jesus Jews among them. And the followers of Jesus themselves turned Jews not of their party into the very children of Satan! Only family could turn on each other with such bile, forgetting in their fury their own most sacred principles. (A

suggested test: at a family gathering, suggest that the attitudes toward hated Uncle X, obnoxious Aunt Y, or a part of
the clan no one acknowledges violates God's teachings. *N.B.*:
Wear Kevlar!)

But what of Jesus' own action in the Temple that day? Did
he not violate his own teachings on non-violence and love,
even of enemy? Could he not see that such violence committed even in the outer parts of the sacred Temple could only
have dangerous consequences for him?

The text raises these important questions, and Mark does
address them in the same chapter as the "cleansing." That
scene, which I would now like to refer to as "The Inclusioning of the Temple," is set in the frame of another story, told in
two parts. And a curious story it is.

After his entry into Jerusalem and brief visit to the
Temple, the text describes Jesus as hungry. He approaches
a fig tree, but "when he reached it he found nothing but
leaves; for it was not the season for figs." Nonetheless Jesus
curses the tree: "May no one ever again eat fruit from you,"
whereupon he leaves the city (Mark 11:12–14). Upon his return the next morning, the fig tree he had cursed had withered "from the roots up." The disciples are amazed. Jesus
responds,

> "Have faith in God. Truly, I tell you, if anyone says to
> this mountain, 'Be lifted from your place and hurled
> into the sea' and has no inward doubts, but believes
> that it will happen, it will be done for him. I tell you,
> then, whatever you ask for in prayer, believe that you
> have received it and it will be yours.
>
> "And when you stand in prayer, if you have griev-
> ances against anyone, forgive him, so that your Father
> in heaven may forgive you the wrongs you have done."
> (Mark 11:22–25)

Why does Mark set off the story of Jesus' encounter with the Temple's exclusionary policies with this account of the cursing of the fig tree, which seems to portray Jesus as a petulant child? Such an action, again, seems most strange for a preacher of non-violence and love.

Let us recall that Jesus had first gone into the Temple, but Mark tells us that "it was already late," and so Jesus withdrew for the night to Bethany with the Twelve (Mark 11:11). Yet in their brief visit surely they must have seen the written warnings promising death to anyone who violated the ritual purity of the Temple. To Jesus and his followers, those signs must have seemed to say, "And this means you." Still angry, Jesus curses an unresponsive fig tree, but let us not forget that the tree was not at fault. Figs were out of season; the tree was not ready.

The next morning after the ruckus, Mark makes sure to return us to that tree. Overnight it seems to have died. Jesus' response to this is a teaching on faith, prayer, and forgiveness.

Taken in the light of our discussion of the "inclusioning" scene, several things become apparent. In much the same way that the fig tree is not ready, Mark portrays the Jewish establishment as not being ready to respond to the teachings of Jesus. Nonetheless, Jesus is so angered by their narrow interpretation of Torah that he lashes out, acting in contradiction to his own first principles.

If indeed the leadership had investigated Jesus, they must have known of his teachings on absolute non-violence; this would have led him to seem much less of a threat. Once, however, he appears at the Temple with a crew of outcasts and begins to wreck the Court of the Gentiles, it must have appeared more like the start of coup than a statement of universal love. Jesus had gone too far too fast.

What's more, it appears that he himself realizes this. In the second half of the fig tree story, Jesus speaks of faith, assuring his disciples that it can move mountains. Is there a self-criticism implied here? Is Mark portraying a Jesus who now wishes that he had relied more on faith, rather than reacting as he did to the exclusion of so many from the inner Temple?

Such a view is further reinforced by Jesus' final words in this section. He instructs his hearers to forgive any grievance against anyone as they pray, that God might forgive them as well. Is Jesus once more reflecting upon himself and his actions in the Court of the Gentiles? Had he first practiced such forgiveness in this ultimate house of prayer, might things have turned out quite differently?

CHAPTER 4

The God of Jesus of Nazareth

God is a staircase that ascends
To a place that is no longer there, or isn't there yet.
Yehuda Amichai[25]

THE GROWING SPLIT IN THE JEWISH FAMILY OVER THE CAUSE
of the Roman destruction of the Great Temple and the actions
needed in its aftermath itself depends on an even more fundamental question: What type of God is God?

The Pharisees of post-Temple Judaism chose to emphasize
a view of God as the giver of *mitzvoth*, and through those
mitzvoth, as a preserver of the Jewish people even in their ad-
versity. The Torah given by God, rather than a Temple built
by Herod, made a Jew a Jew. Holding to this view, Pharisaical
Judaism proved very successful, for Judaism did survive,
not only in the world of polytheism, but even in the much
more threatening universe of Christian dominance. However,
one horrific result of most family splits is the complete dis-
identification of each group with its counterpart, often leading to demonization. In the case of Christians and Jews, it
surely must be said that a Christian understanding of their
own thorough Jewishness and a reading of the Gospels in this
light might have prevented so much horror.

If, indeed, the lesson, drawn by the Jesus Jews from the
Jewish prophets, of Mark's Temple scene is that there must be
no outcasts, what effect might that understanding have had
on relations between these two sides of the Jewish family?
As it is, I think it can be fairly said that the emphasis on a
strict interpretation of Torah by the post-Temple leadership

permitted Judaism to last long enough to itself produce different branches, some far more faithful to the words of Isaiah
56 than the institution named for the Galilean who quoted
them. On the other hand, the God of the Jesus Jews, the God
of Jesus of Nazareth, seems to have been one more casualty of
the family split, that element among the "repressed" most in
need of "return." A further examination of Mark's Gospel will
demonstrate that Christians past and present have had little
understanding of the God of Christ, the very God who most
Christians believe Jesus to be!

After the scene with the money-changers and animal sellers, Jesus decides to take another tack. Apparently he has left
the city; Mark 11:27 describes him as coming "once more to
Jerusalem," and for the remainder of Chapters 11 and 12, Jesus
engages in the much more traditional approach of disputation
or debate.

Much has been made in Christian preaching over the centuries of the "treacherous" Pharisees, scribes, and Sadducees
engaging Jesus in tricky questions. In truth, public religious and
philosophical disputations were the completely accepted and
commonplace means of investigating and discussing a point; the
disputations between the great rabbis Hillel and Shammai, for
example, are classics of Jewish spiritual thought. In entering
into this form, Jesus was taking a more mainstream approach
after the disruptive, more "fringe" actions of the previous day.
This sort of public debate was what a spiritual teacher was expected to do.

Outside its Jewish context, one question in this long disputation can seem particularly puzzling; it occurs in Mark
12:35–37:

As he taught them in the Temple, Jesus went on to say,
"How can the scribes maintain that the Messiah is a son
of David? It was David himself who said, inspired by
the Holy Spirit, 'The Lord said to my Lord, "Sit at my

right hand, until I put your enemies under your feet.'"
If David calls him 'Lord,' how can he be David's son?"
There was a large crowd listening eagerly.

This is indeed a very odd passage, with the all the "Lords"
floating about! But it represents the key moment in the disputation, one in which Jesus' view of God is clearly (at least,
for a Jewish audience) expounded, a view which the people
listening apparently appreciated greatly.

Jesus' statement is directed specifically toward scribes.
Scribes were a particularly important class in the Jewish world;
not only could they read and write when the overwhelming majority could not, but their primary job was to create Torah scrolls, as well as scrolls of other books of Tanakh.
Painstakingly, the scribe would copy every sacred letter; one
error, even the slightest, would mean that the entire scroll
would be destroyed and the whole project begun again. Indeed, Jewish custom maintained, and still does, that, taken
together, the words (and spaces!) of Torah spell out the very
identity of God. It was standard for scribes to have the entire
five books, if not the whole Tanakh, committed to memory.

As a Jew, Jesus knows this; in his own way he is showing
the scribes that he knows as much about Torah as they do (an
essential move for an itinerant preacher from the boondocks
in disputation with leading Torah scholars of his day). And,
with their background, the scribes, for their part, understand
exactly the point that Jesus is making, a point to which they
do not respond.

The lines that Jesus quotes come from Psalm 110, verse 1,
often translated, "The Lord said to my Lord, 'Sit at my right
hand while I make your enemies your footstool.'" This was
the way that most Jews in their synagogue or at the Temple
would have heard the verse. But scribes, who would have had
to often copy that verse, as well as Jesus (who must have been
able to read Hebrew) knew differently.

The Hebrew word for "The Lord" is *Adonai*. It is a very well-known term in Judeo-Christian circles, and its translation, "The Lord," is probably the term most commonly used to describe God. The only problem is that the word itself appears relatively rarely in the Hebrew scriptures.

If one were to go to Jewish worship service, at one point the Torah scroll would be taken from its tabernacle and read. One might notice that in some congregations, a silver pointer is used by the reader to help keep his/her place in the lines. Careful observation will show this reader occasionally lifting the pointer, called a *yad*, from the page. On those occasions the word *Adonai*, or perhaps *ha Shem* ("the Name") will be read or chanted. If someone who could read biblical Hebrew were to examine that same passage, however, he/she would most likely not find either of those words there. Rather, they would read a word made up of the Hebrew letters *yod*, *heh*, *vod*, and *heh*, comprising the name of God commonly described as "Yahweh."

In actuality, no one knows how the Sacred Tetragram is pronounced. Hebrew uses no written vowels, and biblical Hebrew doesn't even employ the marks that its modern counterpart displays to signify vowel sounds. Indeed, throughout Jewish history, this four-letter construction was considered so sacred that no one other than the high priest in the Temple was permitted to say it aloud. With the passing of that active priesthood after 70 CE and throughout all the ensuing centuries, the actual pronunciation of this name of God was lost. Had it been preserved, however, it still would have been considered by traditional Jews too sacred to utter. Instead, *Adonai*, the Lord, became the term of choice to be used in place of YHVH, though *Adonai* itself is hardly ever used at all in the written Hebrew original, and is only spoken and written as "the Lord" in English translations.

Jews of Jesus' and Mark's day would have been very familiar with this customary terminology; the pronunciation had not yet been lost, but the custom of substituting *Adonai* in speech was well established. The vast majority, never having actually read the Torah, would thus be uncertain where *Adonai* was actually used or where it was just a customary substitute. Subsequently, they probably would have usually thought of their God as the Lord, a being primarily of power and mastery.

In his disputation, Jesus (who already knows the answer to his question) is challenging the religious establishment of his day to state aloud the true case, to remind "the crowd" of the scriptural name of God. For the actual text of the psalm reads, "YHVH said to my Lord . . . ." Why is this important? Why should Jesus care?

For the answer, we must go to the place where this name of God is first revealed to humans, the "Burning Bush" episode of Exodus 3. Recall that Moses, having killed an Egyptian in defense of a Hebrew, has fled from Egypt and settled in Midian, where he has married the daughter of the local king and had at least one son. While tending flocks, Moses sees a mysterious light; upon investigation it proves to be a bush aflame but not consumed, out of which the voice of God speaks, commanding Moses to return to Egypt to lead the Jewish people to freedom.

Moses is most reluctant; after all, he is now settled in Midian, is in line to succeed his sonless father-in-law as king, and he has committed a capital crime in Egypt. In a sort of test, he asks God, "When I come to the Israelites and say to them, 'The God of your fathers has sent me to you,' and they ask me, 'What is his name?' what shall I say to them?" (Exod. 3:13).

There is an apparent reference here to the practice of referring to the Jewish God by titles, such as *Elohim* (the Master) or *Adonai*. Moses wishes to know God's actual name, the way in which God identifies God's self. The response?

And God said to Moses, *Ehyeh-Asher-Ehyeh*. He continued, "Thus shall you say to the Israelites, '*Ehyeh* sent me to you.'" And God further said to Moses, "Thus

shall you speak to the Israelites: 'YHVH, the God of
your fathers, the God of Abraham, the God of Isaac,
the God of Jacob, has sent me to you.' This shall be
my name forever. This my appellation for all eternity."
(Exod. 3:14–15)

The first utterance of the name, rendered above in Hebrew
transliteration, is often translated into English as "I Am Who
Am," or "I Am That I Am." Again, we are presented here with
the problem of seeing a Jewish text with non-Jewish eyes.
The Torah, of course, is written in biblical Hebrew, and biblical Hebrew *has no present tense* of the verb. Unusual as it
may seem to us, biblical Hebrew uses past (or perfect) tense
and future (or imperfect), but no present. Thus it is literally
impossible to say "am" in this ancient language! The phrase
Ehyeh-Asher-Ehyeh is rather in future or imperfect tense;
a more accurate English rendering would read, "I Will Be
Whatever I Will Be" (the term *Asher* is indefinite).

One can only imagine Moses' response (or lack thereof) to
this answer to his question. God's name, God's identity, is "I
Will Be Whatever I Will Be"? What could that possibly mean?
Does it say anything at all? But God persists: "Thus shall you
say to the Israelites, 'I Will Be' sent me to you."

What is one to make of a God named I Will Be Whatever
I Will Be? Clearly, this is a God who cannot be defined, can
hardly be described. This God cannot be put in a box, cannot
be predicted or controlled through incantation or ritual. God
will be whatever God will be, and there is nothing humans
can do about it; this divine being is one of infinite possibility,
even contrariness from a human perspective. God's ways are
impossible to foresee, God's nature is impossible to pin down;
the moment one says something definite about this God, one
violates the Name. *Ehyeh* is a God about whom one can never
say never or always. Only whatever.

In short, the God of the Name (*ha Shem*) is not a name, not
a noun at all, but a *verb*—specifically, the verb *to be* in the

first person, imperfect tense. The God of the Jews and of the Jewish Jesus is not first and foremost a lawgiver, a provider of definitions, rather God is a *process*, a constant opening-out into an indefinite, unlimited future.

Even to call such a God "the Lord" can present a difficulty, as the prophet Elijah found in 1 Kings 19. In a vision on Mount Horeb (Sinai), God causes, in order, a mighty wind, an earthquake, and a fire to appear before Elijah. The text insists that God was not in any of them. Finally, Elijah hears a "soft murmuring sound," and hides his head in his cloak in the presence of God (1 Kings 19:11–13). Here "I Will Be" presents divinity in anything but the trappings of lordship, of power and might.

The mysterious term YHVH becomes more accessible in the light of the burning bush. Although no one can be completely certain, the four letters are consistent with the third-person, singular rendering of *Ehyeh*: "He Will Be."

Apparently, Mark's Jesus wishes the scribes in his audience to point out his "mistake" by clarifying that "The Lord" which is the grammatical subject of the psalm's verse is actually not there, but rather a respectful replacement for the Tetragram. Jesus wants to move away from a concept of God as a Near-Eastern despot, a "Lord," and toward a more Jewish understanding, a fuller experience of I Will Be Whatever I Will Be. When this part of the disputation is linked to the earlier occurrence with the money-changers and animal sellers, a pattern begins to emerge.

The scribes do not answer Jesus, and at this the disputation ends; for Mark this clearly represents "match point" for Jesus. Why did they not respond?

Mark seems to be telling his Jewish audience that the scribes, and symbolically the Judean religious establishment, were not willing to remind the people of "God's name forever," this God whom Jesus characteristically called "Abba," or "Dad." No one in a Jewish context would have the slightest problem with identifying God as father; after all, he was the creator of humankind. In insisting in this very public Temple disputation on a God who is first and foremost He Will Be Whatever He Will Be, Jesus reminds his audience that they are children of *Ehyeh*, made in this God's image and likeness. If all people are the image of this Father, then their name as well must be I Will Be Whatever I Will Be (on a human scale).

People, the images of God, likewise then cannot be put in a convenient box, cannot be judged, categorized, or labeled. This is precisely the message of Isaiah 56: God welcomes even those castigated by the *mitzvoth*. I Will Be Whatever I Will Be produced the Torah; God is not bound by it (more on this later). God will be *whatever* God will be!

Mark relates this phase of the disputation in an effort to bolster his side's argument in the Jewish family struggle. The judging of individuals made in the image of I Will Be Whatever I Will Be is self-contradictory. Hence, for Mark, it was the failure of the Jewish establishment to live out this inclusion that caused the downfall of Jerusalem and the Temple, in a reversal of the events of Isaiah's time.

In this way, Mark presents Jesus as a true radical, one who wishes to return to the "roots" (*radicis* in Latin) of his faith. Basic realities, not titles, concern Jesus. He wishes to return to the word which *Adonai* merely stands for. Over and over again in Mark's Gospel (and, I would maintain, in the other three as well), Jesus' belief in the Tetragram, in God as "He Will Be," determines the course of his life and teaching. It is a centrality that Christianity, in its dis-identification with and de-monization of its own Jewish center, has lost, and with it a full understanding of the Jewish Jesus, his ministry and mission. In the interest of its recovery, let us trace the growth of this idea in the Jesus of Mark's Gospel.

CHAPTER 5

(In) the Beginning

I found myself
Suddenly, and too early in life,
Like the inner wall of a house
Which has become an outside wall.

Yehuda Amichai[26]

MARK'S GOSPEL OPENS WITH THIS SENTENCE: "THE BEGINNING of the gospel of Jesus Christ, the Son of God" (Mark 1:1). Even this simple line opens itself much more fully when read with Jewish eyes, the eyes of its intended audience.

To open a piece with the phrase "the beginning" will immediately produce in a Jewish reader or hearer an echo of the first line of the Torah: "In the beginning" (Gen. 1:1). The Hebrew word for beginning, *bresheit*, is also its name for the book of Genesis. Much is implied by the use of this term with a Jewish audience.

First, it indicates strongly that the writer feels he is creating, not just an account of a life, but actual sacred scripture. In his book *Liberating the Gospels, Reading the Bible with Jewish Eyes*, Bishop Spong, relying heavily on the work of Michael Goulder, maintains that the synoptic gospels should be understood as liturgical and lectionary books.[27] The Jesus Jews, still identifying themselves as Jews, would attend service in their synagogues. Spong argues that the episodes of the synoptic gospels were ordered so as to parallel and converse with the traditional Torah portions, or *parashat*, for those services; in other words, in the synagogues of Jesus Jews, the Torah reading would be followed by the appropriate Gospel reading.

If this were the case, then those creating or compiling those episodes would surely have seen their work as that of creating scripture. The phrase "the beginning" would have indicated the use of the opening of Mark's Gospel in conjunction with the phrase "In the beginning" from *Bresheit* 1—the reading that begins the first Torah portion of the Jewish Year.

That *parasha* itself, of course, speaks of creation, and it is easy to see from a reading of Mark's opening scenes that this gospel will portray its events and teaching as a new act of creation, a new beginning, especially for the Jewish people, who have lost their Temple and must redefine themselves.

Mark writes of "the beginning of the Gospel," i.e., "good news as brought by a messenger." Here, too, Jewish echoes are strong. Considering the situation concerning Jerusalem and the Temple, the term "good news" would surely bring to a Jewish ear the line from Isaiah 52:7, "How welcome on the mountains are the footsteps of the herald announcing happiness, heralding good fortune, announcing victory, telling Zion your God is King." This song of the triumph of Judea and the Jewish God over their enemies, as has been previously discussed, calls to mind God's salvation of Jerusalem from the Assyrians, and is linked to Jesus' quotation from that same Isaiah during the "cleansing" of the Temple. The "good news" is that YHVH reigns; I Will Be Whatever I Will Be is God (with all that this means for inclusion).

Goodness and Sin

In addition to the terms "beginning" and "news," we must also look at the word "good" with Jewish eyes, or more specifically, Torah eyes, the terms to which a true "radical" like Jesus would have wanted to return. What does it mean to be "good" in Torah?

Most Christians, I fear, would say that, for Jews, goodness means strict obedience to Torah law; this "party line" was propagated in the days of the family split, and is still heard today. Post-70 Judaism did emphasize the Torah and *mitzvoth* as a way of saving Jewish life, but Jesus was a pre-70 Jew, and Mark is laboring mightily to show him as returning to a more basic Torah approach, especially regarding such an essential idea as "goodness."

The first use of the word "good" (*tov* in Hebrew) in the Jewish scripture comes very early, in Genesis 1, verses 3 and 4: "God said, 'Let there be light,' and there was light. God saw that the light was good." The same word, *tov*, is also used for moral goodness in biblical Hebrew. As the first creation story progresses, the word *tov* continues to be used until a pattern develops. Generally speaking, God seems to create in four steps: first God "speaks" something into being; next it is "so." Following this, God "sees" this creation, and then sees that it is "good."

Here we find a key to the notion of goodness in Torah. Remember that this is Genesis 1; the commandments will not be given until Exodus 20. Thus, whatever goodness may or may not be, it is not yet about following the *mitzvoth*. Rather, the four steps of God's creation reveal a very different understanding of goodness, evil, and sin.

First, let us ask what it means to be "so." God says, "Let the earth sprout vegetation," and skyscrapers don't shoot up! He says, "Let the earth bring forth every kind of living creature," and bicycles don't appear! To be "so" in Torah terms means to be *exactly* what one *is* as God has created one, no more, no less.

Now, being just "so" may seem like a fairly easy task for a tree or an animal. Human beings, however, seem to very often have trouble "being so," being who we truly are as God made us. The next step calls for seeing that "so-ness," for true knowledge of who and what we are. But there is even a step beyond this. It is not sufficient for us to see who we are as God made us; we must see, as God does, that it is *good* for us to be exactly that. Self-knowledge is hard enough. How many among us do see ourselves, only to despair at what we see or even despise ourselves, wishing always to be something different?

Here in Genesis we have a Torah definition of goodness which is process, befitting a God who is process. To be good in terms of this God is to see and rejoice in who and what we truly are, as this unfolds over time. Conversely, we also see here the meaning of evil in Torah terms. It is not essentially, the breaking of *mitzvoth*. If we follow the four steps backwards, we find that the opposite of goodness is instead to be blind to who we truly are as God made us, or, even worse, to see our true nature, but not consider it good.

The Hebrew word for sin, *chet*, at root has nothing to do with religion or morality. It is rather a term from archery or javelin, and means "to miss the mark." In Torah, sin has much more to do with inaccuracy than with the breaking of a law. If one sees something as good when it is not, and acts accordingly, one has been inaccurate. If one does not recognize the true nature of someone (or of oneself) and acts upon that false view, of course the results will not be positive.

The various commandments of Torah are like the proverbial finger pointing at the moon. One should not steal, because to take someone's possessions from him/her does not recognize the true reality of ownership. But even beyond this, if one truly sees oneself as essentially good, who would ever steal from another? Who would ever covet if he or she were fine as they are?

On the other hand, if one sees oneself as inadequate, as essentially less than others, this important inaccuracy will produce all sorts of harmful emotions and actions. Such people (and who is not among them?) may find themselves, for instance, bent on acquiring many possessions to make themselves feel successful, leading to covetousness and theft. The anger generated by self-hate is what produces violence.

In Torah terms, terms that Mark's Jesus is promulgating, the primary state of "so" for human beings is their status as the image and likeness of YHVH. People will be whatever they will

be, as God made them. This status of every human as an image/
likeness of YHVH makes our judging of other individuals (and
of ourselves) out of the question. Specifically, Jesus' identification with those on the bottom of the judgment scale—
prostitutes, tax gatherers, the very poor, the illegitimate—and
his wide acceptance of competing interests—Hellenized Jews
and Hebraic Jews, zealots and former collaborationists, even
Gentiles and Samaritans—all flows from this view of God as
Ehyeh and the Genesis 1 definition of goodness.

Such a view of "goodness" does not mean that Jesus does
not believe in sin. Often he advises those he counsels or heals
to "sin no more." But, as a true radical, Jesus returns to the
root Torah-notion of what sin is; he looks to the moon, not
to the legal finger pointing to it. Due largely to the judgmentalism of human society, various groups and classes of people
find their basic goodness as an image of God denied from day
one. (As a child of "apparent" dubious parentage, Jesus would
have known this phenomenon first-hand.) As a faith, Judaism
did not hold to reward of punishment in an afterlife; subsequently many Jews believed that reward or punishment came
in this life, giving rise to the all-too-convenient notion that
the poor deserved their lot.

The term "good" in "good news" needs to be reexamined
in this context if it is to be true to its basic Jewishness. The
"news" is the reestablishment of the basic Torah concept of
"goodness," as we see exemplified in the life and teachings of
Jesus the Anointed ("Christ"), "the son of God."

Anointing

The term "Christ" (Greek "Christos") is a translation of the
Hebrew *messiach*, or "anointed," and again, is a term that needs
re-Judaization for Christians. Several different types of people
were anointed in Jewish life and history, notably priests, prophets, kings, and corpses. In Judaism, priests came exclusively
from the tribe of Levi; in both gospel genealogies (Matthew's

and Luke's), Jesus is described as a member of the tribe of Judah. His "anointing" would not be as priest. As for prophet and king: Jesus is described as descendant of King David, himself a member of the tribe of Judah, and it is clear that he sees himself, and that many others see him, as a prophet.

In contemporary life, we tend to think of a prophet as one who foretells the future, but this was not primarily the case for the Judaism of Jesus' day. The Hebrew term for prophet, *nev'ar*, means "to speak" or "to speak for." A prophet was one who spoke for God, on God's behalf, sometimes carrying a message about the future, but more often exhortations about the present. It is clear that Jesus considers himself to speak for the God named *Ehyeh-Asher-Ehyeh*.

Still, where, if anywhere, do we see an actual anointing of Jesus of Nazareth as either king or prophet? In Mark 14, Jesus is at meal with a man described as "Simon the leper." A woman enters and anoints Jesus' head with costly oil. Some of those present reprimand her for extravagance, but Jesus praises her, claiming that she anticipates his burial (Mark 14:3–9).

There are several notable elements to this story from a Jewish point of view. First, Jesus is visiting and sharing a meal with a leper. Lepers were among the list of Torah outcasts; the fact that this Simon had not been forced from the company of others or into a leper colony must have meant that he was a man of considerable wealth and influence. Even so, considering the dominant fear of leprosy, chances are that he would have had few visitors. True to his vision of God, Jesus does not condemn this man for simply being who he will be.

Second, Jesus' anointing comes at the hands of a woman. Although women were by no means outcasts in Torah terms, in Jewish society, as in most ancient cultures, they were relegated to a second-class status, at best. In Mark, Jesus does not have women among his inner circle of Twelve, but it is plain that women did occupy an important place in his movement. A woman, Mary of Magdala, is the first to encounter the risen Jesus. When the disciples come upon Jesus having a rather prolonged conversation with a Samaritan woman, they are "amazed," not that he was speaking with a Samaritan, but with a woman, and only to this woman does Jesus plainly and directly state that he is the Messiah (John 4:4–26).

The story of Jesus' anointing by a woman is repeated, with variations, in all four of the gospels. In John, the site shifts to the home of Lazarus, and there Mary, the host's sister, anoints Jesus; in Luke, the woman is an unnamed "sinner" (John 12:1–8). The point in any case is well made: Jesus' embrace of non-judgmentalism is emphasized by the role of the marginalized and the outcast in his anointing.

A further point is made by the apparent unwillingness of those present to respond to the anointing positively, for, after all, the Hebrew term for "Anointed" is *messiach*. For a Jew in Jesus' very public position to be anointed had specific ramifications that any Jew would have recognized. By implication, the Gospel writers are showing that Simon the Leper, who is a Pharisee, cannot get past his own beliefs even when they damage him, even when Jesus reaches beyond those Torah boundaries to him.

The Torah says that those with leprosy were to be expelled from the camp of Israel; in later times, they had to dwell outside of any city or town, including Jerusalem.[28] In other words, Simon would never have been able to enter the Temple in Jerusalem, and, if the Torah were kept, anyone having contact even with a leper's house was to be considered also unclean. The season of the holy days, during which Jesus visits Simon, must have been a particularly lonely and bitter time for this man, but Jesus disregards all the injunctions and visits him nonetheless.

Still, with all this, Mark's Simon does not rejoice and join in the obvious Jewish meaning of the woman's anointing of Jesus; in Luke, he even doubts Jesus' status as prophet, saying to himself that ". . . he should know who and what sort of woman is touching him, that she is a sinner" (Luke 7:39).

Here we see another illustration of the family split to which

Mark's Gospel responds. The "other side of the family," the Pharisees and their supporters, refuse to recognize the anointing of a man as inclusive as Jesus, even when they themselves are the beneficiaries of such inclusion, and, in a sort of perverse hierarchy of outcasts, Simon looks down upon the woman anointing Jesus, even calling Jesus' authenticity as prophet into question. In each gospel account of this anointing, Jesus makes comment about his impending death, implying that he knew well the possible results of his stand of radical inclusion.

In Jewish tradition, there are ways other than a physical anointing with oil to be commissioned as prophet. Often we are told only that "the word of YHVH came to" the individual; Isaiah is made prophet by the touch of a burning ember to his lips by a winged seraph (Isa. 6:6–7). Mark's Gospel portrays Jesus as having that sort of experience of the divine during his baptism by his cousin, John.

Baptism and the Baptist

During his lifetime and for several centuries thereafter there remained a strong belief on the part of many Jews that John himself was the *messiach*. As late as the Gospel of John (90s–100s CE), the writer felt the necessity to reinforce the Baptist's position as "not himself the light," but someone who had come to "bear witness to the light" (John 1:8). After its introduction, Mark's Gospel begins, not with Jesus, but with John the Baptist:

> In the prophet Isaiah it stands written:
> I am sending my herald ahead of you;
> he will prepare your way.
> A voice cries in the wilderness,
> "Prepare the way of the Lord;
> clear a straight path for him." (Mark 1:2–3)

Mark also begins by emphasizing John's non-messianic role. He also immediately establishes a link between Jesus, John, and the prophet Isaiah whose stand on inclusion and the place of *mitzvoth* in Jewish life is so crucial to the post-70 position of the Jesus Jews. The quote in question is from Isaiah 40:

Comfort, oh comfort My people,
Says your God.
Speak tenderly to Jerusalem,
And declare to her
That her term of service is over,
That her iniquity is expiated;
For she has received at the hand of the Lord
Double for all her sins.

A voice rings out:
"Clear in the desert
A road for the Lord!
Level in the wilderness
A highway for out God!" (Isa. 40:1–3)

If one takes Mark's quote from Isaiah in its historical context, we see it joined clearly to the siege of Jerusalem, or perhaps to two sieges—the one which the city survived (but not without great cost) and the one which, to the Jews of Jesus' day, Isaiah had foreseen, the Babylonian victory of Jeremiah's day. In either case, by opening with Isaiah, Mark launches his first foray in the fight for the future of Judaism: John the Baptist was preparing the way for a return to a vision of God and of inclusion which, if accepted, could have altered the bleak future of Jerusalem and the Jewish people, just as had happened in Isaiah's time. But he himself is only the herald of this change; its principal messenger is Jesus.

Mark portrays John as a sort of runaway Essene. He lived in the desert apart from all, as did the Essenes, but unlike those early monastics, John takes an active role in the affairs of men and women, proclaiming "a baptism of repentance" (Mark 1:4). Again, one needs to examine this phenomenon with Jewish eyes; the idea of being submerged in water "in token of repentance" was not new with John or with the Jesus Jews. It follows the time-honored Jewish tradition of *tevilah*.

Tevilah in Hebrew means "immersion," and it has always been a staple of Jewish life. The Torah specifies several circumstances under which people should participate in this ritual immersion, including the contraction of leprosy (Lev. 13:3), the discharge of any bodily fluid, including semen during intercourse, menstruation (Lev. 15:2–19), childbirth (Lev. 12:2), and contact with a corpse (Lev. 22:4). In addition, *tevilah* became commonplace for those who considered themselves in a state of sin and who had followed the Torah prescriptions regarding this state, to engage in *tevilah* as a symbol of their new state without that sin, of their "cleanness." Traditionally, *tevilah* could occur anywhere there was a natural body of water—a pond, lake, ocean, or, in the case of John's work, the Jordan River. In modern Judaism, a pool, called a *mikveh*, constructed for the purpose, is usually used.

Jewish tradition maintains that forgiveness for acts committed between human beings must be sought at that level; only the types of sins one might commit against God, as described in Torah, could be forgiven by God, and such forgiveness would be accomplished according to ritual detailed in Torah, involving sacrifice, sin-offering, etc. *Tevilah* does not forgive sins; it is meant rather as a symbolic, personal reinforcement for the sinner once his/her sins have been forgiven. It is better to think of this ritual washing not as Jewish confession, but rather as a spiritual commencement ceremony. The graduate has already earned the degree; the ceremony is meant as public sign and affirmation of this.

Going down into and re-emerging from a body of water clearly would have further significance for a Jew: it would recall the waters of pre-creation in Genesis 1:1, as well as the passing of the Jewish people through the Red Sea to escape bondage and through the Jordan to enter the Land of the Promise. In each case, new life, a rebirth, was symbolized. John's proclamation that he baptized with water, but that his successor would baptize with the Holy Spirit (Mark 1:8) is a rather straightforward reference to the spirit of God sweeping over the waters in the first creation account (Gen. 1:2).

For John, then, to preach a *tevilah* of repentance means two things: First, he is urging his fellow Jews to seek forgiveness, from God or from each other, for any sin they may have committed, and, second, to reinforce that forgiveness by a public act of *tevilah*. It may safely be assumed that men who were (merely) seeking ritual cleansing after events such as those described in Leviticus could also have used John's natural *mikveh*, as well as they could have any other.

To this spot comes Jesus in Mark 1:9. It is his first appearance in that gospel, and in it he seeks *tevilah*! Matthew portrays John as protesting this, "It is I who should be baptized by you." Jesus merely responds that "it is right to do all that God requires" (Matt. 3:13–17). However, Mark, the earliest canonical gospel, says nothing of such a protest. It is interesting to note that God, in the Torah, does not require of the people *tevilah* for the forgiveness of sin; the high priest only would immerse himself in preparation for Yom Kippur, that is, Day of Atonement, services. God requires *tevilah* only for some states of ritual or personal impurity.

Son of God

Mark describes the scene of Jesus' *tevilah* in this way:

> It was at this time that Jesus came from Nazareth in
> Galilee to be baptized by John. As he was coming out
> of the water, he saw the heavens break open and the

Spirit descend on him, like a dove. And a voice from heaven: "You are my beloved son; in you I take delight." (Mark 1:9–11)

To Mark's Jewish audience, the reference to Genesis 1 would be obvious and one already associated with *tevilah*: in the forgiveness of sin or the restoration of ritual purity, human beings are made anew, given new life. This idea of re-creation must have rung with both irony and hope in the dark light of the events of 70. Could the Jewish people be recreated, reinvigorated? Did the Jesus Jews offer a means toward this?

Particularly fascinating is the voice from heaven, stating that Jesus is God's delighted-in son. As with all things in Mark, this, too, has a particular Jewish resonance.

Looking ahead to Luke's gospel (written about ten years after Mark's), we see a genealogy of Jesus, beginning with Jesus himself and tracing his lineage back through kings and patriarchs to Adam. The writer uses the repeated phrase "son of" to outline his background; as the list approaches its close, we encounter:

Shem, son of Noah, son of Lamech, son of Methuselah, son of Enoch, son of Jared, son of Mahalaleel, son of Cainan, son of Enosh, son of Seth, son of Adam, *son of God. (italics mine)* (Luke 3:36–38)

That Adam should be called "son of God" is no surprise, as he is God's direct creation, and had no human father. It is significant, however, that the first sentence of Mark describes Jesus as the son of God. Combine this with the images of creation and exodus, and one can see Mark making very early the point that Jesus represents a new Adam, a new beginning for Jews and for humanity as a whole. The intriguing question does remain: Why did Jesus seek *tevilah*? The voice from heaven may offer a clue.

Jesus' affinity for the outcasts, the sinners, the unclean is well established in the gospels. What is often overlooked is the possibility of Jesus' membership in that marginalized group himself. As someone of dubious parentage, one described as a "son of Mary" rather than of a father, Jesus might well have been seen by those who knew him as another possible son of Alphaeus. As such, the Torah injunction would have been clear: Deuteronomy 23:2 forbids membership in the Jewish people to such a one. It must be emphasized that the text indicates anyone *conceived* outside of wedlock; the marital status of the woman at the time of the birth is irrelevant. If there had been suspicions that Jesus' mother had been pregnant before her marriage, unproven suspicions alone might not have been enough to "outcast" Jesus, but certainly enough to cast a pall over his life, to marginalize him, especially true if Jesus were a member of the ultra-strict *natzorim* clan. The twenty-first century is by no means the originator of the sentiment "People *will* talk."

In this sense, Jesus' seeking of *tevilah* from his cousin John takes on new dimensions. If Jesus was viewed by himself or others as illegitimate, ritual immersion would not negate the Torah injunction against him. Still, it might represent a symbolic act on Jesus' part, a surrender of the life of someone troubled by acts outside of his control to a God he hoped would embrace him nonetheless. Perhaps for Jesus son of Mary, Jesus son of Alphaeus, God was the only father he could hope for. The fact that he approaches a family member for this immersion, someone highly likely to know his story, only increases the poignancy of the act.

John, we can see, has plainly departed from the Essenes in preaching and offering *tevilah* to the public; traditionally, Essenes separated themselves in closed communities, convinced, not unlike modern survivalists, that the world was doomed to an imminent Armageddon, one from which the Essenes would emerge to lead people back to strict Torah righteousness. For John, someone of clear Essenic tendencies, to leave his desert of ritual purity and essentially evangelize would indicate a softening of this view of the outcast, for to the Essenes, almost everyone was ritually impure, almost everyone was an outcast.

From this perspective, we hear the voice of God in this scene as one of nearly heartbreaking importance: "You are my beloved son; in you I take delight." Jesus the illegitimate is embraced by God as a "beloved son," but not only that, as a source of God's delight! Small wonder Jesus would identify God as "Abba," "Daddy." The God of Moses, the God of Isaiah, the God whose name is I Will Be Whatever I Will Be is not bound by anything, including the Torah. As the Genesis imagery indicates, Jesus is being re-created; he is being freed from bondage and delivered into the land of promise. He is a new Adam, and no less legitimate than he.

In his Marcan role as symbol of the Jewish people, after his *tevilah* Jesus is "at once" driven by the Spirit into the wilderness for forty days, where he is tempted by Satan (Mark 1:12–13). What could this temptation consist of? Although latter gospels give detail, Mark does not. Could we imagine that Jesus struggles with his newfound sonship? After all, it runs contrary to Torah, and Jesus is a *natzor*? If it is really true that the "outcast" such as he have a place among God's people, what then should Jesus do with this knowledge? What meaning can it have for others who are marginalized?

This wilderness experience, of course, parallels that of the Jewish exodus from Egypt. Just as important, however, is the view of Jesus as symbol of Israel in Mark's day. Just as Jesus was "driven" into the wilderness and tempted, just so the Jewish people were then experiencing a time of wilderness, in which there was great hardship and no Temple, a time when they would be "tempted" by the Pharisaic response to the events of 70. Significantly, the destruction of Jerusalem and the Temple occur approximately forty years after Jesus' execution. In the context of the fractious debate in the Jewish family, Mark seems to be asking that Jesus' lead be followed, and that his life serve as a model in the controversy over how to now be the people of God.

But how did that model come to be formed? What were the circumstances and experiences that formed Jesus the Anointed, embracer of the outcast?

CHAPTER 6

Becoming What He Will Be

There were three who always walked with the Lord.
Mary, his mother; Mary, her sister;
And Miriam of Magdala, who was called his companion;
For Miriam is his sister, his mother, his companion.

Jean-Yves Leloup[29]

IN THE FIRST CHAPTER OF MARK'S GOSPEL, JESUS' PUBLIC LIFE
is introduced by a single phrase of great importance: "After
John had been arrested . . ." (Mark 1:14). Mark sees no need
to describe the circumstances of that arrest here, as his audience would have no doubt already known them. Rather, the
point being made here is one of respect and succession.

Before the arrest, Jesus was last seen going into the wilderness; now he "comes into Galilee" proclaiming "the Gospel
of God" (Mark 1:14). Apparently, Jesus had been elsewhere,
presumably the wilderness, at the time of John's arrest. In any
event, he does not decide to begin his work until John is no
longer able to do his. This reinforces the notion that Jesus was
essentially a follower of John and took up his mantle when his
cousin was arrested, coming out of the desert as had John.

Upon arriving on the scene, Jesus now proclaims, "The
time has arrived; the kingdom of God is upon you. Repent
and believe the Gospel" (Mark 1:15). In the tradition of John
and the Essenes, Jesus insists that the time of great conflagra-
tion has arrived, a point surely not lost on Mark's post-70 audience. However, the gospel, the "good news" that Jesus will
preach will prove to be somewhat of a departure from John's
message.

The Hebrew term for repentance, *charatah*, means literally to "take a new path." The path which Jesus will espouse is in many ways quite new and in others a return to basics: he will call people back to I Will Be Whatever I Will Be, and to a vision of an outcast-less society, à la Isaiah and the salvation of the Temple in that prophet's day. Jesus does not baptize, for it is precisely the labeling of people as unclean that he will work against. Apparently John, an Essene at heart, preaches a return to strict observance of the *mitzvoth*, running afoul of the royal authority when he insists on that observance for all. Herod Philip, one of the sons of Herod the Great, had been granted by Rome reign over the region of Judea, and his brother, Herod Antipas, had been named tetrarch of Galilee. Philip's wife, Herodias, had left him for Herod, who married her in direct contravention of Torah: "Do not uncover the nakedness of your brother's wife" (Lev. 18:16). The only exception to this *mitzvah* would occur if the first husband had died, leaving his brother a responsibility to marry the widow in order to care for her and "raise children to his brother" (Deut. 25:5). Herodias' first husband was very much alive; John the Baptist publicly criticized this new marriage as being against Torah, and ultimately paid for this with his life (Mark 6:14–28).

Discipleship

Jesus' first four disciples are called in this chapter: Simon and his brother Andrew plying their trade as fishermen; another set of brothers, James and John, mending nets. Of these four, three are men with traditional Hebrew names (Shimon, "to hear," and Jacob—in English, James, and John, "gracious"), as well as one with a Greek name (Andrew—"manly"). Mark implicitly makes the point with this inclusiveness that Hellenization, with its tendencies toward a more liberal, more assimilated form of Judaism, apparently does not bother Jesus, nor does the more traditional approach. There are no outcasts.

John's Gospel maintains that Andrew was a disciple of John the Baptist, who sought out Jesus after John's description of him as "the Lamb of God" (John 1:35–40). In that gospel, Andrew brings his brother to Jesus. Mark, however, tells a different story; here it is Jesus who approaches the two brothers at their work, and not until after the arrest of John the Baptist. In Mark's version, disciples do not leave the Baptist in order to follow Jesus; rather, Jesus is taking up the work of his imprisoned cousin. Apparently Andrew, for one, had returned to his workaday life, since it would seem highly unlikely that anyone who ran afoul of a Herod would leave prison alive. This would account for the enthusiasm with which Andrew, at least, immediately left his nets and followed Jesus; it might have well been the re-mustering of a cause thought lost, but now regrouping for another try, which touched a chord in him, and perhaps in his brother as well.

As for James and John, Jesus seems not only to know them, but actually to be related. Their father was a fisherman named Zebedee, with whom they worked (Mark 1:19–20). In his chapter fifteen, Mark names some of the women standing at the foot of Jesus' cross: Mary of Magdala, Mary the mother of James and Joses, and Salome (Mark 15:40). Jesus' own mother is not mentioned. This could be meant to show James, Joses, and Salome all as children of this Mary, or Salome as a separate character. Matthew's Gospel puts the same two Marys at the scene as well as a third unnamed woman, "the mother of Zebedee's sons" (Matt. 27:55). John is the only Evangelist to have Mary, Jesus' mother, present; with her are her unnamed sister, as well as Mary of Magdala, and a woman described as "Mary, wife of Cleopas" (John 19:25). If we therefore take all three Gospels' indication of familial relationship together, it is possible to conclude that Salome is indeed the mother of James and John, and likewise the sister of Jesus' mother, and thus his aunt. James and John then would be Jesus' first cousins, and, as such, related to John the Baptist as well.

There is another possibility, however. As we have already

seen, a James and a Joses are listed among Jesus' brothers in Mark 6:3, the same spot in which Jesus is rather caustically referred to as the son of Mary, rather than of a father. Although John is the only gospel writer to place Jesus' mother at the crucifixion, Mark and Matthew do put "Mary, the mother of James and Joses," there. Mark even calls her the mother of the "younger" James, clearly implying that this woman is Jesus' mother as well. Because of the lack of punctuation in the Greek, the Salome listed in Mark could be seen as yet another child of that Mary, a sister to James and Joses. If this were the case, Jesus would have been an uncle to James and John.

But the intricacies of possibility continue. Matthew's description of the women at the cross includes Mary of Magdala, "Mary the mother of 'James' and 'Joses' and the mother of the sons of Zebedee" (Matt. 27:56), and once again, there is no punctuation to help clarify. Is Matthew maintaining that Mary the mother of James and Joses and the mother of Zebedee's sons are the same woman? If so, why would he not name the mother of James and John, when he did so for the other two women? And, if such is the case, then James and John would be Jesus' half-brothers.

Looking at Matthew and Mark, therefore, Jesus could be uncle, cousin, or half-brother to these two disciples.

John, for his part, however, muddies the waters further by adding that a sister to Jesus' mother was present on Golgotha. Here there is no mention of a James, Joses, or Salome. Rather the text reads, "his mother was standing with her sister, Mary wife of Cleopas, and Mary of Magdala" (John 19:25). There are several possible interpretations of this text. One is that there were four women present at the crucifixion: (1) Jesus' mother, (2) her unnamed sister, (3) Mary, wife of Cleopas, and (4) Mary Magdalene. However, the text could also be read to mean that Mary, wife of Cleopas, is sister to Mary, mother of Jesus. But this would seem highly unlikely; would one nuclear family be apt to name give two daughters the same name?

One clue to this mystery may well lie in John's use of the

term Cleopas or Clopas. This Greek word, related to "alphaeus," is likewise a Hellenic version of the Hebrew *chalpai,* meaning "unknown." Whoever John's Mary is, her husband was "unknown," a polite way of describing her as a woman of questionable sexual morals. As we have already seen, the term "alphaeus" is used to describe the father of the apostle James the Less, apparently brother to Joses and Jesus, and a son of Mary.

I would like to raise the perhaps startling possibility that a literary device is being used by these writers, and that, in fact, all these Mary's—Mary the mother of Jesus, Mary the mother of James and Joses, Mary the wife of unknown, and Mary of Magdala—are *the same woman,* as is the mother of Zebedee's sons. She also may be the same woman who anoints Jesus, at least in Luke's Gospel.

In light of the single identity of Mary, mother of Jesus, and Mary, mother of James, Joses, and Salome, the fact that the apostle James the Less is called "son of unknown" would seem to make a statement about the perceived moral status of his mother. If his mother, Mary, had indeed conceived more than one child out of wedlock, small wonder then for her to be called "Mary, wife of unknown."

The fourth Mary, Mary of Magdala, presents her own set of circumstances. Magdala was a very ancient town in Galilee, north of Tiberias, on the western shore of the lake. Talmud, the most important and sacred of Jewish texts after Scripture, states that the town was eventually destroyed by the Romans in response to the moral depravity of its residents.[30] Traditionally, Mary of Magdala, Mary Magdalene, has been identified with the aforementioned "sinful" woman in Luke 7 who anointed Jesus' feet with oil and with her tears, probably based on Mark's description of Mary of Magdala as having been exorcised of seven demons by Jesus (Mark 16:9). But this woman is never actually named.

Considering the Talmudic description of Magdala as a center of moral depravity, it is not difficult to imagine the type of behavior that might have characterized Mary of Magdala, described as possessed of seven demons. The number seven in Jewish custom indicates totality, as there were seven days of creation. So, then, to describe Mary as seven-times possessed is to indicate total depravity, from which sexual conduct would certainly not be excluded. In short, Magdala was a "red-light town," and Mary of Magdala what would have been described in a quainter age as "a fallen women."

To view this information in its entirety: We are presented with four characters, all of the same name, in a series of works written as Jewish scripture, a literary form known for its rich symbolic content. One of these women has at least two sons named James and Joses; the second has a famous son who has brothers by that same name—and both women are named Mary! One among the inner circle of this famous figure is likewise named James, described as a brother to that figure; he is of questionable birth (son of unknown).

Additionally, the mother of James and Joses could also have two more sons, another James and a John, by a man named Zebedee. As far as the world knows, the famous figure himself was conceived outside of wedlock, his own townsfolk describing him as "son of" his mother, not of his father as would be traditional. In one account this woman is awarded a sister of the exact same name, whose husband is called "unknown." The one consistent element in all of this is the fourth Mary, Mary of Magdala, the term "Magdala" or "Magdalene" being synonymous with moral depravity. She is the only Mary present in all three versions of the crucifixion in which the women are named.

The literary evidence seems to indicate four different "takes" on *the same woman*: She is Mary, mother of Jesus the Messiah, a son who, as far as the world knew, was conceived out of wedlock and thus a Torah outcast; she is likewise Mary, mother as well of James, Joses, Simon, Judah, and daughters, the first by an unknown father, making her children outcast as well. She may also be the mother of Zebedee's sons, and, depending on the nature of that relationship, those two apostles might also fall under the same Torah proscription. She is Mary, the sister whose husband is likewise unknown. And finally she is Mary Magdalene, the sexual sinner.

It is not impossible to envision a scenario in which all these Mary's are one. Perhaps Mary, once pregnant with Jesus outside of marriage, receives the accompanying reputation. Tradition has it that Joseph, Mary's husband, dies relatively early in Jesus' life; the New Testament never shows him present beyond Jesus' twelfth year. He is not mentioned in Jesus' adulthood; indeed, when the family attempts to see Jesus its members are described only as "his mother and his brothers" (Mark 3:31).

With such a reputation, the chances of Mary entering into another marriage would have been slim. Already branded a whore, she does what she must do to maintain herself and her son. She has other children, their fathers "unknown." The term "Magdalene" need not necessarily signify a resident of the town of Magdala, but could have become a euphemism for a "loose woman," the sort the town was famed for. Could it be that the gospel writers, in an attempt to reinforce Jesus' status as the embracer of the outcast and sinner, are all subtly indicating that God chose just such a sinner as the mother of the Anointed?

One further piece of scriptural evidence seems to place a seal on the concept of four Marys as one. In his genealogy of Jesus, Matthew lists Jesus' direct ancestors from Abraham to Joseph, husband of Mary. Almost all the names on the long list are male, with five exceptions: (1) Tamar, mother of Perez and Zerah by Judah, son of the patriarch Jacob; (2) Rahab, the Canaanite prostitute; (3) Ruth, Boaz's wife; (4) "the wife of Uriah the Hittite," that is, Bathsheba, mother of King Solomon, and finally (5) Mary herself. Clearly, all the forefathers of Jesus had mothers; why then are only these five singled out by Matthew in this way? (Matt. 1:1–16).

Tamar, the main figure in the 38th chapter of Genesis, is, at first, part of a marriage arranged by Judah for his son, Er. Er dies, however, and, at Judah's insistence, and in keeping with the *mitzvah*, Onan, Er's younger brother, marries Tamar. Once again, the husband dies. Judah tells Tamar to return to her father's house as a widow, promising his youngest son as a husband as soon as he comes of age, a promise Judah fails to keep. Tamar then disguises herself as sacred prostitute, common in Canaanite religion, and waits by the roadside for Judah, who avails himself of her services. Judah promises the prostitute a kid goat in payment, and the disguised Tamar keeps Judah's identifying seal, cord, and staff as a pledge of this deal. She then disappears before the debt can be settled.

Not long after, it is reported to Judah that his daughter-in-law had "played the harlot" and was pregnant. She is about to be burned alive, when the seal, cord, and staff are brought forth. Judah, himself now a widower, must keep and care for Tamar, although the text is quick to add that "he was not intimate with her again" (Gen. 38:1–26).

The story of Rahab appears in Chapter 2 of the book of Joshua. Joshua had sent two spies into the region of Jericho, where they "lodged" in the house of Rahab, a prostitute. Somehow the king of Jericho discovered this, and sent men to apprehend them. Rahab hid the spies, telling the soldiers that they had already left and then informed the spies of the general paralysis of the city, awestruck at the success of Israel from the Red Sea incident to the present. She asked that she and her family be spared in return for the aid she had given the spies; they agreed. When Jericho fell, Rahab the prostitute and her family were thus the sole survivors and were given membership in the community of Israel.

The biblical figure Ruth, from the book of the same name, hardly seems to fit the pattern of the previous two women. Indeed, Ruth the Moabitess has been held up since antiquity as a model of the loyal and virtuous woman who, after the death of her husband, refuses to leave her Jewish mother-in-law, Naomi. Accompanying her back to Israel, Ruth gleans the fields of one of Naomi's relative, the well-off Boaz. At this point in the story, Naomi gives Ruth some rather unusual instructions:

> "This evening he [Boaz] will be winnowing barley on the threshing floor. So bathe, anoint yourself, dress up, and go down to the threshing floor. Do not make yourself known to the man before he has finished eating and drinking. But when he lies down, take notice of the place where he does so. Then go, uncover and uncover his feet and lie down. He will tell you what to do."
> (Ruth 3:2–4 NAB)

It does not take a great deal of imagination to get the point of Naomi's advice. She knows that Boaz has already noticed the attractive Ruth, who is considerably younger than he. Naomi basically tells her daughter-in-law to crawl into bed with him. One must remember that in ancient times, and indeed in most time periods before our own, men and women led almost completely separate existences. "Dating" as we know it would have been unthinkable to almost everyone from antiquity through to the early twentieth century. Most marriages were arranged, and the idea of a woman "lying down" with a man and uncovering any part of his body would have earned her the reputation as a whore. Naomi is taking a dreadful chance with Ruth's future. Luckily for both of them, Boaz is as virtuous as Ruth. When he awakens and demands an explanation, Ruth answers that she is his kinswoman and asks that he "spread the corner of his cloak" over her, a sign of coming under one's protection. Boaz, as a kinsman of Ruth's dead husband, has the Torah responsibility to marry Ruth and raise children to his dead kin, a responsibility he accepts (Ruth 3:7–14). Of course, Ruth has left him little choice; if they had been seen or if word had leaked out about their encounter, both their reputations would have been irreparably damaged, hers more than his, in this male-dominated environment; but

Boaz, too, would have been cast in a bad light, as one who took unfair advantage of an impoverished woman gleaning his fields, as well as a man unwilling to do his Torah duty to his dead relative.

The story of David and Bathsheba is well known. Strolling on the high, flat rooftop of his palace, David spies Bathsheba bathing and is taken by her beauty. Upon inquiry he finds that she is the wife of one of his commanders in the field, Uriah the Hittite. Nonetheless, David summons Bathsheba; "she came to him and he lay with her." Soon she finds herself pregnant. David tries to cover up his paternity by recalling Uriah from the front, supposedly for a report on the progress of the war. He then urges Uriah to go home, but Uriah refuses, renouncing the comforts of home for himself while his men suffer hardship in the field. The next night, David continues to scheme to hide his fault. He gets Uriah drunk, but still Uriah refuses to enter his home or to sleep with his wife. David then conspires with his chief general, Joab, to place Uriah in the front line, with orders to Joab to fall back "so that he may be killed." With Uriah dead, David marries Bathsheba (2 Sam. 11).

Although the prophet Nathan later upbraids David for his behavior and David repents, the child conceived of the illicit union dies in infancy. Still Bathsheba remains David's wife, and becomes the mother of his son, Solomon, who succeeds him. The royal line of the house of David proceeds through Bathsheba, and indeed it is who she makes possible the Solomonic Golden Age of Israel.

There is no account of Bathsheba's reaction to David's original proposition. There is no mention of her protesting, and there are instances in Jewish scripture in which women do just that in similar circumstances. At the same time, David is an absolute monarch. How free was Bathsheba to refuse him?

Tamar, Rahab, Ruth, Bathsheba: of all the women in Jesus' remote ancestry, only these are mentioned by name in Matthew's genealogy—not the great matriarchs, such as Sarah or Rebecca or Rachel. The first three women in Matthew's list are not even Jews, and the fourth was married to a Gentile. Even more significant is the type of tie that binds them all: sexual impropriety or immorality, by the standards of the times. Tamar, disguised as a prostitute, conceives of her own father-in-law; Rahab is a prostitute by profession; Ruth throws herself, body-first, at Boaz; Bathsheba cheats on her husband and indirectly causes his death. And the fifth and final woman on the list? Mary, the mother of Jesus!

An even closer look reveals another bond between these women: each was virtually forced into their defining acts by the circumstances of their lives. Tamar has been abandoned by Judah after being twice a widow to his sons; he had failed to follow the Torah in regard to Tamar and his third son. Ruth is in the direst of circumstances, trying to support her mother-in-law, and is again seeking only what the Torah describes as her right. Bathsheba is under the heavy pressure of sexual advance by an all-powerful male. And Rahab, who was "in the business," had so little identification with the people of Jericho, with their likely attitude toward her, that she actually aids the Israelites in their complete destruction of the city.

In short, each of these women was an outcast; all bent or broke the *mitzvoth*. But without them, the cause of Israel would have been far less advanced. Without Rahab's help, the spies would have been captured, interrogated, and who knows what havoc could then have been wreaked on the Israelites? From Tamar and Ruth eventually comes King David, and from Bathsheba the legendary King Solomon. And from Mary comes Jesus, the Anointed.

The statement being made about Mary by her inclusion in Matthew's list would be obvious to all Jews hearing the Gospel. None of the previous four female ancestors were merely *believed* to be sexually improper or worse, when in fact they were not. They each had clearly done what they had done; were what they were. There is more to Mary's place in Matthew's genealogy than the mistaken judgment by her peers that it is by another human being that she is with child illegitimately, for there is also in this group of five the unmistakable connection of victimization, by men, by power, by society. God used these victims, these outcasts—all five of them—throughout Jewish history to further the cause of Jewish life in roles that only they can fulfill. They had to be whatever they would be.

Please note that nothing in this hypothesis concerning Mary necessarily excludes the reality of the incarnation. Mary's declaration in Luke's Annunciation scene that she had not "known" a man need not indicate absolute virginity, but simply that she had not the *recent* sexual relations necessary for pregnancy (Luke 1:34). Matthew, the assembler of the genealogy we have been examining, merely states that "she found she was with child through the Holy Spirit" (Matt. 1:18).

So the possibilities abound. Was Mary widowed, like Tamar and Ruth, and like them thus forced to use her body for survival? Was she, like Bathsheba, pressured by someone of power in her community? Or was she, like Rahab, a prostitute forced into that life by a reputation that followed the conception of Christ? Or was that her occupation all along? We cannot know. What we can say with a measure of certainty is that she must have experienced to some degree the life of an outcast and that her children would have experienced it with her.

Should we be surprised that from such a basis arose the compensatory idea of the perpetual Virgin Mary, the mother ever pure, the Immaculate Conception? How often have popular historical figures, from Richard the Lionhearted (who ignored his duty at home for plunder and slaughter in Palestine) to Bonnie and Clyde, from Evita Peron to the womanizing John Kennedy, been raised to the status of near sainthood? In their perceived championing of the poor and downtrodden, all else is forgotten or transformed into untouchable virtue.

Nor should it come as a surprise that a son of such a mother should himself grow to become the champion of the outcast, the spiritual teacher who welcomed prostitutes, traitors, sinners of all sorts, even to the point of proclaiming, with the prophet Isaiah, that the fate of the Temple itself hung on their acceptance and full inclusion.

CHAPTER 7

Torah Without Margins

I want a God who is like a window I can open
so I'll see the sky even when I'm inside.
Yehuda Amichai[31]

JESUS' MISSION TO REACH OUT TO THE MARGINALIZED IN
Jewish life—indeed, to remove those margins altogether—is
characterized specifically by two types of actions: preaching,
especially via parables, and healing. Both these activities move
very quickly to center stage in the first chapter of Mark.

In Mark 1:21 Jesus, with his small band of as yet four disciples, moves to Capernaum, an interesting choice. Capernaum
was a border town in the territory of Herod Antipas but close
to the Tetrarchy of Herod Philip. With John the Baptist in one
of Antipas' prisons, Jesus chooses as his headquarters a town
still within that ruler's borders, thus showing no retreat, but
with easy access to the region ruled by Antipas' bitter enemy.
If Jesus were to ever feel threatened, as would be the case, he
could walk a few miles to safety and feel secure that Philip
would never turn him over to the man who'd stolen Philip's
wife. Not to mention that Capernaum was a very mixed town
in terms of its population of Jews and Gentiles; additionally it
housed a garrison of mercenary soldiers, men from all over the
Roman Empire.[32] Such a location would fit Jesus' message of
inclusion for all, even one's enemies.

When he decides to begin preaching, Jesus does so in a
Capernaum synagogue on the sabbath[33] in quite a departure
from the Essenic John, preaching and facilitating *tevilah* at the
riverside. Most Essenes would not venture into a synagogue, at

least one not their own, since they felt that Jewish society had become hopelessly unclean. Jesus, on the other hand, begins his public life in a mainstay of Jewish life, the synagogue or house of study. The discussions of the scriptures that characterized the life there would give him adequate opportunity to state his views. Thus Jesus clearly does not see himself operating outside the mainstream of Jewish life; his apparent wish is to bring everyone, the "insider" and the outcast, together.

With this setting in place, Mark goes on to note that "there was a man in their synagogue possessed by an unclean spirit" (Mark 1:23). But what exactly does this mean in its Jewish context—"an unclean spirit"?

The Hebrew word for "spirit" is *ruach*; it is also the word for "wind." It is first found in Genesis 1:2 where the *Ruach Elohim*, the Spirit of God, is described as hovering over the waters of pre-creation. In Jewish tradition, this spirit is identified with the *Ruach HaKadosh*, the Holy Spirit. *Kadosh* is the Hebrew for "holy" and literally means "separate," "set apart," or "special" (think of the good china that your mother only used on special occasions). *Ruach HaKadosh* is the spirit of being set apart, being special.

Further related to this scripturally is the scene in Genesis 2 in which God blows the breath of life into the clay model of a person God had just made. It is that breath that makes the statue a *nefesh chaiah*, "a thing with a soul" (Gen. 2:7). It is important to note here that God first creates only one person, only later drawing a second from him. The Talmud states that this was done "so that no one might say to his fellow: 'My father was greater than yours.'"[34]

We have already discussed the notion of cleanness and uncleanness in Jewish scripture. Uncleanness as a condition could be "contracted" from things associated with the loss in or from one's body of a force associated with life or death (menstruation, ejaculation, leprosy, childbirth). Additionally, belonging to a category of people disallowed from Jewish life, such as the foreigner, the eunuch, or the "illegitimately" conceived, would make one effectively "unclean." Apparently, that which made people special, *kadosh*, was linked to the life force breathed into them at creation and/or to inclusion in the community of Israel.

In the Jewish context of the Gospel, then, for someone to be "possessed of an unclean spirit" or "a spirit of uncleanness" would mean to be consistently in a state of uncleanness. The "unclean spirit" is the opposite of *Ruach HaKadosh*; it separates not because of specialness, but because of inferiority. It creates opposite camps, rancor and divisiveness. To be possessed by *this* spirit means, in effect, to be a perpetual outcast.

We have already seen evidence that Jesus belonged to just such a category; many of the people he called most certainly did. Few, if any, would think to ask the circumstances under which that status would have been achieved: poverty, societal cruelty, accidents of birth. Jesus, in keeping with the spirit of Isaiah 56, is claiming that the God whose name is I Will Be Whatever I Will Be is calling once more for the abolition of these categories, for inclusion of the outcasts. All neighbors are to be loved as oneself.

In this story in Mark 1 and consistently throughout the gospels, it is the "unclean spirits" who recognize Jesus as someone holy, someone *kadosh*. "What do you want with us, Jesus of Nazareth?" the spirit shrieks. "Have you come to destroy us? I know who you are—the Holy One of God" (Mark 1:24). There is something telling here; those possessed of uncleanness instinctively seem to know Jesus as the anointed one, the Christ. He is *their* messiah. When Jesus commands the unclean spirit to leave an individual, he is in essence nullifying that person's outcast status. As far as we can see, nothing else has changed. Jesus does not command such an individual to radically change his or her life; he does not address the circumstances that led to the state of uncleanness. He merely removes the spirit of uncleanness from that individual's life.

Plainly, one can see that along with the ritual-oriented state of being "unclean" must come a self-defeating attitude, a pervading sense of being *existentially* unclean, of living as a lesser human being. The demeaning attitudes of any society toward its outcasts are always debilitating, dehumanizing. Such a person soon comes to be possessed of a certain spirit, a hopeless, self-despising spirit, which only increases the likelihood of this person engaging in further acts of "uncleanness" and sin. Why not? In the eyes of society, he or she is already unforgivably cast out; "If he were truly a prophet, he would know what manner of woman touches him, that she is a sinner" (Luke 7:39). In "healing" those possessed of an unclean spirit, therefore, Jesus is clearly healing not just their bodies but their soul as well, their spirit, their self and sense of self. The "good news" is that they, too, are children of I Will Be Whatever I Will Be; as such they are unjudgeable and welcomed in the Kingdom of God, as Isaiah insisted.

Twice in Mark's "coming to Capernaum" story, he states that "Jesus spoke with authority," as teacher and as healer. And well he should, for Jesus the Jew is an outcast who has come to see his own ultimate, inviolate worth as a child of God. As he later states, the devil may not be able to drive out the devil, but only someone who has been outcast him or herself knows the healing words and actions needed to drive the spirit of worthlessness *from* the outcast. That "spirit" spoke the truth: Jesus has come to destroy it, to destroy the whole idea of being unclean and outcast. And that spirit protests; any psychologist could predict that we tend to cling tenaciously to our self-images, even to the most negative and harmful ones. They are, after all, who we believe ourselves to be. Losing those images is like losing our life. But Jesus' work is to enable the outcasts to lose that life, that he or she may find life.

Nowhere is this better illustrated than in Jesus' call of his next disciple, Levi, also called Matthew, in Mark 2:

> Once more he went out to the lakeside. All the crowd came to him there, and he taught them. As he went along, he saw Levi son of Alphaeus at his seat in the

custom-house, and said to him, "Follow me"; and he
rose and followed him. (Mark 2:13–14)

Mark does not say what Jesus is teaching the crowd as he
walks along—or does he? Seeing this text with Jewish eyes
would explain much. We already know what "alphaeus" means;
Levi is twice outcast, once by the attitudes toward "illegitimacy" that seem to have characterized every culture, and second by the Torah injunction prohibiting him from membership
in the assembly of Israel, even his children to the tenth generation. Mark does not describe him as being literally possessed
of the spirit of uncleanness, but does he need to? Not only
"son of Alphaeus," Levi is also a traitor collecting taxes for the
Roman oppressor, the brutal, occupying Gentile power. So he
is thrice cursed! But why shouldn't he do so? He is outcast due
to something over which he had no control; why should he
care for those who despise him for no reason? It is this man,
Levi the bastard, the traitor, that Jesus calls to follow him, and
in quick order Levi does so. He may have heard of the young
teacher, the successor to the Baptist, who had been preaching
in the region of the lake. Perhaps Levi had heard something
of Jesus' background as well, of his questionable parentage?
Bad news travels fast. But so, apparently, does the Good News.
Now this Jesus stood before him, a spiritual teacher of growing reputation, the successor to the highly respected Baptist,
someone sprung from the same background as himself, calling Levi without condition, without reproach. "Follow me," he
says, and to the outcast, those simple words mean acceptance,
validation, homecoming. Levi "rose and followed," perhaps because the weight that had kept him down for so long had finally been lifted (Mark 2:13–14).

Parables

A paragraph later, Jesus offers the following analogies to explain his actions:

"No one sews a patch of unshrunk cloth to an old garment; if he does the patch tears away from it, the new
from the old, and leaves a bigger hole. No one puts
new wine into old wineskins; if he does then wine and
skins are both lost. New wine goes into fresh skins."
(2:21–22)

This, Jesus' first parable in Mark's Gospel, in the tradition
of Jewish parablists before and since, contains a seeming contradiction. At first Jesus seems to be suggesting that, to repair
a torn garment, one must use a similarly old and shrunken
patch; otherwise, at its first washing, the patch will shrink
and tear away from the garment. If Judaism, its life and practice, is that coat, then Jesus seems to be advocating a rather
conservative approach to mending it. Only the tried-and-true
will make good patches for the problems of Jewish life; this
would seem much more like the suggestion of a post-70 Pharisee.
Indeed, in the latter verses of Mark 1, Jesus, upon healing a
leper, almost the archetype of uncleanness, instructs him to
"go and show yourself to the priest, and make the offering
laid down by Moses for your cleansing; that will certify the
cure" (Mark 1:44).

But the parable shifts. The effervescence, the liveliness of
new wine will burst an old wineskin. New wineskins for new
wine! Here Jesus seems to be advocating tossing out all the
old forms of Judaism in favor of something radically new.
Which is it? Old patches or new wineskins? Which is Jesus, a
conservative or a liberal?

In typical I-Will-Be-Whatever-I-Will-Be style, Jesus' first
parable advocates both or perhaps doing both at the same time.
Jesus seems to be making the point that his teachings, his approach to Jewish life, are both old cloth and new wineskin.
The idea of God as YHVH is indeed an old one and a concept
central to the Jewish experience. Certainly the exhortations
of Isaiah are far from new. At the same time, Jesus is refocus-
ing these concepts, calling them back to centrality, asking the

Jewish community to return to those basic principles which, over time, had become hidden beneath layers of legalism and prejudice. Jesus is applying the patches of YHVH, Isaiah, Jeremiah, and the Creation accounts so thoroughly, so completely, to Jewish life that they become a "new" skin, capable of accommodating the renewed energy of all God's people.

Through this parable, Jesus also rejects such convenient and damaging labels as "liberal" or "conservative." Just as he will in his choice of apostles, Jesus rises above such pigeon-holes, preferring instead the inclusiveness implied by the name of God: *Ehyeh-Asher-Ehyeh*. And through his telling of this parable, Mark tries to assure the survivors of 70 that Jesus does not mean to do away with the Torah and traditions of their people, but to renew both for a new, post-Temple age.

This is an effort that continues throughout Mark's Gospel. Many of the scenes involving this issue revolve around the keeping of the sabbath.

Shabbat

Hallowing *shabbat* was and still remains the quintessential Jewish practice. Even before the giving of the Torah and the *mitzvoth*, Moses commands the newly liberated Israelites to rest on the sabbath, a foreign concept indeed for slaves of pharaoh (Exod. 16:23). It must have been simultaneously more central and difficult to Jews after the failed revolution of 70 CE. Indeed, more Jews than ever were living outside of Judea, where it was extremely difficult to keep a sabbath which Gentile society did not recognize. (How often have I been in study groups where returning travelers have moaned, "It is so much easier to keep *shabbat* in Israel!")

Directly following the parable of the wineskins, Mark relates an incident in which Jesus and his disciples are walking through a cornfield on the sabbath; the disciples began to pluck some of the ears. The Pharisees upbraid Jesus: "Why are they doing what is forbidden on the sabbath?" (Mark 2:24).

At this, Jesus reminds his critics of the story of David and the "show bread," bread used as a temple offering. "He went into the house of God, in the time of Abiathar, the high priest, and ate the sacred bread, though no one but a priest is allowed to eat it, and even gave it to his men" (Mark 2:26). As laid out in Leviticus 24:5–9, each sabbath the priests were to place twelve loaves in the Holy of Holies; the loaves were to remain there for the week as a public offering to God. On the next sabbath, they would be replaced by twelve fresh loaves; the old loaves were eaten only by the priests.

The first book of Samuel describes the incident to which Jesus refers. David, under threat of death from King Saul, flees to a pre-arranged site where he will meet some of his men. On the way, he comes to the shrine at Nob and asks its priest for bread for himself and his men. The priest has nothing but the show bread which had just been replaced by new loaves. After being assured that David and his men are ritually clean (that is, "kept away from women"), the priest gives David the bread meant only for himself and his fellow priests.

There are several key elements to Jesus' use of this story. First, we should note that Jesus and his followers are out walking in a field on the sabbath, a day on which one must rest. The Pharisees, however, do not criticize them for this, presuming perhaps that they were either going to or coming from synagogue, action permitted on *shabbat*. David, however, was also taking action on the sabbath; he was fleeing for his life. The priest in the story, however, does not know this. David tells him that he is on a secret mission for the king.

Jesus' use of this story is multi-purposed. It makes his point that the *mitzvoth* do not take precedence over the legitimate needs of people. David was not chastised by God in any way for eating the bread reserved for priests. In addition, using a Davidic story reinforces Jesus' place as the Anointed, a son of and successor to David. Lastly, it is a barb against his critics: Jesus implies that their motives toward him are as hostile as

Saul's toward David, and that he, Jesus, is therefore just as permitted to break sabbath procedure as was David.

The section and the chapter close, then, with Jesus' words, "The sabbath was made for man, not man for the sabbath; so the Son of Man is lord even of the sabbath" (Mark 2:27–28). More here than a simple declaration, there is here also a resonant echo from Jewish history, recorded in the Books of Maccabees, that most Jews of Jesus' day and certainly of Mark's would have heard. Though not part of the canon of Jewish scriptures, as they are for some Christian denominations, the stories in Maccabees were well known among the Jewish people, who, even in Jesus' day, celebrated the Festival of Lights, Chanukah, to commemorate the rededication of the Temple after its defilement by the Syrian Greeks, heirs to Alexander. Any tales concerning harm to and especially restoration of the Temple must have seemed particularly poignant to Jews of Mark's day, the principal audience for his Gospel.

At the death of Alexander the Great, his empire was divided into three parts; the section containing Judea fell to his general, Antiochus. One of his descendants, Antiochus Epiphanes, ruled during the time of the Maccabees. 2 Maccabees, Chapter 5, tells of his quelling of a supposed uprising in Jerusalem. Antiochus ordered his troops to "cut down unsparingly everyone they met, and to slaughter those who took refuge in houses" (2 Macc. 5:12, *Revised English Bible*). After three days, forty thousand Jews lay dead and a like number sold as slaves.

As if this weren't bad enough, Antiochus "had the audacity to enter the most holy temple on earth," stealing the sacred vessels and the votive offerings in the Temple (2 Macc. 5:16). The writer then goes on to explain:

> He did not understand that the sins of the people had
> for a short time angered the Lord, and that this was
> the reason why the Temple was left to its fate . . . *For*
> *the Lord did not choose the people for the sake of the*

sanctuary; he chose the sanctuary for the sake of the people. That was why the sanctuary itself had its part in the misfortunes that befell the nation and afterward shared in its good fortune; it was abandoned when the Almighty was roused to anger, but restored again in all its splendor when the great Master was reconciled with His people. (2 Macc. 5:17–20) (*italics mine*)

Jesus' assertion that "The sabbath is made for man not man for the sabbath," is a restatement of a principle from 2 Maccabees. In reminding his audience so pointedly of these words and the circumstances of 2 Maccabees, Mark's Jesus addresses the burning question of the day. The people have precedence over the Temple; the latter exists for the former, not the reverse.

In this later time of Caesar as in the earlier days of Antiochus, the sins of the Jewish people were seen to have led to the ruin of the Temple. But by applying the words of 2 Maccabees to the sabbath, Jesus is insisting that the *mitzvoth* in general were made for people, not vice versa. Just as David's circumstances allowed him to violate the rule of the show bread without recrimination, so too the circumstances of the outcast must always be taken into consideration. People must be in charge of the *mitzvoth*, not the *mitzvoth* in charge of the people.

Jesus asserts that the "son of man" is lord over the sabbath, and by extension, over all the *mitzvoth*. The term "son of man" is an interesting one, and in Hebrew simply means a person, a human being, generically understood. Jesus is maintaining that he, as a human being, and indeed, all people, are the lords over religious law, ritual, and practice. Anything less leads to the oppression which he and all outcasts knew only too well.

Additionally, the term would have great resonance for a Jewish audience that has just lost its Temple and capital. Ezekiel and Daniel, writing in exile in Babylon, both use the term "son of man." God addresses Ezekiel with this term as he urges him to point out the faults of the Jewish people that led to the destruction of Solomon's Temple, the razing of Jerusalem, and the Jewish captivity. Ezekiel, "son of man," is also given a message of hope and ultimate restoration. Similarly, in Chapter 7 of Daniel, the prophet sees a vision of four fabulous beasts, usually interpreted in Judaism to represent the empires of Babylon, Persia, Alexander, and Rome, each of which eventually fell. Then as Daniel looks on,

> One like a son of man
> came with the clouds of heaven;
> he reached the Ancient of Days
> and was presented to Him.
> Dominion, glory and kingship were given to him;
> All peoples and every nation of every language must
>   serve him.
> His dominion is an everlasting dominion . . .
>   (Dan. 7:13–14 NAB)

As the four empires were basically bestial in nature, inhuman and oppressive, the kingdom of God would be, in contrast, both human and humane in its dealings. As the beasts in this vision stood for empire, so too, "the son of man" stands for a kingdom as well, and is not solely an individual person. The passage from Daniel does seem to indicate that this "son of man" will serve as a ruler also, a leader or dynasty for this more humane kingdom.

Jesus appears to be using the term "son of man" in all three ways. First, he means simply "a human being": "the sabbath is made for man." At the same time, considering the post-70 circumstances, Mark wishes to portray Jesus as another Ezekiel or Daniel, one who is empowered by God to point out to the people the causes of their dire circumstance and offer hope for restoration.

Clearly, this latter use of the term is linked to the first.

The position of the Jesus Jews was that an attitude toward the *mitzvoth* of "man was made for the sabbath" or "choosing the people for the sake of the sanctuary" had led to the outcasting of significant parts of Jewish society, which, they held, had displeased God greatly. Jesus, as a son of David and heir of that dynasty, is the leader who would change this system, his teachings thus ensuring a return to God's favor that Pharisaism, according to the Jesus Jews, could not deliver.

No Outcasts Means *No Outcasts*

. . . And I said to myself,
Otherness is all. Otherness is love.
   Yehuda Amichai[35]

REFLECTING THE POST-70 "FAMILY SPLIT," MARK SHOWS JESUS'
teaching and practice to be particularly threatening to the
Jewish establishment. In Mark 3:1–6, after a second healing on
the sabbath, the text states that "the Pharisees on leaving the
synagogue began plotting with the men of Herod's party to
bring about Jesus' death" (Mark 3:6). In the previous "healing on the sabbath" scene, the actual healing of a paralytic is
preceded by Jesus' saying, "My son, your sins are forgiven"
(Mark 2:5). Immediately Jesus is accused of blasphemy, as in
Jewish tradition only God could forgive sins. Jesus then continues, "To convince you that the son of man has authority on
earth to forgive sins," and orders the man to walk.

The man in question suffers from paralysis; the figure in
the second sabbath healing has a withered arm. In both cases,
the ability to move, to do, is impaired, to say the least. As a
son of man, Jesus forgives the first man's sin; he does not here
use the phrase "son of God." The second man is likewise not
put off until after the sabbath. Plainly what is needed here is
human forgiveness, a change of attitude on the part of those
around these men with regards to their value, their "sinfulness," especially as compared to that of religious observance.

Society's attitude toward the sick and handicapped, the belief that they are being punished for some sin of their own or
of their parents is what compounds the sense of disability and

paralysis in such people. The prizing of religious observance over human life by extension weakens and paralyzes the society. A change in that perception, introduced by a respected public figure such as Jesus, makes all the difference in the lives of those afflicted individuals and could do the same for the society as a whole.

The reaction to these healings by a group of scribes who "had come down from Jerusalem" was to pronounce Jesus in league with the devil, and hence able to drive out demons (Mark 3:22). Jesus' response that a house divided against itself could not stand was, as many know, adopted by Abraham Lincoln in the anti-slavery cause, a usage more telling than Lincoln himself probably knew. Josephus, in the fourth and fifth chapters of his *Jewish Wars*, describes the several factions among the revolutionaries that turned on each other at various times during the conflict and thus greatly weakened the Jewish cause. Mark in his Gospel makes sure to remind his audience of the ill effects that such divisions could have on the post-70 Jewish people. The Jesus Jews were an important but distinct minority in Jewish life, and any attempt on the part of the more powerful Pharisee movement to excommunicate them (as later did occur) could only, in Mark's view, weaken the nation further.

This exchange with the Jerusalem scribes closes with Jesus' rather cryptic words, "Truly I tell you, every sin and every slander can be forgiven, but whoever sins against the Holy Spirit can never be forgiven" (Mark 3:28–29). Odd words, from the welcomer of all outcasts! But we must here remember the meaning of the phrase "Holy Spirit" in Judaism. As previously discussed, the *Ruach HaKadosh* is "the spirit of being set apart" of "specialness," but never of division or superiority/ inferiority. This spirit broods over the waters of pre-creation, and then goes on to create distinction between light and darkness, waters above and below, sea and land, different types of beings, and ultimately to form one human individual (not tribes, classes, or castes) out of the dust of the earth and God's very breath.

What, then, does it mean to sin against *Ruach HaKadosh*? An understanding of this fundamentally Jewish term shows us that the creation of any type of division, of distinction in terms of basic human worth, of "outcastness" would be to "miss the mark" with regard to the nature of reality and the spirit of its creator. Considering his Jewish background and the mission he has taken on, Jesus views such an attitude of exclusion and its resultant actions as the one unforgivable sin.

In this chapter of Mark's Gospel, the outcast nature of Jesus' life and work is further heightened by yet another form of rejection. Jesus' family, hearing of all his activity, "set out to take charge of him. 'He is out of his mind,' they said" (Mark 3:21). It is no wonder that, upon being notified of their arrival, Jesus asks, "'Who are my mother and who are my brothers?' Then looking around at those who were sitting in the circle about him he said, 'Here are my mother and my brothers. Whoever does the will of God is my brother and sister and mother'" (Mark 3:32–35).

Indeed, beyond family and caste, Jesus takes his commitment to inclusion to still another level, that of preaching and healing in Gentile territory. In Mark this first sojourn into a non-Jewish area occurs after Jesus tells a number of parables to a group of people, "so large that he had to get into a boat on the lake and sit there, with the whole crowd on the beach right down to the water's edge" (Mark 4:1). His crossing into a Gentile region could here be an attempt to find some temporary breathing room, but just as likely is the possibility that Mark wishes to show some of the parables in action. This is an oft-repeated pattern in Mark: after a pronouncement or parable, the audience is then given an example of its efficacy in the flesh. In this case, the connections are not hard to make; Jesus has just recounted the parables of the sower and the different types of soil, of the seed growing all on its own, and of the mustard seed, explaining to the disciples that the different types of soil in the first parable represent the types of hearers of "the word." In the second, he compares the kingdom of God to a seed the sower spreads, which "sprouts and grows—how he does not know" (Mark 4:27). Lastly, the kingdom is compared to a mustard seed, remarkably small, but wide-spreading. Immediately after preaching these parables, which takes up most of Mark 4, Jesus takes to a boat to cross the Sea of Galilee to enter Gentile land.

At best Jesus has had a mixed response to his teaching in Galilee, not only from scribes and Pharisees but from his own family, who believed him insane. Now he may very well be looking for more fertile ground upon which to sow his words. Gentiles were considered beyond the pale by Jews of Jesus' day, in that they did not possess the Torah and were not God's chosen people. A Talmudic legend tells that, at the revelation at Mt. Sinai all the nations and peoples of the earth were given the opportunity to accept the Torah and its way of life. Only the Jews responded positively. Yet, behind all this "chosenness" a specific fear has haunted Jewish life since the days of Abraham: assimilation. The Jews have always been a people in the minority; indeed, for many centuries they were the only monotheists in a polytheistic universe. The risk to Jewish identity, the danger of being swallowed up by the majority cultures, has always been great.

Abraham steadfastly refused to find a wife for his son Isaac from among the Canaanites, instead sending his servant back to Charran for that purpose; neither did Jacob marry from among the local people. Much later, when the Jewish exiles returned from Babylon, Ezra, the new Jewish governor appointed by the Persian king, issued this decree: Any Jews or the descendants of Jews who had fled to the hills or otherwise escaped deportation to Babylon and who had married Gentile wives were to divorce them immediately or be cut off from the Jewish people. We have already seen that proceeding beyond the Temple's Portico of the Gentiles meant instant death for any foreigner, even if they were Roman citizens. Titus, the general who razed Jerusalem, could not believe that the Jews could revolt after being granted such a privilege.[36]

Consistently, however, Jesus demonstrates that for him "no outcasts" means exactly that. As incomprehensible as it would have been to the Jewish people of his day to consider Gentiles the "good soil" of the parable—how could they be, without the cultivation of the Torah—Jesus' second parable and his subsequent journey to Gentile country illustrate literally that the seed grows even in what is considered darkness, even if the "enlightened" cannot fathom how.

Finally, the parable of the mustard seed makes the point further. A tenacious and fast-spreading variety of weed, the mustard plant was the bane of farmers and an excellent symbol of the "undesirable" Gentiles living in Galilee and Judea in particular. Despite various attempts over the course of Jewish history to uproot or convert them, such people still remained. How would they respond to Jesus' message?

Going beyond Isaiah's earlier exhortation to the Jews of his day to welcome the foreigner, the outcast, and the ritually unclean, Jesus now extends to foreigners a personal invitation into "the kingdom of God." This truly radical departure from the Judaism of his day is then symbolized in the difficulties of his making the crossing of the Sea of Galilee:

> That day in the evening he said to them, "Let us cross
> to the other side of the lake." So they left the crowd
> and took him with them in the boat in which he had
> been sitting; and some other boats went with him.
> A fierce squall blew up and the waves broke over the
> boat until it was all but swamped. Now he was in the
> stern asleep on a cushion; they roused him and said,
> "Teacher, we are sinking. Do you not care?" He awoke

and rebuked the wind, and said to the sea, "Silence! Be still!" The wind dropped and there was dead calm. (Mark 4:35–39)

The reaction of the natural elements, which seem to try to prevent Jesus from reaching the other side of the lake, implies subtly that Jesus' outreach to the Gentiles is not "natural," that to extend membership in the community of the Jewish God to non-Jews is not the way things should be.

Jesus is blissfully asleep through the tumult, but the disciples fear for their lives in a boat that seems on the verge of capsizing. This "lifeboat view" of life—that there is room for only so many on the lifeboat of any given community, and any more would swamp the boat for everyone—is one way to justify restrictions. If non-Jews were given equal status to Jews in God's sight, what would become of Judaism, already a minority, and now, post-70, struggling for its life and in danger of capsizing in a Gentile sea?

Jesus silences the storm with a word and accuses the disciples of cowardice and of lacking faith, a symbolic rebuke of all those who so greatly feared assimilation and who were insisting, in Mark's day, on a stricter interpretation of the *mitzvoth* and a less open form of Judaism. The story portrays Jesus as affirming that Judaism is stronger than that, and that faith in God, not lifeboat exclusions, will ensure the continuation of the Jewish people.

An important note should be added here. Nowhere in Josephus' history of the Jewish wars is there any mention of a role by the non-Jewish residents of the province. After the fall of Jerusalem, the emperor Titus proclaimed that no Jews could live in the area of Jerusalem any longer. Only Jews are thus singled out; the many Gentile inhabitants are permitted to remain, and indeed, more Gentiles actually move into the area. After the final Jewish revolt, the Bar Kochba rebellion (132–135 CE), Jews came to be expelled entirely from the Roman province of Judea; the region's name was officially changed to Philistia. Once again, Gentiles were not expelled, and many took over the homes and properties abandoned by the fleeing Jews.

This war by Rome against Judean rebelliousness, so central to an understanding of all the Gospels and of Mark's in particular, was truly a *Jewish* war, one in which few of the non-Roman Gentile residents of the Holy Land took part. None of the bordering provinces joined the Jewish people in their attempt to liberate themselves, and many Gentiles profited from the suppression of Judea. To Mark's Jewish audience, the Gentile people to whom Jesus is reaching out must have seemed like cowards, collaborators, traitors in their midst, which makes the incidents of Jesus' ministry to them that much more a statement of radical inclusion. Thus there is a political element in Mark's post-70 backdrop and debate, one of blame and guilt. If Jews had earlier followed the lead of an Isaiah and loosened their attitudes toward Gentiles, would those Gentiles then have acted differently during the rebellion? Would the addition of these people and of the neighboring peoples have tipped the scales in favor of the revolution? Would Judaism, now so bereft in a Gentile world, have a better chance if it were less scornful of that world? Might there be an opportunity for the resurrection of Judea and a rebuilding of the Temple, if Rome saw a kinder, gentler, more inclusive Judaism emerging?

In any event, Jesus and his disciples do arrive safely on the eastern shore of the lake, "the country of the Gerasenes" (Mark 5:1). This general area was known as the Decapolis, from the ten Greco-Roman cities that thrived there. The term "Gerasene" does not indicate a particular tribe or race, rather, it is a Greek version of a catchall term in Hebrew, *Gerashim*, which means "strange" or "foreign people." Both the Talmud and the early Christian writer Origen identify these people as being the descendants of the seven indigenous nations who had inhabited Canaan at the time of the Hebrew invasion, and who had been largely but not entirely driven from the land.[37]

The book of Joshua names them as the Canaanites, Hittites, Hivites, Perizzites, Girgashites, Amorites, and Jebusites (Josh. 3:10). We have already discussed a further forced conversion/ expulsion of such people in and from Galilee by the Maccabees kings.

Upon arriving in this foreign territory, Jesus is immediately met by a man "possessed by an unclean spirit" who "came up from among the tombs where he made his home" (Mark 5:2). Clear symbolism is at work here. To Jews of the day, *all* Gentiles, as pagans, were unclean *all* the time, and in a state of permanent spiritual deadness. And yet, they are strong and resilient: "Nobody could control him any longer, even chains were useless . . ." (Mark 5:3–4).

The rest of the scene mirrors the events in Mark 1. The man possessed recognizes Jesus as "son of the Most High God," and again the spirit is identified as plural; when asked its name, it replies, "My name is Legion, there are so many of us" (Mark 5:6–9). In this case, however, the "spirit(s)" beg for mercy, asking to be sent into a herd of local pigs. Jesus complies, and the pigs rushed over the edge of a cliff and into the sea.

The use of pigs is the perfect symbol for the chasm between Jews and Gentiles. Even today, those who know little of Jewish practice are aware that Jews do not eat pork. Even among very liberal Jews who do not generally keep *kashrut* or kosher, avoidance of pork products still occurs; as a kind of basic sign of one's Jewishness. The pig for Jews is the epitomic unclean animal.

Jesus allows the request of the spirits of uncleanness to enter into a herd of swine, and the herd immediately destroys itself. One would think that just the opposite would be the case, as the spirits had specifically requested safe residence in the herd. The episode, however, seems to be pointing in an entirely different direction. A spirit of uncleanness, being possessed by a pervasive sense of worthlessness and marginalization, is always a spirit of death. The Gerasene possessed by this spirit lives in a cemetery; pigs—which, one would think, should thrive on such a spirit—instead seek to end their lives.

This episode makes it clear that a sense of worthlessness is self-destructive and deadly for everyone, Jew and Gentile. The ripple effect of such a spirit of worthlessness within a significant number of outcasts could be potentially devastating to an entire society—a significant fact for post-70 Jews. Rather than risk further financial loss, the Gerasenes beg Jesus to leave them; they show no wonder or joy at the healing of the outcast.

The message in this sequence of stories should not be lost on the reader: Mark is quite consciously constructing an equation between the Jewish and Gentile peoples; the two incidents parallel each other. Mark seems to be implying that the attitude Jesus encounters on his own side of the lake is little better: that loss of the outcast means financial loss for the Jewish society of Jesus' day. To the outcast, then as now, were relegated all the worst jobs of society; one may be outcast for being a prostitute, but if there were no outcasts, who would be the prostitutes? Who would collect the taxes? What would become of the role of women if menstruation and childbirth were not viewed as unclean?

At the very least, Mark seems to be indicating that for too many in Jewish life the *mitzvoth* have become the equivalent of a Gerasene pig. People care more for the strict enforcement of the *mitzvoth* than for human life. For his part, the man healed wishes to follow Jesus, presumably returning with him to Jewish territory; and, had Jesus asked it of him, the grateful man might well have converted to Judaism. But Jesus tells him that it is perfectly fine for him to stay in a land of Gentiles, a land of ritual uncleanness. He urges the man to tell his own people "what the Lord in his mercy has done for you" (Mark 5:18–19).

These themes continue to be elaborated symbolically as Jesus returns to the more Jewish side of the Sea of Galilee. Here he is immediately met by a local synagogue president named Jairus, a name that would certainly send up a red flag for those in Mark's audience. "Jairus" is an obvious Latin name, a name in the language of the hated conqueror, those who would later destroy Jerusalem and the Temple. However, this man is also a Jew, as he is a synagogue official, though it is unlikely that he is a convert, for he would have most likely adopted a Hebrew name and almost certainly not have been made synagogue president. It seems most likely that Jairus is a Latinized Jew, one who either had been given his Latin name at birth or had assumed it in an effort to pursue a more Roman identity. It may have been to the benefit of that synagogue in its dealings with the Roman authorities to have Jairus at its head. At the same time, given the religious and political context, such a synagogue would doubtless have run the risk of being seen by many Jews as a Quisling establishment, a sort of a "Vichy synagogue."

Nonetheless, Jairus' plea to Jesus is heart-wrenching: "My little daughter is at death's door. I beg you to come and lay your hands on her so that her life may be saved" (Mark 5:23). Jesus consents; the crowd that accompanies him includes a second figure in need of help, "a woman who had suffered from hemorrhages for twelve years" (Mark 5:25). Reluctant to speak with Jesus, she just touches his "cloak," hoping that this will produce a healing, and in fact her action is successful. She is indeed healed. This woman represents one more example of the blameless outcast; according to the *mitzvoth*, her hemorrhages made her unclean—for twelve years! Through no fault of her own, this woman faced a future as a permanent outcast. Although the woman may have heard of Jesus' proclivity for the outcast, he is still a Jewish spiritual teacher. Naturally she hesitates to approach him in her unclean state and settles for contact with Jesus' "cloak."

Matthew's Gospel is even more specific; here the woman reaches for "the tassel" of Jesus' cloak, a detail that helps our understanding tremendously (Matt. 9:20). Jews are commanded by the Torah to "wear fringes on the corners of your garments, look at them, and remember all of God's commands and do them" (Num. 15:38–39). In Jesus' day *tzitzit* (fringes or tassels) would be attached to the four corners of the outer garment that most people wrapped around themselves. Over the centuries as this type of clothing disappeared, Jews took to wearing an undergarment with tassels, a custom still maintained by many orthodox Jews. Likewise, the *tallit*, the Jewish prayer shawl, also features these tassels.

The fact that the woman reached specifically for Jesus' tassel to be healed is a very significant detail, for the wearing of *tzitzit* is a specific Torah command for all Jews, and something that would distinguish a Jew from other peoples. The woman, then, is reaching out to Jesus *as a Jew*, appealing to Jesus' basic Jewishness. "Is this really what it means to be a Jew?" she symbolically asks. "To reject another simply because she is ill?"

Further, the *mitzvah* concerning tassels calls upon Jews to use the *tzitzit* as a reminder to do *all* God's commands. When Jesus is later asked to name the greatest *mitzvah* of all, he does not respond that all the commands are equal and thus must be valued equally. Rather he insists that the command to love God and to love neighbor as self takes precedence over all others; Matthew adds the words, "the whole law and the prophets depends on these two commandments" (Matt. 22:40). To be so strict about the laws of ritual impurity as to outcast a person who is ill, thereby ignoring the command to love, is essentially un-Jewish.

Attention to Every Word

Jesus does give the woman a bit of a scare. He feels the "power" going out of him and asks, "Who touched my clothes?" The disciples respond, "You see the crowd pressing around you and yet you ask 'Who touched me?'" (Mark 5:31). The slight difference in Jesus' words and that of his disciples is nonetheless telling. "Who touched *my clothes*?" Jesus asked. "You ask, 'Who touched *me*?'" say the disciples. Are we making too much of a slight change in wording? Not at all.

The collection of stories and teachings that would become known as the synoptic gospels involved a process of consciously creating scripture in its Jewish sense. Anyone who has ever participated in a Torah study knows how painstakingly each phrase, each word, can be examined for nuances and shades of meaning.

Many Christians, particularly in Catholicism and Orthodoxy, often are completely unaware of the second commandment forbidding images (Exod. 20:4). Although this *mitzvah* seems to apply particularly to things carved, it has cast a bit of a pall over images in general. Hence, Judaism and Jewish life have always poured much of its creative energy into *words* rather than pictures. God creates by means of words. The most sacred object in Judaism is not a statue, a flame, or a relic of some great patriarch; rather it is the Torah, a collection of words. This emphasis has even survived the "family split," as Jesus is often referred to as the Word of God or the Word made flesh.

In studying any Jewish scripture, then, great attention is paid to individual words, their context, and their relationships to each other. (My friend and teacher Rabbi Alan Ullman tells the story of one of his students who was describing his study to a second, more elderly rabbi. "We've spent weeks on one paragraph of Torah," the student said. The rabbi responded, "Tell Ullman, 'What's your hurry?'")

Jesus wishes to know who touched the tassels of his garment, who touched his essential Jewishness, and with it a Jew's dedication to all the *mitzvoth*. It is from this that his "power" comes, the power to heal the effects of outcastness. The disciples *say* it differently because they *see* it differently; for them, it is Jesus himself, the figure of the man, which works the miracles. For Jesus, however, it is never about personal power. He consistently rejects any cult of personality, often forbidding those he's healed to speak of the event and refusing all attempts to make him king. It is not so much Jesus the man but Jesus *the Jew*, and in that sense, the power of Judaism itself, freed from parochialism, which heals and liberates.

This distinction is further reflected in the fate of the woman who has been healed. She comes forward and falls at Jesus' feet, trembling. Jesus says to her, "Your faith has healed you" (Mark 5:34). These words have often been interpreted in a way similar to the view held by the disciples: that the woman's faith in *Jesus* has healed her. But Jesus did not ask, "Who touched me?" but rather, "Who touched my clothes?" The woman had touched the Torah-commanded tassels of his cloak; she had made contact with Jesus' essential Jewishness. Her faith as a Jew had healed her.

In the middle of all this, a messenger arrives from the home of Jairus: "Your daughter has died; why trouble the teacher anymore?" Jesus, overhearing this, responds, "Do not be afraid. Simply have faith" (Mark 5:35–36). Jesus' response is intriguing; Jairus has just heard of his child's death, but Jesus does not say to him, "Do not despair," or "Do not lose hope." Rather it is "Do not be afraid." Of what would this man be afraid? As a Latinized Jew, he would have been someone looked down upon by many as someone trying to cozy up to the conquerors. He certainly would have been someone outside of the mainstream of Jewish life and probably had moved far from the world of "faith healers" or even of traditional Jewish practice. For him to approach this very Jewish teacher must have been extremely difficult.

Imagine for a moment a very pragmatic Jew. Perhaps he believes in God, but does not "buy into" the rites, practices, or mindset of Judaism. Yes, he may actually have a membership in a congregation; he may give great sums to it, might even become its president. But essentially, he sees himself as a modern man, a person of the fast-track, high-tech, money-management world of the twenty-first century, with nothing in common with folks in *tallits* who will not work all seven days a week or who refrain from certain foods. And suddenly his child becomes deathly ill. All the money and technology of the modern world cannot save her. In his desperation, he looks to his roots, to his religion. Everything else has failed. Can the faith make her well?

Imagine further the scorn of others on both sides of the question when he decides to employ his old faith in this matter. His secularist peers will see him as a sell-out, as someone who is acting like a desperate fool. What will he try next—witch doctors? Filling the daughter's room with crystals? And those Jews whom he has avoided all these years, those whose *minyan* (prayer community) he has never joined, with whom he never prayed or studied Torah, how will they feel when this man comes around only in his time of trial? Money or not, would they not be inclined to label him a spiritual opportunist, a hypocrite?

Even the messenger from Jairus' house says, "Your daughter is dead. Do not bother the teacher further." With a patronizing "Give it up," he seems to be saying, "Religion cannot help, as we all knew. Why bother anymore?" But Jesus' response to Jairus is "Do not fear." Even if he has outcast himself from the people of Israel, do not fear. Do not fear those who laugh, or those who judge. And the daughter is healed, as Jesus instructs her to do what he feels everyone in his hearing needed to do: "Wake up."

The Return Home

Shortly thereafter, at the beginning of Mark's sixth chapter, Jesus returns to Nazareth. We have already discussed the reaction of the people there to him, the insult intended in their description of him merely as "the son of Mary," rather than of a father. They also tick off the names of his brothers, one of whom, James, we know as "father unknown." Those in his home place remind him in no uncertain terms that he is an outcast, no matter what great feats he might work. In our

own time there is a crude riddle: "What do you call a successful, wealthy, cultured, family-oriented black man?" Answer:
"A nigger." I have heard the same "joke" told about Jews,
Hispanics, and gays. It makes no difference to many in his day
what accomplishments Jesus had made; he was a "misbegotten"
and, as such, a permanent outcast. Period.

Jesus' reaction to this exclusionary contempt is twofold.
The first is an act of defiance: rather than allowing himself to
be diminished by this attitude, Jesus expands his work. He
instructs the Twelve to go out in pairs and spread his message
of radical inclusion, anointing the sick and healing them of
"demons" (Mark 6:6–13). Rather than capitulate, Jesus effectively increases his campaign's efforts twelvefold.

At the same time, Jesus *is* negatively affected by all that
has happened. He tries to get away alone with his disciples,
but the crowds find them, and here Jesus works the feat usually called the Multiplication of the Loaves and Fishes.

The story is well known. The disciples approach Jesus,
saying, "'This is a remote place and it is already late; send the
people off to the farms and villages round about, to buy themselves something to eat.' 'Give them something to eat your-
selves,' he answered" (Mark 6:35–37).

Here we see a tendency that has begun to manifest itself
ever since the sending off of the disciples to preach and heal
on their own. For the remainder of Mark's Gospel, Jesus attempts to convince his disciples that they, too, can do what
he does, that the power he displays is one of awareness rather
than gift. Jesus as "son of man" and "son of God" is a human
being who has fully recognized his kinship with God, fully
actualizing his potential as an image and likeness of God. If
the disciples do the same, he seems to be saying, then they
too could work wonders.

The disciples are incredulous; how can they find food for
so many people in such an out-of-the-way spot? All they have
with them are five loaves and two fish. The number seven is

a consistent metaphor in Jewish thought; it is a reminder of the seven days of creation. Specifically here, we see a division into five and two: living creatures, including fish, are created after Day Five of Creation. By invoking such a familiar Jewish metaphor, Mark indicates that a re-creating is at work here. Everyone in the crowd eats his or her fill, and still twelve baskets of food are left over. The number twelve is also significant, alluding to the twelve tribes of Israel.

All these symbols would not be lost to Mark's Jewish audience. During his time, the Jewish people were being forced to re-create themselves or to face extinction as a separate ethnicity. Mark seems to be pointing out through such subtle allusions the approach and philosophy of Jesus, that of radical inclusion, can accomplish such re-creation and wholeness for Judaism.

This point is further reinforced two chapters later, when Jesus repeats the exact same feat, but this time, importantly, in Gentile territory. The two events are nearly identical; here there are seven loaves with a few fish. The disciples offer the same excuses. But after this multiplication, seven baskets filled with food are left over, again a significant number (Mark 8:1–10). Jesus is in Gentile territory and, as previously noted, there were seven Canaanite peoples that had been conquered and/or expelled from ancient Canaan by Joshua and the invading Hebrews.

Once again the point is quite clear: Jesus makes no distinction between Jew and Gentile. The non-Jews are nourished as abundantly as Jews—all seven peoples, all twelve tribes, no outcasts.

In the intervening chapter between these parallel miracles, Mark presents the Pharisees' reaction to the multiplication event. Considering the family quarrel in response to which Mark's Gospel is written, that reaction is predictable. Rather than marveling at the miracle or understanding its underlying message, the Pharisees are portrayed as nitpicking about ritual practice. This particular group of Pharisees is not local; it

has come up to Galilee from Jerusalem. Jesus is being investigated. These Pharisees complain that some of Jesus' disciples
did not follow the practice of ritual washings before eating
(Mark 7:1–2).

It is important to note here that the practice in question is
not commanded by the Torah, at least not for all. The ritual
washing of hands, as compared to complete immersion in a
mikveh, was commanded only of the priests before sacrificing. Why then do the Pharisees make such an issue of Jesus'
disciples, none of whom are mentioned as priests, eating with
unwashed hands?

There are two answers to this question; the first involves
the approach to Judaism taken by Pharisees as opposed to
Sadducees. The Sadducees were the Temple party, the group
within Judaism that most emphasized Temple ritual. Although
there were priests in all religious parties, the Sadducee party
was particularly priest-oriented, as only the priest could offer
Temple sacrifice. The Pharisees, by contrast, tended to (re-
spectfully) downplay the importance of the Temple, in favor
of Torah. Although they would never deny the Torah-defined
role of the priest, they tended to emphasize God's description
of the *entire* Jewish people as "a kingdom of priests, a holy
nation" (Exod. 19:6). Hence the practice of the Pharisees was
to keep all the customs that the priests kept. They taught that
each meal should be viewed as a sacrifice of thanksgiving to
God, and that all Jews, as priestly people, should follow the
ritual of washing before eating.

There would be little point in the Pharisees' criticism of
Jesus' disciples if they had not expected them to be different. In other words, these Pharisees from Jerusalem, according to whatever information they already possessed, expected
Jesus to be more Pharisee than not. They may have come to
Galilee looking for an ally in their long-running feud with the
Sadducees. In Jewish life of Jesus' day, the Pharisees were the
liberal party; they may have heard that Jesus, too, emphasized
living the Torah over keeping Temple ritual. Their reaction is

therefore one of surprise and disappointment that he does not share their ritual practice.

Second, in understanding the Pharisees' criticism, we must constantly keep in mind Mark's post-70 audience. Once the Temple has been destroyed, the question of sacrifices becomes moot. Yet, sacrifice is commanded by the Torah. In this post-Temple universe, the leading rabbis (all Pharisees) solidified and broadened the idea of all people as priests and every meal as a sacrifice. The ritual washing of hands began to grow in importance for everyday Jews as a substitutional way of keeping the *mitzvoth* regarding priestly sacrifice.

For the poor, for the peasants and manual laborers, demonstrating a certain laxity with practices such as washing would have been almost a matter of necessity. The land of Israel is largely composed of scrub desert; convenient sources of water are not abundant. For those Jews in Mark's day expelled from and working outside of Judea, the practice of lengthy and involved ritual washing was hardly a practical one. Those who work with their hands for a living could easily find themselves forgoing this ritual washing out in the fields, etc. There was much work to do and little time dedicated to the morning and noon meals. In short, Mark portrays the Pharisees as being unsympathetic to the plight of the poor worker.

For this reason, Jesus lashes out at this delegation from Jerusalem: "How right Isaiah was when he prophesied about you hypocrites in these words: 'This people pays me lip-service, but their heart is far from me. They teach as doctrine the commandments of men'" (Mark 7:6–7). This is a frontal assault on the Pharisees of Mark's day, those who were in competition with the Jesus Jews for leadership of post-70 Judaism. A requirement for non-priests to ritually wash before each meal is not in the Torah, and so Mark uses this fact to portray the Pharisees as disregarding the Scripture, substituting their own notions for the *mitzvoth*, and making the lives of post-70 Jews more difficult in the process.

Jesus then offers a further example of this practice:

"Moses said, 'Honor your father and mother,' and again, 'Anyone who curses his father or mother shall be put to death.' But you hold that if someone says to his father or mother, 'Anything I have which might have been used for your benefit is *corban*' (that is, set aside for God), he is no longer required to do anything for his father or mother." (Mark 7:10–12)

The practice of *corban* is likewise not in Torah. Over the centuries, the idea had emerged that one could dedicate a certain portion of one's wealth for use by the Temple either in one's lifetime or as a bequest to be fulfilled after one's death. The latter was more often the case. In this way, the person kept the wealth on hand and actually could use it as long as the amount was replenished before his or her death or otherwise guaranteed, by value of property, for instance.

In this way, *corban* became almost a form of bankruptcy protection, as creditors were forbidden to take wealth set aside for the Temple. Once an amount was declared *corban*, the Temple was entitled to it, and could attach it as debt for someone's heirs.

In his rebuke, Jesus takes more of a swipe at the Sadducees, the Temple party, than at the Pharisees, almost as if, having demonstrated his differences with the Pharisees, he did not then wish to be automatically considered a Sadducee either.

But Jesus takes the matter one step further, declaring, "Listen to me, all of you and understand this: Nothing that goes into a person from outside can defile him; no, it is the things that come out of a person that defile him" (Mark 7:14–16). At this point, Jesus takes a radical step away from the Judaism of his day. He does not merely insist that the contents of the human heart and the actions that spring from it *also* can make a person unclean; he seems to be saying that the rules of *kashrut* (or kosher) mean nothing.

It should be recalled that, according to *The Acts of the Apostles*, Peter received just this sort of revelation not long after Jesus' death. In a vision, Peter sees something that "looked like a great sheet of sailcloth." In it he sees all manner of non-kosher animals. A voice urges him to "Get up, kill, and eat." Peter refuses, saying, "No, Lord! Never have I eaten what is profane or unclean." The voice replies, "It is not for you to call profane what God counts clean" (Acts 10:9–16). Immediately thereafter, Peter is called to the house of a Roman centurion who wishes to hear his message. Peter responds, "I need not tell you that a Jew is forbidden by his religion to visit or associate with anyone of another race. Yet God has shown me clearly that I must not call anyone profane or unclean" (Acts 10:28).

In his book *Living Judaism*, Rabbi Wayne Dosick lists "identity" as one of the principal reasons for the existence and keeping of *kashrut*:

> One of the most intimate acts of human existence is sharing food and eating a meal with another person. The biblical insistence that Jews eat in a specific, prescribed manner made it virtually impossible for them to share meals with their pagan neighbors—who, of course, would not be eating kosher food—where they might be influenced to adopt pagan beliefs and customs.[38]

Added to the examination of this passage from Mark must be the post-70 considerations. The destruction of Jerusalem and the expulsion of its population meant that more and more Jews would be living outside of Judea in a hostile Roman universe. It would be increasingly difficult, if not impossible, to keep kosher or to avoid mingling with Gentiles in such a way that guaranteed ritual purity. Of course, Judaism never held that Gentiles were inferior to Jews. But because contact with someone who may have broken one of the cleanliness *mitzvoth* could make another unclean, the practice of non-mingling of which Peter speaks became important for observant Jews.

Taken together, all these elements shed a somewhat different light on Jesus' statement regarding *kashrut*, ritual purity,
custom, and the *mitzvoth* in general. Mark's Jesus is advocating a shift in, but not a loss of, identity for the Jewish people
in the wake of the failed revolt. In many ways, the Jewish life
Jesus seems to be advocating resembles that of contemporary
Reform and Reconstructionist Judaism, as well as of the more
progressive wing of the Conservative movement. Many modern Jews feel the same as Jesus about the kosher laws, and
Reform and Reconstructionist Judaism rarely, if at all, employ
these practices. Many who consider themselves good Jews do
not follow *kashrut* or do so only in rudimentary form—not
eating pork, perhaps, or leaving cheese off the hamburger. Only
the most extreme Orthodox would assert that such people are
not truly Jews.

Jesus clearly is of the view that tying Jewish identity so
closely to *mitzvoth* such as the kosher laws, rules governing
ritual purity or related Torah commands, does not make Jews
kadosh, set apart in a positive way, holy. Rather, he wishes to
emphasize the types of *mitzvoth* found in the *Shema*—to love
God and neighbor completely—and in the Decalogue, such
as the honoring of parents. Keeping these more fundamental
commandments would truly set the Jewish people apart in the
most positive of fashions and attract others to Judaism. The
nature of "what comes out from within" cannot only make
one unclean; it can also make one holy.

Further, Jesus sees a danger in a legalistic identity particularly as regards customs *not* found in Torah. When one's very
existence is understood in terms of rules and rituals, there
is a natural tendency to expand them, and it becomes easy
for customs not based in Torah to become almost as important as *mitzvoth* themselves. Those from a Roman Catholic
background may well remember the overweening emphasis in
Catholic life on not eating meat on Friday or, for women, on
never entering a church without a hat. Some Protestants may
likewise identify with the pressure to tithe, which can often be

so difficult for the poor, or with a ban against dancing of any sort or from attendance at even a children's film. For many Catholics, fasting from meat on the fifth day defined them to the world as a Catholic. (As a New Englander, I can almost hear Jesus railing against those of us who "fulfilled the rule" by feasting on lobster!) How many women attended Mass with Kleenex bobby-pinned to their hair, because in church a bare-headed Catholic woman was almost no Catholic at all? Wouldn't it be infinitely preferable for people to identify a member of a particular Christian denomination as someone remarkable for his or her love and compassion, rather than by matters of custom and history, whether they involve Friday's menu, dancing the tango, or the place of pope, hellfire, or pledge of allegiance in his or her life?

In his treatment of Jewish denominations, Rabbi Dosick writes,

> . . . Jewish "labels" mean very little. It does not matter if a Jew calls himself or herself Orthodox, Conservative, Reconstructionist, or Reform; religious or secular; a "good Jew" or a "bad Jew."
>
> There is only one designation that counts: a *serious* Jew.[39]

Jesus is indeed a serious Jew; it would also appear that he was a Jew ahead of his time. I think it is fair to say that strict adherence to the *mitzvoth* has not been a long-term necessity for Jewish survival. A more Reformist or Reconstructionist approach to Judaism has not led to the demise of Jewish life for those communities; on the contrary, they continue to be dynamic and alive. They are Jewish denominations into which Jesus would have easily fit. During his lifetime, however, no such Jewish movements other than his own existed.

Thus, having posed a threat to or angered virtually all the major players in Jewish life, and doubtless conscious of the fate of the Baptist, Mark's Jesus now retreats to the safety of Gentile territory.

Jesus Among the Gentiles

In Tyre, a principal city of Phoenicia, Jesus actually finds a house to stay in. Mark states that Jesus' intention was "to remain unrecognized, but that was impossible" (Mark 7:24). A woman whose daughter was possessed of an unclean spirit comes to Jesus for help. Mark seems anxious for his audience to know that "she was a Gentile, a Phoenician of Syria" (Mark 7:26). Jesus replies to her plea in what appears to be a most uncharacteristic manner: "Let the children be satisfied first; it is not right to take the children's bread and throw it to the dogs" (Mark 7:27). Is Jesus, champion of the outcast, now outcasting another?

Two important considerations need to be kept in mind when treating this story. First we must consider Jesus, the human being. In a certain sense, he is on the run. He has crossed the border into Gentile territory largely because of his encounters with the Jewish religious leadership and Herod's suspicions that he is John returned. No doubt, Jesus is fully cognizant of what happened to John and could well happen to him. He is not anxious for martyrdom.

He crosses into Phoenician territory apparently hoping to lie low for a while. He even finds a dwelling for himself, something unusual in his later lifetime. These plans for peace and refuge are shattered, however, by the entrance of this woman seeking a healing for her daughter. Jesus is trying, for once, to avoid trouble; he is already in great difficulty for treating the outcast, the sinner, the Gentile, as equal to a "righteous" Jew; he now is faced with (1) a woman, and (2) a Gentile (3) involved with an unclean spirit. Jesus' initial reaction to her is undoubtedly harsh, but it is a harshness probably rooted in exhaustion, anxiety, and fear. Will his response get back to the Jewish authorities and back them off? Could his harshness here be a mode of very human self-protection?

Beyond this we once again take the post-70 context into account. Proclaiming all peoples equal before the God of all peoples was a difficult sell in Mark's time. Was there to be no special status for the Chosen People? Mark shows Jesus asserting a primary role for Jews, insisting that they be the first to have the opportunity to be "satisfied"; they are not the only ones, merely the first. Mark could reasonably argue that this opportunity had continued to be given, up to and including the time of the disaster of 70. Now that the Jewish people were to be largely scattered among the Gentiles, the time to share the table, rather than view Gentiles as dogs feeding on crumbs, had arrived.

The response of the woman does not take issue with Jesus on either of these points. She does not rail against him, nor does she storm off in a huff. Rather, she reinforces the special status of the Jewish people: "Even the dogs under the table eat of the children's scraps" (Mark 7:28). Her response, too, needs to be seen in the light of Mark's times. The great post-70 fear was that of assimilation and thus the end of the Jewish people. Mark puts forth this Phoenician woman, therefore, as an archetype of the Gentile response to the message of the Jewish Jesus. She does not say, "What do you mean, dogs? My faith and way of life are every bit as good as yours." On the contrary, she recognizes the worth of Judaism and Jewish life.

As we see from Acts of the Apostles and the letters of Paul, all of which predate Mark's Gospel, the type of Gentile who responded to the Jesus message was usually a Jewish proselyte, someone, often a woman, profoundly attracted to Judaism, but who had not converted. By the first century CE there was already widespread disaffection, especially among the educated classes, with polytheism. The works of Aristotle and Plato, though not denying the existence of the classical gods, clearly maintained that they were not the ultimate, causal, or final power in the universe. The Greek and Roman gods and goddesses, with their pettiness, feuds, trysts, and jealousies, seemed to many thinking people to be little more than overgrown, powerful children.

Consequently, a significant number of Gentiles were interested in the monotheism of Judaism, and would even come to the local synagogue, where Paul would meet them; but they drew the line at conversion. For a man, there were obvious and physically painful reasons for doing so, but beyond the obvious impediment that circumcision presented was the attitude we saw earlier manifested by Peter. To become a Jew was not only to join a religion but to take on a new nationality, one that insisted on never mingling with Gentiles if one could help it. Conversion would mean totally cutting oneself off from one's family and race, a price very few were prepared to pay.

The type of Judaism represented by Jesus and subsequently preached by Paul, Barnabas, Silas, and others seemed to remove such barriers. This form of Judaism welcomed the foreigner and did not employ the rules of *kashrut* or ritual impurity; no cutting-off of anyone or anything was required. Thus many Gentiles who embraced the Jesus Movement early on were for the most part already enamored of Judaism, and on Jesus' terms were quite willing to join and support it, not subvert or destroy it. (Reader, ask yourself: If you were to convert to Judaism, with a still non-Jewish extended family, while working and living in a non-Jewish world, which form would you be most likely to choose? The strictness of Orthodoxy? Or Reform or Reconstructionism?)

In short, the Phoenician woman is used by Mark to address an issue of his day: the role of Gentiles in this still largely Jewish Jesus Movement. The apparent harshness of Jesus' remark corresponds to the fears and concerns evident throughout *Acts* and Paul's letters regarding the relationship between these two groups; the equally extreme but opposite reaction of the woman is meant to help quell those fears. Mark has Jesus resolve the tension in the end by saying, "For saying

that, go, and you will find the demon has left your daughter"
(Mark 7:29).

When Jesus decides to journey back toward Galilee, he goes
by way of another major Phoenician city, Sidon. This fact means
little to a contemporary reader, but spoke volumes to Mark's
audience. Getting to Galilee from Tyre via Sidon is something
like journeying from London to Normandy via Scotland!
Sidon is twenty-five miles north of Tyre, while Galilee is considerably south of that city. Mark further notes that Jesus
ended up "well within the territory of the Decapolis" (Mark
7:31), a Gentile region outside the control of either Herod. So
to reach the Galilee area, Jesus first travels in the opposite direction, then heads west and south, around the northern rim
of the lake, and finally into the Decapolis. In other words, it is
a circuitous route that no sane person would take, *unless* he or
she were trying not to be spotted, tracked, or captured on the
way. Clearly Jesus feels like a hunted man.

Once in the Decapolis, however, the now-familiar pattern
repeats itself: the locals bring to Jesus a man who is deaf and
speech-impaired. Jesus takes him aside, away from the crowds,
puts his fingers in the man's ears and touches spittle to the
man's tongue, at which his hearing is restored and the impediment to his speech removed (Mark 7:31–35). These actions,
especially the latter of the two, may strike contemporary readers as strange, but they are symbolic of the man's status as a
Gentile. To Jews of the time, Gentiles were people who could
not or would not hear the word of God revealed in Torah.
Therefore, any words they themselves might utter would be
considered handicapped by this ignorance. Add to this consideration the overwhelming significance of words for the
Jewish people—who are forbidden the use of images by the
God who creates by using words—and the image of Gentiles
as "word-impaired" becomes clearer.

Jesus further stops the deaf man's ears, indicating that he
should not be outcast even if he could hear the Torah, and
simultaneously places spit upon the man's tongue. Spit was

to show disapproval in ancient Jewish life. When a child was guilty of ignoring the command to honor mother and father, the parent would spit upon him or her (Num. 12:14). If a widow was faced with the adamant refusal of her brother-in-law to marry her, as the *mitzvah* commanded, she was to spit in his face (Deut. 25:9). Here, using what may at first seem to be very odd symbolic gestures, Jesus turns the practice on its head, using a sign of rebuffing as one of healing.

Later, still in the Decapolis, Jesus works the second multiplication of loaves and then he returns to Jewish territory, crossing the Lake to Dalmanutha, on its western shore. Immediately he is met by Pharisees who "came out and argued with him. To test him, they asked him for a sign from heaven" (Mark 8:11), a curious request. Have not the healings and multiplications been "sign" enough? But the term "sign from heaven" had a very specific meaning for Jews of Jesus' day.

As previously stated, debate, especially religious debate, was nothing new in Jewish life; as the old Jewish saying had it: "Three Jews, five opinions." Even within movements such as the Pharisees', factions existed, with often bitter and contentious disagreements. Two of the best-known schools of Jewish thought were led by the famous scholars Hillel and Shammai. Whether these men lived just before or during the life of Jesus is unknown, but the fact that the first was *Nasi*, or Sanhedrin president and the second *Av Bet Din*, or vice president, and that neither are mentioned in the Christian scripture lends credence to the idea that both had passed from the scene before Jesus' public life had begun.

Although they were considered equals in scholarship and wisdom, Hillel was known as the more liberal, gracious, and compassionate, Shammai the more conservative, strict, and rigid. Hillel and his followers tended to emphasize a more human-oriented approach to Torah; Shammai and his school saw the *mitzvoth* as immutable mandates from heaven. For example, the question was raised, "When does Shabbat begin?" Shammai answered, "When three stars appear in the sky on

Friday evening." Hillel's response was, "When man recites the *Kiddush*" (the opening *shabbat* prayer). Actually, there is no external difference between the two answers, since *Kiddush* is recited at the appearance of the three stars. But the difference in focus is pivotal. For Shammai, the sabbath is built into the natural order of things by God. For Hillel, the sabbath is nothing unless it is recognized by human beings.

In the numerous stories about debates such as these, the matter in question often is settled by a *bat kol* or "voice from heaven." In one famous tale, after long and bitter presentation by both sides on a certain point, a "voice" from on high is heard saying, "Both are the word of the living God, but the law follows the teachings of Hillel" on the matter.

For those in some of the more dogmatic or fundamentalist denominations of Christianity, the notion that two diametrically opposed positions could both be "the word of the living God" may be a difficult idea to understand. But Judaism has traditionally not been a dogmatic faith. Neither the Hillelists nor the Shammaists expected or demanded that their point of view be consistently adopted by the Sanhedrin or by universal Judaism.

In the rare instances that Judaism lapsed into sectarianism and schism it was usually a result of extreme stress on the Jewish community. Such, unfortunately, was the case at the aforementioned Council of Yavneh (Jamnia), in which anyone who claimed that the Messiah had already come was condemned. Still, this in itself was a teaching and nothing more; Judaism did not and still does not have an "enforcement arm." In other words, if Jesus Jews still considered themselves Jews and attended a synagogue as such, no one from a central office in Yavneh would show up to expel them or to shut that synagogue down. Though it was possible, by vote of the members, to expel someone or some group from a particular synagogue, it was not nor is it possible, even now, to expel dissenters from Judaism itself; people could merely move on to another synagogue or form their own. For several centuries after Jamnia,

Jesus Jews continued to pray in synagogues with other Jews, as well as in those they themselves had founded as Jews.

The situation may be compared to the state of affairs in Roman Catholicism, admittedly a dogma-oriented institution. Formal Catholic teaching condemns practices such as birth control and states that voters should not support pro-choice candidates. It is clear that many practicing Catholics ignore these edicts. Still, no one is met at the church door by an official with an oath to sign on these matters, ready to expel anyone who refuses to sign.

Christians for two millennia have endeavored to imitate Christ—in all but his inclusive Judaism. Nowhere in the Gospel does Jesus ever "enforce" any of his teachings, not the most central truth, the most beneficial practice. He never expels any of his error-prone disciples, not even his own betrayer. Rather, in the tradition of his Jewish faith, Jesus teaches, *just teaches*, and believes that if the teaching is truly "the word of God" it will not need enforcement; it will grow like the parable's seed in the night, one knows not how. In Judaism, one does not need to enforce the faith as taught; one's faith is *in* the teachings. Put another way, Jesus was clearly much more a Hillelist in his approach than a Shammaist. The important Jewish historian Joseph Klausner in his *Jesus of Nazareth* emphasizes just that; for him and many other Jews, Paul, not Jesus, was the actual founder of what came to be called Christianity, for those Christian teachings that seem to contradict a more basic Judaism originated with his epistles and with his actions and attitudes as recorded in Acts of the Apostles.[40]

In any event, in asking for a "sign from heaven," the Pharisees are seeking just the sort of voice which, in Jewish legend, intervened in other religious debates. Jesus' response is to "sigh deeply" and say, "Why does this generation ask for a sign? Truly I tell you, no sign will be given it" (Mark 8:12). But what was wrong with the Pharisees asking for exactly the type of sign that had, according to tradition, been experienced at other instances of Jewish debate? The answer would have been a plain one to the audience of Mark's day, made up of Jews and Jewish proselytes, and represents just one more example of the need among Christians for restored Jewish eyes, for although God's voice would sometimes intervene in such discussions, nowhere do we find anyone in those debates asking, let alone demanding, that his opposing partner produce a heavenly voice. In fact, in almost every case, the *bet kol* comes unbidden, seemingly interrupting debate. Rarely did individual members or the Sanhedrin as a whole even pray and ask God for this voice; it was understood that it was up to the participants to sort out the questions, that God resides with his people. Jesus could have very well responded, "Why don't *you* produce a sign from heaven confirming *your* point of view as correct?" Rather he just sighs at the attitude that anyone could or should produce such a sign on demand to settle a point of religious debate, an extraordinarily un-Jewish idea.

In another example, the Talmud tells the story of the very conservative Rabbi Eliezer ben Hyrcanus (second century CE) trying to prevail in a religious debate and calling upon the heavens to uphold the rightness of his position. Exactly that seems to happen: a carob tree miraculously uproots itself and begins to fly, a river runs backwards, the walls of the synagogue begin to buckle. Finally a *bat kol* is heard attacking those who opposed Eliezer. Nonetheless, one of those challengers rises and says, "The Torah is not in heaven, and we pay no attention to heavenly voices." Rabbi Eliezer's point loses the day and he himself is disbarred from the assembly of scholars.[41] To the group of Pharisees questioning Jesus, no sign would be given, precisely *because* one had been demanded. The Torah was not in heaven, but had been given to men and women. It is up to human beings, God's images and likenesses, to sort out the issues presented by the spiritual life.

While crossing to Bethsaida in the tetrarchy of Philip on the northern shore of the lake, Jesus warns his disciples to be "on guard against the leaven of the Pharisees and the leaven of Herod" (Mark 8:15); by this he means Herod Antipas, who ruled Galilee. When the disciples are at a loss to understand, Jesus says,

> "Have you forgotten? When I broke the five loaves among the five thousand, how many basketfuls of pieces did you pick up?" "Twelve," they said. "And how many when I broke the seven loaves among four thousand?" "Seven," they answered. He said to them, "Do you still not understand?" (Mark 8:18–21)

What is there *to* understand? Leaven is used, of course, to raise dough, to increase its mass, in essence to make it grow. With this symbol, Jesus is cautioning his disciples (and Mark his own contemporaries) that there are many ways to "grow" faith and a people. Not all of them yield the same results. The "leaven" of the Jesus approach, however, produces benefits to overflowing, for Jews and Gentiles alike, represented by the numbers twelve and seven. The leaven of the Pharisees and of Herod, Mark is implying, created only the explosion of the revolution with its disastrous consequences for the Jewish people at the hands of Gentiles. Mark is sure to emphasize this point, that only that which benefits *both* Jews and Gentiles jointly will save the Jewish people in their post-70 universe. Rather than worrying about assimilation, they should have faith enough in themselves as Jews to be open to those once outcast, as they themselves are now outcast from Jerusalem.

CHAPTER 9

The Approach to Jerusalem

the shape of a dome, of a tower, of a flat or sloping roof,
all are bubbles before bursting. And God
takes the prophet who happens to be near him at the moment
and as if with a wooden spoon he stirs it up, stirs and stirs.

Yehuda Amichai[42]

MARK'S EIGHTH CHAPTER IS THE MIDWAY POINT OF HIS sixteen-chapter gospel. In it, a new tone, a new feel is introduced regarding Jesus' attitude toward himself, one that can only be described as "doom-ridden." From here on, more and more often he speaks about his death, trying to prepare his disciples for it and to help them understand its significance. He is walking, with no illusions to the contrary, into his own demise. This shift of tone is first seen in verse 27, when Jesus asks his disciples the opinion of the people regarding him: "Who do people say that I am?" (Mark 8:27). The initial response portrays Jesus as a reincarnated prophet, perhaps Elijah or John the Baptist. But Jesus then asks, "And you, who do you say that I am?" Peter responds, "You are the Messiah."

Jesus gives his disciples strict orders to tell no one about him and further explains that "the son of man" would endure great suffering, be rejected by the Jewish establishment, be executed, but would also rise in three days. The text insists that "he spoke about this plainly" (Mark 8:27–32), and that Peter, he of the messianic response, then "took hold of him and began to rebuke him" (Mark 8:32).

The image is enough to make the pious gasp; Peter actually grabs Jesus in an apparent attempt, as the saying goes, to "shake some sense" into him. Jesus turns and looks, not at Peter, but at the rest of the disciples. "Out of my sight, Satan," he says. "You think as men think, not as God thinks" (Mark 8:32–33).

In a few short verses, Peter has gone from hero to goat. Still, we must not misinterpret Jesus' use of the term "Satan," as the meaning of this word in the Jewish world of Mark's audience was far different than it is in our own day. Our images of Satan, with his horns, pointy tail, and pitchfork, were wholly foreign to the Judaism of Jesus; our contemporary picture of Satan grew primarily from the conceptualization of "demons" and "evil spirits" in the polytheistic religions that Christianity met, converted, and to a significant degree absorbed. The Jewish Satan was a different creature altogether.

The Hebrew word *sa'tan* literally means "adversary" or "accuser" and is usually found in the Jewish scripture as *ha sa'tan*, "the satan." His role is one of prosecuting attorney or the one who asks the difficult questions. His most prominent role is played in the book of Job, where he is one of the "divine beings" who present themselves before the Lord (Job 1:6). In response to God's question, *ha sa'tan* states that he has been "roaming all over the earth." When God then boasts about his upright servant, Job, *ha sa'tan* fulfills his function as prosecuting attorney of the heavenly court, claiming "but lay your hand upon all that he has and he will blaspheme you to your face" (Job 1:6–11), a scene that is repeated at the beginning of Chapter 2, after Job's initial misfortunes. Once again the accuser does his job, and God agrees to further test *ha sa'tan*'s contention on Job's very body.

Nowhere in the book of Job does God condemn or even scold *ha sa'tan*. Even after all of Job's trials find him still blameless, and all is restored to him, there is no final scene in which Satan gets his comeuppance. Rather *ha sa'tan* is fully a part of the heavenly court, not lord of an infernal one. The concept is quite foreign to classical Judaism, although tinges of it do filter in from neighboring cultures, and later from

Christianity and Islam. Nowhere in Torah, the most sacred element in Judaism, does "Satan" even appear; the snake in the Garden of Eden is never identified as this accuser. In Jewish thought, *ha sa'tan* is a being whose specialty is the bursting of bubbles, who points out instantly that which no one wants to consider. His is the gadfly voice that keeps on insisting, "Oh, get real!"—an avowed pessimist, a spoilsport to be sure, but hardly evil personified. Satan's job in Judaism is not to lead high-flying spiritual types to hell, but to bring them, proverbially, "back to earth." By Jesus' day, however, other elements, particularly from the culture of Persia, had slowly crept into the picture of *ha sa'tan*, beginning to move him toward being seen as God's enemy, rather than the valued antagonist of classical Judaism. But at the time of Mark's Gospel this transformation was as yet far from complete. When Jesus calls Peter a "satan," he uses the term in its Jewish rather than later Christian context.

The words Peter spoke to Jesus on this occasion Mark does not reveal, but Peter's body language is unmistakable. He is violently upset; the man who had just validated Peter's opinion of him as a Messiah is now speaking of rejection and death. Jesus' use of the word "satan" does say a great deal, though. It does not indicate that Peter is evil or trying to tempt Jesus to betray God or his mission. Rather, Jesus sees him playing the part of prosecuting attorney, clarifying, cutting to the bone of the matter at hand. Does Jesus realize the effect his words have on his disciples, who have left everything to follow him? What of the Jewish people who have waited so long, in such bondage for their Messiah? The disciples have seen Jesus' power firsthand; to seemingly give himself over to death and defeat when he could so easily conquer must seem to them irresponsible and uncaring. What will then become of the outcasts, lifted to a place of hope just to be dashed to pieces? What will happen to the disciples? To him, Peter, himself? We can see why Jesus directs his response, not to Peter directly, but to the disciples as a teaching. Peter is thinking as people do, not as God does—the God whose name is I Will Be Whatever I Will Be. Salvation itself rides on the difference.

As we've already discussed, human beings, as the image and likeness of God, must accept their own ineffability, their own open-ended potential. Human beings, too, will "be whatever they will be." Real sin, for the Jew and therefore the Christian, lies in denying this potential, in stifling it in oneself and condemning it in others. The message of Yeshua, whose name means "'I Will Be' Will Save," is fundamentally that attitude. This understanding of oneself and others will save humankind.

It would be unlikely, then, and self-defeating to imagine that the Messiah would resemble the common preconceptions about him. We have a saying in our study group: "Why did YHVH cross the road?" Answer: "Because everyone believed he never would." The Messiah, Jesus maintains, must be rejected, suffer, die, and rise again. The opposite of I Will Be Whatever I Will Be is "I Will Be Whatever You Want Me to Be." In our study, we came to the conclusion that if the Jewish people had been *expecting* as Messiah a lowly carpenter turned itinerant teacher, God would have sent a wealthy, royal warrior on a white horse! I Will Be Whatever I Will Be is always the entire point.

Jesus next broadens his attention, addressing not only the disciples, but calling "the people to him" and offers the famous call,

"Anyone who wants to be my follower must renounce self; he must take up his cross and follow me. Whoever wants to save his life will lose it, but whoever loses his life for my sake and for the gospel's will save it." (Mark 8:34–35)

The seeming contradictions in this statement reconcile themselves in the light of the sacred Tetragram, for the life to be saved is that of our *true self*, that made in the image and

likeness of YHVH. The life that must be lost is that of convenient labels, categories, social castes, and even that of self-
image. Jesus and his Good News will help rid us of all that
hinders us, but the response of those who wish others and
themselves to be whatever they want them to be will not be a
positive one. Expect crosses.

We have already seen that, in Mark's Gospel, Jesus himself
is accused of being in league with Beelzebub; how unusual
and ironic for him to call one of his chief disciples "Satan."
But, in an odd sort of way, Jesus himself is a *sat'an* in the
Jewish sense of the word, just as his kinsman, John, was before him. He exposes, he strips away the layers of identity and
cultural definition from each person, leaving only that which
is his or her truest self in process.

In the book of Job, the stricken man's so-called Comforters
exasperatedly and angrily demand that Job acknowledge his
guilt before God. After all, God is a just judge; Job *must* have
done something wrong to deserve his fate. The Comforters
have a preconceived definition of God, and according to that
definition, Job deserves his outcast status. How horrified they
would have been to know of the little dare, the bet going on
between *ha sa'tan* and God. But this seemingly ridiculous
situation is exactly the point.

Any set notion, any hard-and-fast conception of I Will Be,
even the most positive, is definitionally inaccurate and thus
harmful. A society that saw God only as the just judge must
be exposed to the God who places wagers with a blameless
man's health and well-being. The God who forbids images must
be a mold-breaker. And that God's Messiah must break that
mold as well.

Transfiguration

This message of unexpected transformation is a scene commonly known as the Transfiguration.

Six days later, Jesus took Peter, James and John with him
and led them up a high mountain by themselves. And in
their presence he was transfigured . . . (Mark 9:2–3)

Jesus' clothes become dazzling white; Elijah and Moses
appear, conversing with him. Then Peter speaks up. "Rabbi, it
is good that we are here. Shall we make three shelters, one for
you, one for Moses, and one for Elijah?" (Mark 9:3–5).

The choice of these two figures from Jewish history may
seem an obvious one. They were each major leaders among
the people of Israel, the first as liberator and lawgiver, the
second the nation's most important prophet. But, considering
the changed, darker tone of Mark's Gospel, there is another
reason that these two figures stand with the Jewish Jesus:
personal failure.

If Abraham is considered the father of the Hebrew people,
then Moses is certainly the founder of the Jewish nation and
of Judaism itself. It was he who led the Jewish people out
of bondage in Egypt. To him was given the Torah on Mount
Sinai, and to Moses God revealed his true name, *Ehyeh Asher
Ehyeh*. For forty years in the desert, Moses molded and transformed a skittish, backward-glancing, unsatisfiable group of ex-
slaves and other outcasts, many of them not Jewish at all, into
a holy nation, a people set apart, as well as a formidable fight-
ing force. As latter-day European kings would use the religion
of Christianity to create political and social unity, Moses used
the practices, commands, restrictions, and spirit of the Torah
to unify and provide an identity for a population that had
had neither. All of this he did at the time of their Exodus, at
great personal risk to himself, as several times his own people
were on the verge of killing him. These events are well known
to all, but perhaps the part of the story that is the most
poignant for Jews is Moses' end, as it speaks of forced exile
and unfulfilled longing for the land of promise.

The Israelite community is in the Sinai and in need of

water. They complain mightily, but the Presence of the Lord appears to Moses, saying, "You and your brother Aaron take the rod and assemble the community, and before their very eyes order the rock to yield its waters" (Num. 20:8).

Moses, however, *strikes* the rock twice, which does produce the required water, but earns Moses a severe reprimand from God, "Because you did not trust me enough to affirm my sanctity in the sight of the Israelite people, therefore you shall not lead this congregation into the land that I give them" (Num. 20:12). This punishment seems awfully harsh for striking a rock twice, especially considering all that Moses has gone through and will still go through on behalf of God's people. But there is much more involved here than simple "lack of faith." God tells Moses and Aaron that there is nothing they have to do to create miracles. All that is needed is their word; they have only to say "Let there be." At Meribah, Moses and Aaron have come to a watershed in their spiritual development. Made in the image and likeness of God, they have reached the stage of actualizing that reality to the point of sharing in God's creative power. Their mere words can make things happen. But Moses and Aaron cannot make the leap. They feel that just being who they are is not enough to affect the changes they need to accomplish. They must *do*, not just *be*. They cannot see what "is so" for them, or if they do see, they do not believe that it is good, sufficient, unimprovable. They do not permit themselves to be whatever they will be. They deny their true promise, and thus cannot enter into the land of promise.

The same spiritual difficulty afflicts the prophet Elijah. In 1 Kings 19:9–11, after enduring many hardships, he is alone and hunted, hiding on Mt. Horeb (Sinai) from Jezebel, the Phoenician wife of the king of Judah, who seeks his life. In a cave on Horeb, the word of the Lord comes to Elijah:

"Why are you here, Elijah?" He replied, "I am moved
by zeal for the Lord, the God of Hosts, for the Israelites

have forsaken your covenant, torn down your altars,
and put your prophets to the sword. I alone am left,
and they are out to take my life." "Come out," He
called, "and stand on the mountain before the Lord."

The scene that follows is among the best known in the
Jewish scriptures. The Lord is to pass by Elijah. First, there is
a "great and mighty wind," but the Lord is not in the wind.
Then comes an earthquake and a fire; still the Lord is in neither. Finally, after the fire, a soft murmuring sound is heard (1
Kings 19:11–12). Some translations offer this as a "still small
voice." The Hebrew, *kol d'mamah dakah*, is difficult to trans-
late succinctly, as the words call for the sound of a gentle
brook flowing.

At this point, God repeats his initial question, "Why are
you here, Elijah?" And Elijah answers in the exact same way
as before, speaking again about his zeal for God, the unfaithful-
ness of the Jewish people, and his own lonely and endangered
situation.

God responds to this by giving Elijah his walking papers:

The Lord said to him, "Go back the way you came, on
the wilderness road of Damascus. When you get there,
anoint Hazael as king of Aram. Also anoint Jehu son
of Nimshi as king of Israel, and anoint Elisha son of
Shaphat of Abel-meholah to succeed you as prophet."
(1 Kings 19:15–16)

What has Elijah done to cause God to relieve him of his
duties as prophet and pass the job on to Elisha? The answer is
found in an earlier incident:

Elijah stepped forward towards all the people and said,
"How long will you sit on the fence? If the Lord is
God, follow him; but if Baal, then follow him." Not a
word did they answer. Then Elijah said, "I am the only

prophet of the Lord still left, but there are four hundred and fifty prophets of Baal. Bring two bulls for us.
Let them choose one for themselves, cut it up, and lay
it on the wood without setting fire to it, and I shall prepare the other and lay it on the wood without setting
fire to it. Then invoke your god by name and I shall invoke the Lord by name; the god who answers with fire,
he is God." The people all shouted their approval.

Elijah said to the prophets of Baal, "Choose one of
the bulls and offer it first, for there are more of you;
invoke your god by name, but do not set fire to the
wood." They took the bull provided for them and offered it, and they invoked Baal by name from morning
until noon, crying, "Baal, answer us!" But there was
no sound, no answer. They danced wildly by the altar
they had set up. At midday Elijah mocked them: "Call
louder, for he is a god. It may be that he is deep in
thought or engaged, or on a journey; or he may have
gone to sleep and must be woken up." They cried still
louder and, as was their custom, gashed themselves
with swords and spears until the blood flowed. All afternoon they raved and ranted till the hour of the regular
offering, but still there was no sound, no answer, no
sign of attention.

Elijah said to the people, "Come here to me," and
they all came to him. He repaired the altar of the Lord
which had been torn down. He took twelve stones, one
for each tribe of the sons of Jacob, him who was named
Israel by the word of the Lord. With these stones
he built an altar in the name of the Lord, and dug a
trench round it big enough to hold two measures of
seed; he arranged the wood, cut up the bull, and laid
it on the wood. Then he said, "Fill four jars with water
and pour it on the whole-offering and on the wood."
They did so; he said, "Do it again." They did it again;

he said, "Do it a third time." They did it a third time,
and the water ran all around the altar and even filled
the trench.

At the hour of the regular offering the prophet
Elijah came forward and prayed, "Lord God of Abraham,
of Isaac, and of Israel, let it be known today that you
are God in Israel and that I am your servant and have
done these things at your command. Answer me, Lord,
answer me and let this people know that you, Lord, are
God and that it is you who have brought them back to
their allegiance." The fire of the Lord fell, consum-
ing the whole-offering, the wood, the stones, and
the earth, and licking up the water in the trench. At
the sight the people all bowed with their faces to the
ground and cried, "The Lord is God, the Lord is God."
Elijah said to them, "Seize the prophets of Baal; let not
one escape." They were seized, and Elijah took them
down to the Kishon and slaughtered them there in the
valley. (1 Kings 18:21–40 REB)

The very last part of the story is the most telling. Elijah has
prayed that God send fire from heaven to demonstrate that
the entire display has been done at God's command; God responds accordingly. Nowhere in the story, however, is there
even a hint that God has ordered the wholesale, cold-blooded
slaughter of four hundred and fifty human beings! In this
Elijah acted entirely on his own.

The outraged reaction from Queen Jezebel is predictable:
". . . she sent this message to Elijah, 'the gods do the same to
me and more, unless by this time tomorrow I have taken your
life as you took theirs'" (1 Kings 19:2). It is not for the showing up of her god, Baal, that Jezebel is outraged, but for the
murders. This is the reason for Elijah's flight to Mount Horeb
and his complaint before God there.

Placed in the context of Jewish scripture, God's response

to Elijah's bitterness is now understandable. Elijah had made the cardinal error for a servant of *Ehyeh Asher Ehyeh*: he has assumed that he knew exactly who God was and what God would want. A great irony here is that all throughout Elijah's earlier prayer at the altar, he uses the term YHVH (translated, as Jewish tradition dictates, as "The Lord"). He calls upon the people over and over to acknowledge that the only God is He Will Be Whatever He Will Be. But in the end he acts on his own to create this God in his own personal image. Like Moses before him, Elijah, too, has been sorely tried; often his life has been at risk in a hostile atmosphere. The God he wishes for is one that will avenge his indignities and wreak bloody havoc upon the servants of other gods. The God Who Would Be Whatever Elijah Would Have Him Be would come with earthquake, wind, and fire. But the one true God reveals himself to Elijah not in any of these, but in the barely audible sound of a running brook. God is here giving Elijah a second chance in what is often called today "a teachable moment." If Elijah had gotten the message, he would have responded quite differently to God's repetition of his question, "Why are you here, Elijah?" An enlightened Elijah would have said something like, "I am here because I blew it. I listened to my-self rather than to you. More, I thought I knew exactly who you were and what you wanted, oh YHVH. I slaughtered the priests of Baal because, if I were God, that is what I would do. I forgot your name, I Will Be Whatever I Will Be; I could not conceive of your being other than how I wished you to be. Acting on that false conception got me into all this trouble, and has brought me here to this mountain. Forgive me, my God." But Elijah doesn't get it. Instead, he repeats his litany of woes and complaints. Thus God realizes that Elijah's effective-ness as prophet is at an end.

These are the two figures who appear with Jesus in the Transfiguration scene, an episode that actually has less to do with transfiguration than with trans-failure, the rising above one's own downfall. One can only imagine the "conversation" among these three men. Did Moses and Elijah warn Jesus as he approached Jerusalem not to trip into their pitfalls and to believe unreservedly in his own God-sustained abilities? Did they exhort him never to forget the ramifications of God's true name? Or did they reassure him that, even if his life were to end in apparent failure, its results would still be successful, as successful as the entry of the Jews into the Promised Land, as the eventual defeat of Jezebel and her illusory gods?

Peter's response to this vision is also an utterly Jewish one: "Let us build three shelters," a comment that suggests that the event probably occurred sometime around the 15th of the Jewish month of Tishri, late September or early October in the Gregorian calendar, around the Jewish feast of Succot (or Booths or Tabernacles). During this festival, an eight-day celebration in biblical times, Jews construct a temporary shelter called a *succah*. The *succah* needs to be strong enough to stand for the entire festival but fragile enough to show that it is not meant to be a permanent home. This *succah*, or booth, represents the temporary dwellings of the Jewish people during their wanderings in Sinai, and further reminds us of the fragile nature of all we construct or create, making Succot a festival of non-attachment. Usually families will eat meals and even sleep in the *succah* during Succot, weather permitting, as its roof is always made only of branches and leaves, to reveal the sun, moon, and stars to those within.

Peter's calling for just such a structure of non-attachment for Moses, Elijah, and Jesus is thus a telling statement. For a moment, Peter, who had just laid hold of Jesus and scolded him, gets a flash of insight. The fact that Jesus, his Messiah, must suffer and die is not the ultimate disaster Peter thinks it must be. After all, Moses and Elijah each endured massive personal "failure," but the work of God did not depend on their personal successes; the Jewish people did enter Canaan, Jezebel was ultimately defeated. The Succot message of the transience of all things is a perfect preparation for what is to come. Even Jesus, as the disciples know him, is temporary;

they must not become "attached." They must center their attention on the beautiful moon, not to the owner of the finger pointing to it. Today, in the now moment, "it is good to be here."

At the close of this scene, a cloud appears, and from it comes a voice repeating in part the words heard at Jesus' baptism by John, "This is my beloved son; listen to him" (Mark 9:7). It is imperative that the disciples take heed of Jesus' predictions concerning his death and his resurrection, for soon the end of all attachment is coming. Jesus will die, the *succah* of the Temple itself will be taken down; the temporary nature of all earthly things will be reinforced. But the God whose name is I Will Be Whatever I Will Be, the God who lit the sun, moon, and stars, will ultimately bring success to God's people. All of them.

Healing

These themes infuse the healing that follows the Transfiguration event as well. Upon his return from the mountain, Jesus encounters a chaotic scene. His disciples are embroiled in argument with a group of scribes, a boy is rolling on the ground foaming at the mouth, and a crowd has gathered. Apparently, Jesus' disciples had attempted unsuccessfully to heal the boy, who is described by his father as, "possessed by a spirit which makes him dumb. Whenever it attacks him, it flings him to the ground, and he foams at the mouth, grinds his teeth and goes rigid" (Mark 9:17–18). In context, two important elements emerge here. First, the boy is possessed of a spirit of muteness, that is, of wordlessness which, in its Jewish context, means a young person bereft of a truly essential characteristic of the human being as an image and likeness of God—the ability to form and use words.

Beyond this, the boy's condition causes him terrible torment, flinging him to the ground with foam at the mouth, until finally he "goes rigid." In other words, under the grip of this spirit the victim appears to be dead, so that when Jesus cures him, the boy at first exhibits all these behaviors, including the rigidity. It is not hard to see in this death-like illness a prefigurement of Jesus' impending demise, a symbolic reinforcement of the message he has been trying to communicate to his disciples. On the one hand, the words Jesus has been using to convince his disciples of the inevitability of his doom, as well as the ultimate triumph contained within it, have not been successful. It is as if he were mute, the power of the word ineffective. But then Mark offers a flesh-and-blood example of this reality in an attempt by Jesus to show by deed what he had failed to teach in word.

The young man's father begs Jesus for his assistance: "If it is at all possible for you, take pity on us and help us." Jesus' response is, "Everything is possible to one who believes." The father's reply has become a by-word of faith: "I believe; help my unbelief" (Mark 9:22–24). Here, then, is the crux of the matter. Jesus possesses the belief—in *Ehyeh Asher Ehyeh*, in the ultimate inclusion of the outcast, in the Good News, and in the fate of the grain of wheat that falls and dies, only to then sprout and spread. His disciples do believe but not enough. Jesus' true problem is how to increase the faith of his disciples. But this problem is not just theirs. We began our investigation of Mark's Gospel with "The Cleansing of the Temple," in which Jesus himself, faced with a situation that angered him greatly, forgot his own belief in non-violence and love and struck out violently at those around him—an act the uselessness of which is symbolized by the futility of cursing a fig tree for being fruitless when it was not fruit season. Now the boy who has been brought to the disciples for healing has been in this condition "from childhood," according to his father (Mark 9:21). The convulsions, the foaming, the flinging to the ground, can all be seen as manifestations of frustration experienced by the boy due to his muteness. Jesus himself, seen from his earliest days as a person of suspect birth, may have experienced just this frustration, especially as his insight into

God and God's Good News grew in him. How to communicate this? How to make people see and understand? Small wonder that, in this very episode, Jesus exclaims aloud, "What an unbelieving generation! How long must I endure you?" (Mark 9:19).

Jesus' healing of the boy is symbolically both an act on behalf of his disciples and an act that demonstrates his own belief in God. He hopes to show to his disciples that, although death may appear to triumph, such is not always the case, especially for "one who believes." The father's words, "I believe, help my unbelief," apply to the disciples and to Jesus himself.

At the close of this incident, Jesus' disciples ask him privately why they could not drive the spirit from the boy. Jesus' answer? "This kind cannot be driven out except by prayer" (Mark 9:29). These words are meant as much for Jesus himself as for his disciples, and certainly, in Mark's context, for the post-70 Jewish community as well.

Prayer

The question of prayer can be a very difficult one. In Mark's Gospel, Jesus does not actually attempt to teach his disciples to pray; the "Our Father" is not a part of this gospel. And although we are told that Jesus prays a blessing over the food that is to be multiplied for the crowds, the words themselves are not recorded. Nor need they be, for everyone in Mark's audience would have been more than familiar with the Jewish blessings at meal. The same, I would maintain, is true of prayer in general.

The most sacred prayer in Judaism, the one with which almost all other prayer begins, is the *Shema*: "*Shema, Israel, Adonai Elohano, Adonai Echad.*" It is found in the Torah in the book of Deuteronomy, the sixth chapter, the fourth verse, and is commonly rendered in English, "Hear, O Israel, the Lord your God, the Lord is one." But, as we have already discussed, neither use of the term "Lord" (*Adonai*) is actually in the Torah but is merely substituted in speech out of respect for the sacred Name. A more accurate translation of the *Shema* would read, "*Hear, O Israel, He Will Be, your God, He Will Be is one.*" The centrality of this prayer in Jesus' life and teaching is confirmed later in Mark's Gospel, when, in response to a question concerning the most important of the *mitzvoth*, Jesus quotes the *Shema* (Mark 12:29–30). For Mark's Jewish audience, the word "prayer" and the sacred *Shema* would be inexorably intertwined; one would hardly think of the one without, or in terms exclusive of, the other. When Jesus then urges prayer upon his disciples (and himself), recognizing that certain types of spirits cannot be altered by any other means, what does he mean? What does Mark mean by including this injunction in his post-70 gospel?

The first requirement, the underlying condition, of Jewish prayer is *to hear, to listen,* to *Shema.* This is what Moses failed to do in the episode with the water from the rock; likewise the sound of the barely heard brook that held the presence of God escaped the understanding of Elijah on Mount Horeb. If the word is sacred, creative, energizing, then listening for and to that word is absolutely essential. What good is a word unheard? And the listening called for here is of the most active variety; response is needed to make the word efficacious. Even the inert elements of pre-creation responded to God's actualizing words: "*V'yahe chein,*" not "*And it was so,*" but, literally, "*It was yes.*"

The first thing needed, then, is to *actively listen,* and true listening requires openness. Elijah presumed that he already knew exactly who God was and what God would want. He "heard" only what he expected to hear, and when he heard nothing, he went on his own presumptions. Moses did not listen to the words of God that all he need do was command the rock to yield water; would this not mean being like God, the temptation to which destroyed the perfection of Eden? Surely

God could not have meant this? And so Moses failed to actualize his ultimate potential.

The term *Shema*, then, is inseparable from the sacred Tetragram, *Yod-Heh-Vav-Heh*, in English, *He Will Be*. God will be whatever God will be, and as God's images, the same is true for us. When we listen to the voice of He Will Be, the voice of limitless reality, of unbounded potential, we listen to the voice of our truest self as well. What is true for God is likewise true for God's images. The listening that the disciples and Jesus must both do is one.

The *Shema* is a call, a reminder. It is written in direct address, and the one addressed is Israel, the Jewish people. But, as with almost everything in Jewish life, therein lies a story.

Israel

Before there was a *people* called Israel, there was *Israel* the individual, the patriarch Jacob, son of Isaac and father of the Twelve Tribes. As the book of Genesis describes, at one point in his life Jacob was in great distress. He was on his way to face his brother, from whose hatred he had fled a number of years before. The evening before the encounter, Jacob has sent his wives, children, and entire entourage on ahead of him. He spends the night in isolation, until a strange encounter occurs:

> A man wrestled with Jacob until the break of dawn.
> When he saw that he had not prevailed against him,
> he wrenched Jacob's hip at its socket, so that the
> socket of his hip was strained as he wrestled with him.
> Then he said, "Let me go for dawn is breaking." But
> he answered, "I will not let you go, unless you bless
> me." Said the other, "What is your name?" He replied,
> "Jacob." Said he, "Your name will no longer be Jacob,
> but Israel, for you have struggled with beings divine
> and human and have been able." (Gen. 32:24–28)

Here we have the essence of the word "Israel," and with it the heart of what it means to be a Jew: to struggle, to wrestle, with God and with human beings, and to be able.

Who is the stranger that wrestles with Jacob? Is he human or divine? The Hebrew text describes him as an *ish*, a man, but he comes out of nowhere, inexplicably begins wrestling with Jacob, speaks to him in a mystic way, gives him a new name as God had done for his grandparents, Abram and Sarai, then is gone. Perhaps the text means us to see the stranger as *both*, to see human beings as the image of God, and to understand the struggle that fulfilling this can entail.

And if to be Israel is to "struggle with God and with people and be able," the question emerges, "Able to do what?" The traditional Jewish answer is "Able to keep struggling, to keep on wrestling." One can easily see the role of a type of prayer that includes such a concept in the life of Jesus and his disciples: "How long must I endure you!" The life of anyone who truly tries to live out his or her full potential as a child of I Will Be Whatever I Will Be will of necessity be fraught with struggle, both with others who feel threatened or challenged and with God who calls us to be our truest selves, despite our own inclinations toward security and ease. We would like to sleep a while, but the stranger comes to wrestle.

In such a light, a translation of the sacred *Shema* could run: "Listen actively, responsively, O you who struggle with He Will Be and with He Will Be's images and are able to go on struggling: He Will Be is your God, and He Will Be is one."

Moreover, the term "one," in Hebrew *echad*, also bears investigating. The term can mean "singular," as in "there is only one God." It can also mean "first"; it is the word used to designate the first day of creation in Genesis 1:5. It can mean "unique," "one of a kind," and it can indicate unity. Genesis 2 states that when a man leaves his father and mother and attaches himself to his wife, the two become *echad* (Gen. 2:24).

To understand that He Will Be, the one with whom we struggle and prove ourselves able, is *echad* is to realize several things. He Will Be is singular, unique; so, too, is each of us as images of He Will Be. He Will Be is the first, the foremost of all that is; in an odd sense, on a created scale, so is each of us. Each human being is "in first place"; we are each unique and each of infinite value in and of ourselves. On the scale of existential worth, life is a universal tie for first. But very importantly, He Will Be is one with each of us. Genesis affirms that we are created differently than all other things, for God breathed his very life into us. There is an *echad*-ness, a oneness between us and God, even as we remain unique. And, as God's images, we share that oneness with all people.

We can then offer one more rendition of the *Shema*: "Listen actively, responsively, O you who struggle with He Will Be and with He Will Be's images and are able to go on struggling: He Will Be is your God, and He Will Be is singular, unique, the foremost, and at one with you. It is your own singularity, uniqueness, highest worth, and oneness with God and each other that you struggle with, and prove able to go on struggling with."

And perhaps truly listening, openly, actively, responsively, *is* the greatest part of that struggle: How else would we ever hear our true name? How easily, otherwise, to mistakenly hear it as "Outcast"?

This powerful spiritual attitude is surely what Mark wanted his audience to adopt. The same applies to the post-70 situation of Mark's Jewish audience. In this time of catastrophic failure, the defeat of Jewish hopes for freedom, the razing of Jerusalem and the destruction of the Temple, the juxtaposition of Moses, Elijah, and Jesus, all seeming personal "failures," must have been particularly poignant for these people. Yet the raising of the boy, as a foreshadowing of Jesus' own resurrection, must have also been a sign of hope. Since his entrance into the waters of the Jordan, Mark's Jesus has been a symbol of the Jewish people, their history and struggle; the doubts, conflicts, and ultimate victory over death that he experiences are meant to be theirs as well.

Taken in this context, the context of its essential Jewishness, its "*Israel*-ness," we can surely see why Jesus speaks of Jewish prayer as the only means of dismissing the type of harmful spirit encountered in Mark 9. It is a spirit not only dangerous to the boy and to his father alone, but to Jesus himself, to his disciples, to the wounded Jewish nation, and to all images of I Will Be. It is a spirit that no longer can engage in the activity of the creating word, of communicating who and what it is and will be, a spirit of frustration and of frustration's violent anger. It is the spirit that nurses the wound in its hip socket and walks away from the struggle of ever turning that wound, via actualizing word, into a source of strength in the struggle, for itself and for all those with whom it is at one. Ultimately, it is the spirit of becoming rigid, of death-in-life.

To cast out this spirit, Jesus reminds himself and his disciples, one must be the opposite of rigid: "I do believe; help my unbelief." In the woundedness of his struggle, the father offers words of actualization of potential, the potential of the image of I Will Be, to Jesus, with whom he is at one as a child of God. "Listen!" he pleads. "I Will Be is our God, and we are God's images. Listen! We are in process, you and I and everyone. I do believe; help my process of belief. And in that process, help your own, for we are *echad*."

"And," the text says, "Jesus took hold of the boy's hands and raised him to his feet and he stood up" (Mark 9:27). And with him, I would suggest, he also lifted his disciples, frustrated by their failure, and himself, at the end of his tether, ready to explode. Jesus, too, returns to his feet, as, symbolically, Mark promises ultimately will be the case with the downcast Jewish people.

Of course. Jews stand to pray.

And Christians are Jews.

CHAPTER 10

A Difficult Question (Made More So)

Around the dead word "we-loved"
covered over by seaweed in the sand
the curious mob crowded.

Yehuda Amichai[43]

AS JESUS LEAVES GALILEE, ENTERS JUDEA, AND APPROACHES
Jerusalem, the audience becomes increasingly more cosmopoli-
tan and refined than in the distant northern region, and the
questions he fields reflect this.

> He taught them as was his practice. He was asked: "Is
> it lawful for a man to divorce his wife?" This question
> was put to test him. (Mark 10:2–3)

At first blush, this seems like a foolish question in its Jewish
context. Divorce *is* permitted by the Torah; every Jew knows
this, and did in Jesus' day. Jesus answers accordingly,

> "What did Moses command you?" They answered,
> "Moses permitted a man to divorce his wife by a certifi-
> cate of dismissal." (Mark 10:4)

This answer is correct—partially. The book of Deuteronomy
states,

> A man takes a wife and possesses her. She fails to please
> him because he finds something obnoxious about her;

he writes her a bill of divorce, hands it to her, and
sends her away from his house. (Deut. 24:1)

At face value, this verse may seem to indicate that a man
may divorce his wife for any reason at all, and, indeed, such
was the opinion of Hillel, who felt that burning the dinner
or breaking a husband's favorite cup was sufficient reason for
him to issue the bill of divorce. Shammai, on the other hand,
felt that only adultery (on the part of the wife, that is) consti-
tuted grounds for divorce. Of course, according to the Torah,
adultery would also result in the woman being executed, usually by stoning.[44]

Mark's Jesus, however, seems to take an even stricter view
than Shammai:

Jesus said to them, "It was because of your stubborn-
ness that he [Moses] made this rule for you. But in the
beginning, at the creation, 'God made them male and
female.' This is why a man leaves his father and mother,
and is united with his wife, and the two become one
flesh. It follows that they are no longer two individuals:
they are one flesh. Therefore what God has joined, one
must not separate." (Mark 10:5–9)

Jesus' disciples are none too pleased with his response; Mark
states that once they had Jesus alone they "questioned him
about this." Jesus' answer remains firm: "Whoever divorces his
wife and remarries commits adultery against her; so, too, if she
divorces her husband and remarries, she commits adultery"
(Mark 10:10–12).

The later Gospels soften this pronouncement. Matthew
adds the phrase "for any cause other than unchastity," and
fleshes out the response of the disciples: "If that is the way
things stand for a man with his wife, it is better not to marry"
(Matt. 19:9–10). The answer of Matthew's Jesus is intriguing:

"This is a course not everyone can accept, but only
those for whom God has appointed it. For while some
are incapable of marriage because they were born so,
or were made so by men, there are others who have
renounced marriage for the sake of the Kingdom of
Heaven. Let those accept who can." (Matt. 19:11–12)

In actuality, Matthew is picking up on a cue in Mark's
text on divorce. In justification of his teaching, Jesus quotes
Genesis 1:27 (the creation of human beings "male and female") and 2:24 (the two becoming one), representing the
approach to marriage and divorce taken by the Essenes, who
so greatly influenced Jesus, if not directly then through his
cousin John.

Central to Essenic spirituality was the idea of attaining spiritual perfection, that is, regaining the original state of Adam.
By a strict adherence to the Torah and the following of their
particular spiritual practices, Essenes believed that one could
"reclimb the ladder" of spiritual perfection from which Adam
had fallen. Indeed, the head of the community was referred
to as *Adam Kadmon*, or "original Adam," a term used to describe Adam before the creation of Eve from his rib.[45] Judaism
had long maintained that originally Adam was neither male
nor female, but both (as Eve was at first "within" Adam). By
this, *Adam Kadmon* is not meant to be seen as a hermaphro-
dite; the masculine and feminine characteristics this concept considers are not external but internal, something more
akin to a Jungian view of human nature. The Genesis verse
Jesus quotes regarding "two becoming one" directly follows
the Creation of Eve account, and so seems to posit a natural,
human yearning to return to the state of *Adam Kadmon*: "This
is why a man leaves mother and father and attaches himself to
his wife" (Gen. 2:24).

Josephus claims that the Essenic communities were overwhelmingly celibate, but investigations at the Qumran sites
have yielded skeletal remains of women and children significant

enough to cast this view into doubt.[46] For some Essenes, marriage and sexual relations would represent a way of doing exactly that which Genesis 2:24 speaks of, regaining the original oneness of male and female, but for the celibate Essenes—"those who renounced marriage for the sake of the Kingdom of Heaven," one presumes that a similar goal was sought by an opposite means: by refusing to participate in the effects of the separation of male from female, and by engaging in practices that today we might call "nurturing their feminine side," they seemed to hope to reverse that separation, to recapture the feminine within themselves. Essenes rejected all aggression; rule-bound to offer hospitality, they refused even to offer animal sacrifice and were noted for their knowledge of healing and for their renunciation of individual possessions as causes of envy and conflict.

Luke has Jesus give even further praise to the Essenes. When asked a question of Byzantine complexity regarding multiple remarriage and the resurrection, Jesus states that,

> "The children of this age marry and remarry, but those who are deemed worthy to attain to the coming age and to the resurrection neither marry nor are given in marriage. They can no longer die, for they are like angels, and they are the children of God for they are the ones who will rise." (Luke 20:34–36)

Angels played an important role in Essenic spirituality. Their secret, sacred texts claimed to contain the true names of all the angels (hence allowing one to call them). According to the Essenes, each person possessed an angel almost as one possessed a soul, with whom one could commune and from whom one could learn. The most spiritually advanced among the Essenes were thought to have completely attained to the original Adamic state, including freedom from death, at least by natural causes.

In these texts, then, is Jesus proposing that everyone join

the Essenes or at least lead an Essenic life with regards to marriage? This would be an extreme teaching indeed, and one that would seem to run counter to the nature of Essenism itself, which called for a complete separation from the rest of the world and from everyday life.

I believe there are three distinct but interrelated purposes in Jesus' answer to the question put to him, "Is it lawful for a man to divorce his wife?" The first is to point out the foolishness of the question and of the controversy that spawned it. The second is to praise the Essenes, and the third is to provide cover for himself as he attempts to respond to questions in the more hostile environment of Judea.

As previously stated, the Torah precept regarding divorce seems very clear. Yet, in the "refined" world of Judea and Jerusalem, it generated controversy. Recall that Deuteronomy states that a man may divorce his wife if "she displeases him because he finds something obnoxious about her." The difficulty of translation is obvious; Everett Fox's version (1995) renders the verse as "if she does not find favor in his eyes— for he finds in her something of 'nakedness'"(Deut. 24:1).[47] Christian translations describe the woman as "offensive" (*Revised English Bible*) or "indecent" (*New American Bible*).

The problem comes not so much with the idea of disfavor, but with the term rendered in English as "obnoxious," "indecent," etc. Following the Jewish Publication Society's translation, the Hebrew term is *evrah*, which literally means "to uncover nakedness." The most frequent and fullest use of the term is found in the book of Leviticus: "None of you shall come near anyone of his own flesh to uncover nakedness: I am YHVH." For the next eleven verses, the text offers a litany of offenses related to *evrah*; one is not to uncover the nakedness of one's father, mother, step-mother, sister, grandson or granddaughter, step-brothers or step-sisters, paternal aunt, maternal aunt, blood uncle, aunt by marriage, sister-in-law, or of a woman and her daughter (Lev. 18:6–11). The connotations are glaringly sexual; the next step after uncovering nakedness is clearly sexual relations, thus, the prohibition. At a stretch, it might, considering the times, be understandable to apply the term *evrah* to inappropriate flirtiness, to a come-on, or an attempt to seduce.

The positions taken by Hillel, Shammai, and their schools, to which Jesus is asked to respond in the Gospel texts, represent extremes in either case. Hillel's stand on the matter seems to ignore the fundamental meaning of *evrah* altogether, focusing instead solely on the term "displeasure"; the burning of a dinner hardly qualifies as an act of uncovering nakedness! Shammai, on the other hand, equates *evrah* with adultery only. If a woman—and the Torah verse applies only to women—were acting in a sexually shameful manner that did not extend to adultery itself, Shammai's opinion would leave her husband no legal recourse at all. Thus limiting *evrah* to the actual act of adultery is the same as making every divorce a death sentence for the woman.

Jesus' response is to by-pass the Hillel-Shammai debate altogether, and to do so with a clarity that both cuts through the sophistication of his questioners and shrewdly puts himself forward as a force not to be underestimated or patronized by the urban establishment. By going to the very beginning, to the creation acts themselves, Jesus is plainly getting back to basics, rather than employing the exegetical gyrations of those in higher places. His words, in effect, are the equivalent of a modern commentator pointing out the silliness of saying, "It depends on what the meaning of *is* is." A semantic bubble is burst, and everyone says, "Of course! How did we ever get caught up in such word games?" At the same time, the strictness of Jesus' pronouncements and their ramifications are enough to make the crowd gasp (as his disciples surely do). The original Torah injunction, the one the experts are murdering to dissect, is actually an easier burden than the alternative, Genesis-based approach. There is an inherent criticism in

Jesus' answer: "When one tries to philosophically tap-dance one's way out of one restriction, the orchestra pit one falls into can be far worse!"

Referring to the Essenes was a stroke of genius, in that this group was by far the most generally respected in Jewish life at that time. Criticizing them would have been the modern equivalent of disparaging Albert Schweitzer or Mother Teresa. Offering the Essenic way as a subtle example serves the dual purpose of being both rebuttal-proof and gasp-producing. As respected as the Essenes were, most Jews would not want to give up all they had to become one. It is similar to the saying, "Everyone wants to go to heaven, but no one wants to die." Every Jew would love to be an *Adam Kadmon*, but become an Essene? Again, Jesus is saying, "If you really want to argue over a simple Torah teaching, there *is* another way . . . ," an alternative that should quiet the semantic controversy.

His answer to the question serves a third purpose of providing him cover in his debates with the Jewish establishment. He does not take the side of either Hillel or Shammai, but instead sides with the book of Genesis and with the Essenes. Neither of the two schools can then identify him as an advocate for its opponent, but rather as a proponent of a movement, highly respected, which prided itself on being above (or beyond) such matters. If Jesus is basically an Essenic preacher, he is little danger to the establishment, as the Essenes never mingled in religious politics and advocated a withdrawal from the world altogether. The public positions that a Schweitzer or a Mother Teresa might take, as pure and ideal as they might be, could be shrugged off with the words, "Such things are perfect, but we are not. We are not like them."

The question remains, however, what did Jesus actually mean by his teaching on divorce? Should it be taken literally? Mark would have all divorce impossible. Matthew would allow it only in the case of infidelity. Luke seems to be saying that this difficult teaching is binding only for those capable of handling it; "Let those accept it who can."

Looking at the teaching in its Jewish context, both in terms of Torah and the times of Jesus, it is reasonable to say that Jesus' response to the divorce question was more ploy and teaching tactic than anything else, an attempt to show the absurdity of the question, and of the effete machinations of the "experts" over a rather straightforward Torah verse.

This view is reinforced by the placement of the episode in Mark's text, directly following a series of extremely hyperbolic statements clearly made by Jesus for effect:

> "If anyone causes the downfall of one of these little
> ones who believe, it would be better for him to be
> thrown into the sea with a millstone round his neck.
> If your hand causes your downfall, cut it off; it is bet-
> ter to enter into life maimed than to keep both hands
> and go to hell, to the unquenchable fire. If your foot
> causes your downfall, cut it off; it is better to enter life
> crippled than to keep both your feet and be thrown
> into hell. And if your eye causes your downfall, tear
> it out . . . ." (Mark 9:42–47)

One could never maintain that Jesus meant these statements literally; yet they set up the divorce question and its answer, which many *have* taken quite literally over the centuries and continue to today. When looked at with Jewish eyes, however, it seems evident that all of these statements are set *in extremis* for the sake of effect, and, as is the case with such statements, a literal interpretation can result only in hardship and would require the sort of theological gyrations that Jesus was condemning. For Christians, this literal interpretation of Jesus' injunction removed from the Jewish context of disputation has resulted in some denominations forbidding divorce under any circumstances, no matter how violent or cruel. Others have established just the kind of contrived, legalistic hoops that Jesus argued against here. Still others live with the lingering, uneasy sense of ignoring a "biblical command" altogether, which requires its own sort of doctrinal tap-dance.

What, then, *is* Jesus' stand on divorce and remarriage? I believe that the most that can be said is, "We don't know." In a style typical of him and of many great Jewish teachers, Jesus uses the opportunity to address the real question within the question: "What is your motive in asking?" The text plainly states that the motive here was not to actually get an answer, but "to test him." Jesus knows this, and his response is meant much more to challenge such a use of the sacred Torah and to hold a mirror to those asking. In this sense, his answer here belongs in the same category as that given to the entrapping question of paying the Roman tax or to the "angels on a pin's head" story of multiple marriage and resurrection (Mark 12:13–27).

What does seem certain in the light of Jesus' entire life and teachings is that he would not have called for the outcasting of anyone. To establish a "rule" that would cause anyone to be placed outside of God's people or that did not take into consideration the circumstances of one's life would have run counter to all that Jesus stood for. After all, many episodes of his life—when the "sinful" woman washes his feet, his conversation with the Samaritan woman who had had many husbands, and the incident with the woman caught in adultery—would have certainly turned out differently had Jesus meant his words on divorce literally. Indeed, Jesus' own thoughts on the whole matter are probably best summed up in his response to that woman brought before him: "Neither do I condemn you" (John 8:11).

Meanwhile, inadequate knowledge of the Jewishness of Jesus, of his world, and of Christianity has for millennia resulted, not in the plucking of eyes and severing of limbs, but in tearing out the hearts of so many in the already-painful situation of failed marriage. Better to go through life bereft of one's heart than to be thrown wholeheartedly into hell? An utterly unjewish, and, therefore, unchristian, sentiment.

CHAPTER 11

The Jerusalem Disputation

> . . . Jews have never been afraid of quarrels. Two Jews
> and three opinions are better than three Jews with no
> opinions. Passionate arguments are better than passionless
> acceptance.
>
> *Elie Wiesel*[48]

AS JESUS PREPARES TO ENTER JERUSALEM FOR PESACH
(Passover), it grows increasingly clear that he has failed to
prepare his disciples for what will follow. An encounter with
a rich, young potential follower and a request from two in
his inner circle leave little doubt of this. In the first instance,
Jesus is approached by a wealthy young man with a very
basic spiritual question: "What must I do to win eternal life?"
(Mark 10:17), to which Jesus answers as would any good Torah
Jew, "You know the commandments: 'Do not murder; do no
steal; do not give false evidence; do not defraud; honor your
father and mother'" (Mark 10:19). The young man is sincere
and ardent; he is kneeling at Jesus' feet. "'But Teacher,' he
replies, 'I have kept all these since I was a boy'" (Mark 10:20).
The text says that Jesus looked at the young man and "his
heart warmed to him. 'One thing you lack,' he said. 'Go, sell
everything you have, and give to the poor, and you will have
treasure in heaven; then come follow me.'" The young man
greets the advice with a heavy heart, for he is a person greatly
attached to his wealth (Mark 10:21–22).

Several important points emerge in this brief encounter.
The view of Jesus as a sort of "engaged Essene" (in the manner of "engaged Buddhism"), one adapting ascetic Essenism

for the masses, is reinforced. Although the Torah continually reminds Jews to place nothing before God, the rejection of possessions and property is not seen as a necessary virtue in Judaism. There has never been a notion of "Holy Poverty" in mainstream Jewish life. This was an Essenic practice, in keeping with that sect's goal of returning to an Adamic state of direct, absolute dependence on God. Note that Jesus does not begin by recommending this course of action to the young man; his first response is merely to suggest that he follow the *mitzvoth*, an answer in accord with the events of the episode directly preceding it: simply keeping the *mitzvoth*, without the contrivances and contortions of the theologians, is sufficiently holy. Moreover, Jesus' first answer also serves to counter critics who might feel Jesus is acting or teaching in a counter-Torah fashion. However, if one were seeking a greater challenge, a deeper experience, then nothing must be more important than that search. Jesus' second answer reveals that a willingness to put aside everything of societal value in one's life (in this case possessions) must be an essential part of discovering one's truest self, who One Truly Will Be.

The reaction of the disciples is all too typical: "What about us?" said Peter. "We have left everything to follow you" (Mark 10:28). Despite all of Jesus' warnings, the signs and symbols concerning his impending doom, his followers still await a big political/social payoff, it seems.

Still, Jesus gives it another try; now on the very road going up to Jerusalem, he once more tells his disciples that

> "The son of man will be handed over to the chief priests and scribes; they will condemn him to death and hand him over to the Gentiles, he will be mocked and spat upon, and flogged and killed; and three days afterwards, he will rise again." (Mark 10:33–34)

Their response? Two of his inmost circle of three, James (the Greater) and John, both witnesses to the Transfiguration, approach and ask a favor: "Allow us to sit with you in your glory, one at your right hand and one at your left" (Mark 10:37). With what can only be viewed as supreme patience, Jesus explains that there can be no will to power for those who seek God; "Whoever wants to be first must be the slave of all" (Mark 10:44).

A ray of hope is added, however, in what will be the final healing miracle of Jesus' career in Mark, the restoration of sight to the blind beggar Bartimaeus. The word "Bartimaeus" means "son of the precious one," a name that could be applied to all children of God, even to blind disciples, and this healing speaks to the ultimate enlightenment of Jesus' circle of followers.

As he approaches the city, it becomes clear that Jesus already has a following in Jerusalem, or at the very least a network available to him, although Mark presents this as Jesus' first visit to the capital. Jesus instructs two of his disciples to go into a village opposite the Mount of Olives; as they enter it they will come upon a colt as yet unridden by anyone. They are simply to untie it and bring it back; if anyone questions them, they are to say, "The Master needs it and will send it back without delay" (Mark 11:3).

Significant here is the use of the term "Master," which Jesus has never before used in reference to himself. There is an important difference between the terms "rabbi" (teacher) and "master." Before the destruction of the Temple there was no ordained rabbinate as we know it today; any respected spiritual teacher could be called "rabbi." The term "master" was more specific and more likely to be used by the Essenes, who referred to their leaders and revered teachers by that title. Further, Josephus writes of the Essenes that "They have no one certain city, but many of them dwell in every city."[49] This would certainly include Jerusalem, with its Essene's Gate. It would seem likely that the colt in question would belong to an Essene, and insofar as the village or city gate was a traditional gathering place for spiritual teachers to offer their thoughts, it would be a very safe bet that one would find an Essenic teacher at their gate. Additionally, the rule of the order mandated absolute hospitality and forbade individual posses-sions; a colt would belong to all Essenes communally and would have to be shared with generosity. The simple words that "a Master needed it" would probably have been sufficient to ob-tain the use of the animal.

The arrival of Jesus in Jerusalem is greeted by throngs of significant size and enthusiasm, once again suggesting that, if nothing else, word of the young preacher had spread there, perhaps propelled by Jerusalem's major Essene contingent and their admirers in the city. In keeping with his primary theme, Mark reports the words shouted by the crowds as Jesus passes:

> Hosanna! Blessed is he who comes in the name of the
> Lord! Blessed is the kingdom of our father David which
> is coming. Hosanna in the heavens! (Mark 11:9–10)

Mark's Jewish audience would no doubt recognize the words of the 118th Psalm, "Blessed is he who enters in the name of the Lord; we bless you from the house of the Lord." The significance of the choice of this psalm would not be lost on them, for it is a psalm of victory, a song of deliverance:

> They surrounded me on every side,
> But in the Lord's name I drove them off.
> They swarmed round me like bees;
> They attacked me, as fire attacks brushwood,
> But in the Lord's name I drove them off . . .
> Listen! Shouts of triumph
> In the camp of the victors! (Ps. 118:11–15 NAB)

Nevertheless, the great irony behind Mark's text is that these words are being offered in the Gospel as Jerusalem lay in ruins and the Temple obliterated. Thus, Mark's implication is

that the revolution might have never occurred and Jerusalem's
Temple would still stand had this enthusiasm for Jesus and
his approach to Jewish life been embraced by the leadership.
Aiming at the Pharisees of Mark's own day and at their position in the family quarrel, Mark asserts that an acceptance of
their solution to the crisis of post-70 Judaism, rather than that
of the Jesus Jews, would result only in more destruction and
hardship for the Jewish people.

It is at this juncture that the "Cleansing (better, the 'Inclusioning') of the Temple" scene occurs. After this explosive
event, things settle down a bit, into the more traditional for-
mat of a "disputation," that is, a public discussion and debate
on a religious topic. Once more it must be emphasized that
this discussion does not represent a particularly prosecuto-
rial move on the part of those questioning Jesus; the disputation was a common and commonly accepted part of Jewish
intellectual life. As a matter of fact, it is Jesus who seems to
initiate the disputation. The day after he turns the Court of
the Gentiles upside down, he returns to the Temple, and is
approached by the chief priests, scribes, and elders, who
ask him, "By what authority are you acting like this? Who
gave you authority to act in this way?" (Mark 11:28). Jesus
responds with what certainly appears to be an invitation to
debate: "I also have a question for you, and if you give me an
answer, I will tell you by what authority I act. The baptism
of John: was it from God or from men? Answer me" (Mark
11:29–30).

Jesus' questioners do not insist on a response to their first
question and apparently accept his invitation to disputation.
But they are at a loss how to respond:

> "What shall we say? If we say, 'From God,' he then
> will say, 'Then why did you not believe him?' Shall
> we say, 'From men?'"—but they were afraid of the
> people, for all held that John was in fact a prophet.
> (Mark 11:31–32)

This incident reflects back on the question on divorce put to Jesus on the Jerusalem road; not a true quest for knowledge or for the best application of Torah prompts such questions as these, but simply a striving for one-upmanship and power, the type of practice that Jesus firmly condemned following the request of Zebedee's sons. With such power plays as their primary goal, Jesus' questioners are unable to come up with a "safe" response: "So they answered, 'We do not know,' to which Jesus says, 'Then I will not tell you either by what authority I act'" (Mark 11:33).

Round One of the Disputation to the Galilean.

Yet, what *is* the answer to Jesus' question on baptism? If the representatives of the Jewish establishment had said, "John's baptism was of God," Jesus could have well criticized them for their non-belief in the Baptist, although the Gospels make no mention of such, or of any official criticism of John. As John's focus seemed to center on Herod, it probably would have seemed politically wise for the religious establishment to just stay out of it. But after making such a criticism, Jesus would have had to have kept his part of the bargain and answer the initial question. The same would have been true if he had received the opposite response, that John's baptism was "of men." However, Jesus, as a master disputationist, could have tailored his response to that of his opponents: if John's work had come "from God," with Jesus as John's heir, then his own work would share that same legitimacy. The response "from men" on the other hand would have given Jesus the perfect opportunity to reiterate his key message, the value of all human beings as images of I Will Be Whatever I Will Be and the need to revere God's presence in them. It would provide the chance for him to appear in a part of the Temple relegated to the outcast, as a champion of the people versus the establishment, a sort of first-century "outside-the-beltway" crusader. We can believe from the way Mark has set this scene that the response of those in the crowd would certainly have been overwhelmingly positive.

In truth, as the text makes it clear that the Jewish establishment did not embrace John but is afraid to criticize his memory publicly, the answer "from men" represents the actual opinion of Jesus' questioners, for this text is plainly geared toward Mark's post-70 audience in the midst of a very public and messy dispute over the future of Judaism. The failure of the revolt, the devastation of Jerusalem, and loss of the Temple did nothing to enhance the people's faith in their leadership. The primary question of the day, "Why did God do this terrible thing to us?" indicted that leadership squarely. If the Jewish people had been doing something to provoke God's wrath or abandonment, it was the Jerusalem establishment that had led them there, hence the perfectly legitimate question rising from the still-smoldering ashes of the Temple: "Why should we listen to you now?" It is a question that the Jesus Jews would obviously hope to exploit to their advantage in the family quarrel.

As evidenced by his own interchanging of the titles "son of man" and "son of God," for Jesus there seems to be little difference between the phrases "of God" and "of people." Although Mark's Gospel does not contain the famous phrase "The Kingdom of God is within you," that sentiment is present in everything his Jesus does. In the power vacuum of post-70 Jewish life, Mark's Jesus is making a strong case for a Judaism centered on and flowing from all the images of I Will Be, not merely the remnants of a failed leadership.

The Vineyard

In response to the leadership's non-answer to his question, Jesus offers a parable:

> "A man planted a vineyard and put a wall around it,
> hewed out a winepress, and built a watchtower; then
> he let it out to vine-growers and went abroad. When
> the season came, he sent a servant to the tenants to

collect from them his share of the produce." (Mark 12:1–2)

In this well-known story, the first servant sent by the owner is beaten and sent away empty-handed, a second is treated just as badly, and a third is killed. Finally the vineyard owner sends his "beloved son," but the tenants murder him as well, in the belief that the death of the heir will leave them in ultimate and sole possession of the vineyard.

At the end, Jesus then asks, "What will the owner do? He will come and put the tenants to death and give the vineyard to others" (Mark 12:9).

The traditional Christian interpretation of this text has been one of successionism, the notion that Christians have now taken the place of the Jews as God's Chosen People. This parable has been used to justify the view of all Jews as killers of "the beloved son and heir," deserving themselves only of displacement and death. Yet, true immersion into the Jewishness of Jesus and the nature of the family split within Judaism alters radically such an anti-Semitic interpretation of the text. In these scenes of direct disputation with the Jewish establishment, Mark will lay bare the differences between the two sides in the family dispute and put forward most pointedly the arguments of the Jesus Jews, primary among which is that the responsibility for the disaster of 70 rests squarely at the Pharisaic establishment's feet.

To begin, we should note the unusual description of the vineyard. It is encircled by a wall; the winepress is hewn into rock, and, most noteworthy, the property includes a watchtower. If anything it seems more like a fort or a city prepared for battle than a winemaking enterprise. The description of the vineyard leaves little doubt that it is meant to be seen as the city of Jerusalem itself, the city of the fabled King David.

The second book of Samuel describes David's capture of Jerusalem from a Canaanite people, the Jebusites. After taking the city, David "fortified the surrounding area, from the Milo inward. David kept growing stronger, for the Lord of hosts was with him" (2 Sam. 5:9–10). The Milo was the citadel of Jerusalem. Over time, however, the political power of the royal house of David had eventually ended with the Jewish exile in Babylon, and descendants of David were not reinstated, even as vassals, when the Persian King Cyrus allowed the return of the exiles to Palestine. Thus the only subsequent rulers with the title of "king" had been the Maccabees, who claimed no blood relationship with David, and the Herods, who were not Jewish by birth. It was generally believed, however, that the Messiah, when he came, would be a descendant of David.

In this light, it can be seen that the "tenants" of Jesus' parable in whose hands David leaves his fortified vineyard are those who followed David in leadership, pointedly those in the present day, including Herod and the very men now questioning Jesus. Herod was certainly responsible for the death of a "servant of David," John the Baptist, himself of Davidic stock through his mother, Elizabeth. And now Jesus, aware of the intentions of this leadership toward his own life, identifies himself as Messiah, heir to David.

Particularly interesting and noteworthy in the context of the family quarrel is the line "This is the heir; come on, let us kill him and the inheritance will be ours" (Mark 12:7). This seems to be putting forth the idea that the Jerusalem establishment would never hand over leadership of the Jewish people even to the Messiah but would rather murder the one whom they recognized as David's heir. In brief, the struggle between Jesus and the Pharisees, and by extension between the Jesus Jews and the Pharisee party of Mark's day, is *not* one of legitimate spiritual differences but only of power, at least on the Pharisees' part.

Of great significance is the closing line of the parable: the owner (David) will in turn put the tenants to death and give the vineyard to others. If the vineyard represents the fortified city of Jerusalem and by extension, Judea in revolt, then it would seem clear that its tenants would not simply give up without making use of those fortifications. Mark is, once again, strongly implying that the ill-fated revolution, the destruction of Jerusalem and loss of the Temple, could have been avoided had Jesus been embraced by the Jewish leadership. The opposite having been the case, David himself, a symbol of Jewish glory and salvation, turns against these leaders and against Jerusalem.

Contrary to the traditional interpretation of this parable offered by a Christianity out of touch with its own Jewishness, the Jewish people as a whole are not indicted here as the killers of the owner's son or as responsible for the loss of the vineyard. In the center of an intense struggle for the minds and hearts of post-70 Jews, Mark would have made as much headway faulting the Jewish people themselves for their fate as one would by blaming the occupants of the World Trade Towers for 9/11. Such a tactic would have been nonsensical. Mark's quarrel is with the remaining post-70 leadership, and it is to them that the parable is addressed, as the text asserts: "They [the Jewish leadership] saw that the parable was aimed at them and wanted to arrest him . . ." (Mark 12:12).

Moreover, the parable does not close with the death of the tenants. Jesus adds the remark, "Have you never heard this text: 'The stone which the builders rejected has become the main corner stone. This is the Lord's doing and it is wonderful in our eyes'?" (Mark 12:10–11). This verse, like those used by the crowds cheering Jesus' arrival into Jerusalem, is taken from Psalm 118. In traditional Jewish belief, all one hundred fifty of the Psalms are thought to have been composed by David himself. Psalm 118 contains some of the most memorable lines in the entire Psalter:

> In distress I called on the Lord;
> The Lord answered me and brought me relief.
> The Lord is on my side,
> I have no fear;
> What can man do to me? (Ps. 118:5–6)

It is better to take refuge in the Lord
Than to trust in mortals;
It is better to take refuge in the Lord
Than to trust in the great. (Ps. 118:8–9)

I shall not die but live
And proclaim the works of the Lord. (Ps. 118:17)

The lines of which Jesus reminds his questioners concerning "the stone which the builders rejected," are similarly misunderstood by Christians as support for the idea that Judaism has fallen from God's favor to be replaced by Christianity. In such a view, Jesus is the stone rejected by the Jewish people, the builders. But a view of the entire parable in its and Christianity's native Jewishness shows how inaccurate this interpretation is. It is the post-Davidic leadership, particularly the Pharisees, whose party now opposes the Jesus Jews, who are the parable's "tenants," those who reject Jesus and his approach to Jewish life, in his day and in the post-70 universe. Just as David was opposed by the leadership of his day (Saul, his children, and those supporting them), not to mention various non-Jewish peoples (Jebusites, Philistines, and others), Jesus in his day and the Jesus Jews in Mark's face vigorous opposition. But through "the Lord's doing," the "gates of victory" eventually open; Jerusalem becomes the City of David. In the same way, Mark is expressing his optimism that the Jews who follow Jesus as Messiah will ultimately carry the day over their Pharisee opponents and emerge victorious in the struggle for Judaism's future.

In all of this we must never lose sight of the one central fact about Mark's Gospel: that it is fundamentally a work of propaganda, meant to sway minds and hearts in the midst of a bitter family quarrel within Judaism. I would repeat here the words quoted from James Carroll, that "to read the New Testament apart from the context of the Roman war against the Jews—as it almost always is—amounts to reading *The*

Diary of a Young Girl without reference to the Holocaust."⁵⁰ By extension, to read Mark's Gospel (indeed, all Christian scripture) as a non-Jewish document is the equivalent of turning Anne Frank into a Gentile and her experiences into those of any other child in occupied Holland. Mark's Gospel is being created in the very crucible of the Jewish War and in the major questions it precipitated; nothing about this Gospel can be accurately understood apart from them.

The Factions

Following this parable, Mark parades forward representatives of the various factions in Jewish leadership to take their turn in the Disputation. The first is a combined group, "a number of Pharisees and men of Herod's party" (Mark 12:13), another illustration of the propagandist nature of Mark. Herod, presumably Herod Agrippa come down from Galilee for Pesach, was no friend of the Jewish religious establishment, nor they of him. His father, the immensely cruel Herod the Great, had not even been a Jew by birth but an Idumean; he and his family had never been accepted by the Jewish people. If any group in Jewish life had a reason to cozy up to the Herods, it was the Sadducees, not the Pharisees. The Sadducees were the more Temple-oriented party, and Herod the Great had built the magnificent new Temple in Jerusalem. As the Herods were Roman appointees and puppets, it was to the benefit of the Sadducees to at least passively support them, and thus minimize the risk of bringing imperial wrath down on the Temple. But here Mark makes sure to link the Pharisees, his day's opponents of the Jesus Jews, with the hated Herod family, as it is their delegation that asks Jesus the question, "Are we or are we not permitted to pay taxes to the Roman emperor? Shall we pay or not?" (Mark 12:14–15).

Of course, this question represents another no-win situation for Jesus. A "yes" to a tax question would not have endeared him to his oppressed fellow-Jews, while a "no" would have certainly brought the Roman authorities quickly down upon his head. But let us examine the question itself from the Torah point of view.

Nothing in the Torah forbids the exacting or the paying of tribute. In the past the Jewish nation had engaged in both practices, demanding tribute of neighboring peoples when it was strong and paying it to others when it was not. There is, therefore, no question that the paying of tribute is "permissible," demeaning certainly, but not forbidden by Torah. The Pharisees and Herodians who are asking the question surely know this.

In response, Jesus asks to see a silver piece. "Whose head is this, and whose inscription?" he asks. "Caesar's," comes the reply. "Pay Caesar what belongs to Caesar, and God what belongs to God," says Jesus (Mark 12:16–17). That Jesus uses a "coin of the tribute" to make his point is of note, for it also aids in answering the question raised by his response: What exactly *does* belong to Caesar? The coin displays an engraved image, that of the head of the Roman state (in Jesus' day, Tiberius). Of course, the making of graven images is a Torah offense, and a very serious one at that, as the Second Commandment points out. Jesus' answer, then, implies that that which is profane, that which is outside the Torah, belongs to the realm of Caesar, by which he manages to take a swipe at the oppressive Roman authority, but in a way subtle enough to avoid immediate trouble with it.

The question still remains: What belongs to God? In this same chapter of Mark, Jesus will strongly remind the Jewish authorities and his entire audience of God's name and the ramifications for those made in God's image. I Will Be Whatever I Will Be is the God of Jesus of Nazareth, the concept that underpins his entire work and message. So perhaps the question should be rephrased: What belongs to I Will Be Whatever I Will Be? What should be "rendered" to such a God?

Several related answers emerge. Graven images are forbidden, because they falsely limit the open-endedness of God. An image contributes to the illusion that we know who and what God is and subsequently can predict or control God's behavior. From there it is a very small step to doing the same for others and for ourselves, with division and outcasting the inevitable result. Nothing that is false can belong to God. We are thus obliged to render unto YHVH everything that is real.

Tribute rankles on several levels, but if that payment is not financially oppressive, perhaps the worst is the feeling of slavery that it produces, the loss of freedom supposed. (Note that Jesus' questioners had not asked if paying *overly burdensome* tribute was permitted by Torah, but tribute in general.) Jesus, in his teachings on non-violence and his recommended attitude toward the Roman occupiers, seems not to be troubled by such things. Freedom for an image of I Will Be has little to do with who rules whom, as Jesus' admonitions concerning rank among his own disciples point out. The freedom to truly actualize one's full potential, to be whatever one will be without the fetters of caste or judgmentalism stunting that process—*this* is what Jesus proclaims. In pointing out the coin of the tribute, Jesus is saying that concern over the question of tribute itself is an unreal one, the type of thing that "the rulers of the Gentiles" worry about. His answer to the question is one more form of saying, "It must not be that way with you" (Mark 10:43).

Of course, the family quarrel is never far below Mark's surface, and by answering in this way, Mark's Jesus is further pointing out the weaknesses of the Jewish leadership, lumping them in with those authority seekers whose primary concern is the non-reality of power, in Jesus' day and in Mark's own.

As a matter of fact, in this answer and the one to the question that follows it, Mark takes aim squarely at that establishment. After the failure of the Pharisees and Herodians in the Disputation, the Sadducees step up to the plate. The Sadducees, "who maintain that there is no resurrection," ask

Jesus the contrived question of a hypothetical widow who has married and lost seven husbands, all brothers, who had married her in obedience to the *mitzvah*. "At the resurrection, when they rise from the dead, whose wife will she be?" (Mark 12:18–23).

Jesus' answer has been partially examined in our discussion on the Essenes. Following his assertion that "When they rise from the dead, men and women do not marry, they are like angels in heaven" (Mark 12:25), Jesus adds the following dictum:

> "As for the resurrection of the dead, have you not
> read in the book of Moses, in the story of the burning
> bush, how God spoke to him and said, 'I am the God of
> Abraham, the God of Isaac, the God of Jacob'? He is not
> God of the dead, but of the living. You are very far from
> the truth." (Mark 12:26–27)

In the culminating question of the Disputation, note the masterful way in which Mark's Jesus leads his audience toward the all-important name of God insisted upon by Jesus. From the very first question regarding John, the idea of the sacredness of people as unjudgeable images of God has led toward an ultimate exploration of that Name itself, unspeakable as it may be. Jesus' bringing the image of the burning bush, the event at which that Name was revealed, into the discussion paves the way for that exploration. And along with this, Mark makes a very strong assertion regarding the future of the Jewish people: God is the God of the living, not the dead. As difficult as it may be, Jews now need to grow beyond the Temple; they must face this future, so radically different from their past, with a spirit of openness to the new. The Jewish people are still alive and they, too, must be whatever they will be, not continue to try to be only what they once were. For Mark, the Jesus Jews and their approach to Jewish life will best serve this purpose.

Even though the Herodians and Sadducees are finished as a power at the time of Mark's Gospel, he makes sure to include and debunk them in his Disputation scene nonetheless. It would seem that Mark does not want to leave his audience with the impression that some other faction in Jewish leadership could have done a better job than the Pharisees. For Mark, post-70 Judaism should clearly be a case of new wineskins for new wine.

The two more points remaining in the Disputation have already been thoroughly examined in this book, the scribe's question concerning the greatest of the *mitzvoth*, and Jesus' defining question to that same group concerning the ancestry of the Messiah. Of all the groups in the Disputation, it is noteworthy that the scribes fare the best. Jesus' answer that the greatest of the *mitzvoth* is to be found in the sacred *Shema* and the second in the love of neighbor is greeted by his questioner with the words, "Well said, teacher . . . that means more than any whole offerings and sacrifices" (Mark 12:32–33). Jesus' response is the exact opposite of that given to the Sadducees: "You are not far from the kingdom of God" (Mark 12:34). To be accurate, Jesus does embarrass the scribes as well in the final question of the Disputation and in an additional, rather scorching critique (Mark 12:37–40). Still, a scribe is the only questioner about whom Jesus has anything positive to say, and he receives high praise indeed. After the destruction of the Temple, the Torah took on even greater importance in Jewish life; though Temples may be razed, the Torah, both in scroll form and, as was often the case with scribes, committed to memory, could go on forever. Thus scribes became even more important figures in the post-70 Jewish world than previously, a fact of which Mark is clearly aware. Following Jesus' praise of the scribe in search of the greatest *mitzvah*, Mark adds, "After that nobody dared ask him any more questions" (Mark 12:34). With this, the Disputation is over, and Jesus' fate is sealed. He has won and by so doing has lost his life.

For Jews, there is great irony in losing by winning. The practice of the disputation did not end with the scene of Mark's event, the Temple. Rather, the practice of disputation was revived by the monarchs of medieval Europe, only the debates were held between Christian and Jewish scholars in Christian countries, refereed and judged by the Christian ruler. As Wylen points out,

> These disputations were ordered for the amusement of the nobility or as a pretext to initiate a new policy of persecution. All interfaith learning and discussion was carried on in a spirit of competition and missionary fervor.[51]

In such debates, the deck was clearly stacked. Jews were not permitted any type of objective study of Christianity from Christian sources; if a Jew approached a priest to learn about Christianity, he was expected to convert. The Christian debater, however, was often himself a Jewish convert, with all the attendant knowledge of a cradle Jew (note, however, that conversion *to* Judaism was punishable by death in medieval Europe). There was no possible way for the Jewish scholars to ever "win" such a disputation. What Christian monarch could risk the consequences of judging against his own Church? In 1240, for example, the Disputation of Paris was held, initiated by a Jewish convert and monk, Nicholas Donin, who had denounced the Talmud as seditious to the king and queen of France. Rabbi Yehiel of Paris and his fellow scholars debated skillfully, but still the Talmud was condemned. Great masses of Talmuds and other Jewish tracts, confiscated from French Jews, were publicly burned all across the kingdom.[52]

Another such disputation occurred in Barcelona in 1253 between Rabbi Moses ben Nahman (Nahmanides) and a convert, Pablo Christiani. The most that any Jewish scholar could hope for was to successfully defend Judaism against the charges made in such a debate, for there was never a question of counter-attacking Christianity, at least not if the Jewish scholar wished to preserve his life and those of the rest of the Jewish community. But even such a small victory had its costs. Rabbi Nahmanides did successfully answer the charges brought against the Jews of his day, but the strain broke his health and his success left his life in danger from outraged Christians. He was forced to flee Spain and died an exile.[53]

It is the height of irony that, while furiously excoriating the Jews for "their" treatment of Jesus, Christians then treated them in exactly the same manner. But this only goes to show the depth of blindness and viciousness to which a family quarrel can sink. The great tragedy here is not only that Christians have thusly treated Jews, but that they have failed to recognize themselves *as* Jews. The Disputations in Paris and Barcelona were no more about obtaining true knowledge than was that in Mark's Jerusalem. Had they been, then each side would have seen their inherent sameness and realized that they were more than brothers engaging in fratricide; they were one people bent on self-genocide. And if Jesus' assurance that "whatever you do to the least of my brothers, you do unto me" is to be believed, then mustn't Christianity ask itself: "Who has truly murdered the heir to the vineyard?"

CHAPTER 12

Last Days

And already the demons of the past are meeting
With the demons of the future and negotiating about me.
Yehuda Amichai[54]

MARK'S THIRTEENTH CHAPTER CENTERS ON JESUS' PREDICTIONS concerning what is called "end times" or "last days." The question for the modern reader is: To which days or times is the text referring?

From its earliest days, Christianity has had a fascination with "the end of the world." Much in the Christian scriptures indicates that even before the family split became permanent, Jesus Jews expected that Christ's return was imminent, and such expectations did not die with the first generation of believers. During the spring of 999 CE, for example, "end-times fever" had grown to the point that many farmers in Christian Europe did not bother to plant their crops—to what end, if the end was about to commence? Some Christian denominations, such as Jehovah's Witnesses and the Seventh Day Adventists, were founded around a specifically predicted date for the Second Coming. The dawning of the year 2000 also saw its share of Christians who believed they were living in "the last days" and still do.

Perhaps nowhere else is the Christian distance from its own Jewishness better displayed than in its treatment of these words of Jesus. Rarely, if ever, does a Sunday sermon on this or a similar gospel text center on the destruction of Jerusalem and its Temple by Rome, despite the opening lines of Chapter 13:

> As he was leaving the temple, one of his disciples exclaimed, "Look, teacher, what huge stones! What fine buildings!" Jesus said to him, "You see these great buildings? Not one stone will be left upon another; they will all be cast down." (Mark 13:1–2)

It is important to Mark in establishing Jesus' place in post-70 Judaism to show him predicting the very event causing the family quarrel. Jesus sees what the Jewish leadership of his day did not; by association, Mark paints the heirs to that leadership as likewise blind.

When asked by Peter, James, John, and Andrew when these awful events will occur, Jesus first warns against following false Messiahs (several claiming messianic status would arise between Jesus' death and the fall of Jerusalem). He also speaks about the persecutions his followers will endure, persecutions described more fully in the Acts of the Apostles.

However, the following words may seem the most obscure to Mark's readers today:

> "But when you see 'the abomination of desolation' usurping a place which is not his (let the reader understand) then those who are in Judaea must take to the hills." (Mark 13:14)

Exactly what readers have understood by the phrase "abomination of desolation" has varied greatly. It has been identified with the antichrist, the papacy, Luther, Calvin, Protestantism in general, Catholicism in general, Hitler, the United States, World Government, the Arab states in conflict with Israel, Islam in general, Satan himself, or any combination of these and others.

Mark's Jewish audience, however, would have had little trouble recognizing Jesus' reference, which is to a statement by the prophet Daniel. In the ninth chapter of the book bearing his name, Daniel, an exile in Babylon after the destruction of Solomon's Temple, offers what Judaism traditionally has understood to be a prophecy concerning the post-exilic future. The angel Gabriel appears to Daniel, telling him that

> Seventy weeks are decreed for your people
> and for your holy city.
> Then transgression will stop and sin will end,
> and guilt will be expiated. (Dan. 9:24 NAB)

In Jewish mystical writing, a week can be used to represent a year, as seven days, the period of creation, can symbolize a totality, a complete set, such as a full year. Indeed, the Jewish people spent approximately seventy years in exile in Babylon.

The text in Daniel then goes on to speak of "one who is anointed and a leader," traditionally understood to indicate Cyrus, the Persian king who conquered the Babylonian empire and permitted the Jewish return to Judea (Dan. 9:25). This royal house is soon "cut down," however, setting the eventual stage for the victories of Alexander the Great and his successors in the east, the Antiochus kings. The stormy relationship between that dynasty, with its brutal program of forced Hellenization, and the Jewish people is chronicled in the books of Maccabees. There we see the family of the same name rise up in revolt against Antiochus IV, a revolt spurred on by a terrible sacrilege committed in the rebuilt Temple of Jerusalem:

> On the fifteenth day of the month Chislev in the year
> one hundred and forty-five, the king erected the
> abomination of desolation upon the altar of holocausts.
> (1 Macc. 1:54)

In the Hebrew original, a play on words exists between the phrase "abomination of desolation" and the term "Lord of heaven," the title the Greeks gave to Olympian Zeus.

Antiochus, in his effort to remake his third of the old Al-
exandrian empire into a totally Greek realm, had declared all
other religions illegal. For Jews, he specifically forbade their
sacrifices to YHVH, mandated work on the Sabbath, turned
all shrines and sanctuaries into centers of Greek worship,
commanded all Torah scrolls to be burned, and outlawed circumcision (1 Macc. 1:41–56). Then, in a crowning indignity
to the Jewish faith, Antiochus gutted the Temple of anything Jewish, raised a statue of Olympian Zeus in the Holy of
Holies, and there sacrificed swine to that god. The story of the
eventual triumph of the Maccabees over Antiochus and the
rededication of the Temple to the service of YHVH provides
the basis for the feast of Chanukah.

This "abomination of desolation" is the focus of Daniel's
prophecies:

> And the people of a leader who will come shall destroy
> the sanctuary. Then the end will come like a torrent;
> until the end there shall be war, the desolation that is
> decreed. For one week he shall make a firm compact
> with the many; half the week he shall abolish sacrifice
> and oblation; On the Temple wing shall be the abomi-
> nation of desolation, until the ruin that is decreed is
> poured out upon the horror. (Dan. 9:26–27 NAB)

Writing in the post-70 universe of Jerusalem's fall and the
Temple's destruction, Mark again raises the specter of "the
abomination of desolation," making sure to warn the reader to
"understand" the image and reference. Josephus' description
leaves little doubt as to what Mark means the reader to understand by that image:

> And now the Romans, upon the flight of the seditious
> into the city, and upon the burning of the holy house
> itself, and of all the buildings round about it, brought

their ensigns to the temple and set them over against its eastern gate; and there did they offer sacrifices to them, and there did they make Titus imperator with the greatest acclamations of joy.[55]

The victorious legions of Rome erected their standards, standards that included graven images of all kinds, then, like Antiochus earlier, sacrificed to these images in the ruined Temple. The abomination repeats itself.

So Mark's prophetic warning to understand the meaning of the phrase "abomination of desolation" ironically ought to resound for Christians as well. As first and foremost a Jewish phrase, rooted in Jewish history, it can be easily missed outside of that context, or worse, become a phrase ripe for fantasy and misuse if separated from its fundamental Jewishness.

Mark's treatment of the "end times" of his Jewish world is an encapsulation of Jesus' vision of the future and his plans for it. It is a common Gospel technique to portray Jesus as predicting events that have already occurred by the time of the writing of the Gospel. Accordingly, we have already seen Mark's Jesus predict the destruction of the Great Temple, with such a catastrophe implying the loss of the entire city of Jerusalem. By doing this, Mark presents a Jesus who could read the times well enough to see the coming revolt against Rome and is insightful enough to recognize its hopelessness. His efforts to spread his philosophy of non-violence and love of enemy are an attempt to stem this tide of revolution, an attempt that he likewise recognizes will fail. In the face of the end of the Jewish world, when the sun, moon, and stars themselves will seem darkened, Jesus and his movement, having taken no part in the revolt, would step forward to assume leadership and set out a direction for a decimated Jewish people. "The son of man" will come "in the clouds with great power" and "gather his chosen from the farthest bounds of earth" to which the war had scattered them (Mark 13:26–27).

It was to be Jesus of Nazareth, not a Yohanan ben Zakkai, who would set the course of Jewish life for centuries to come.

Jesus, however, does not survive this Pesach. At the time of the creation of Mark's Gospel, the disciples of Yeshua and the disciples of Yohanan are already locked in a bitter contest for the future of Judaism, a battle which, absent their charismatic leader, the Jesus Jews will not win. Thus what we see in Mark 13 is how Jesus' anticipated assumption of post-70 Jewish leadership evolves into his followers' anticipation of his immanent return from heaven and, failing that, into an ultimate "end time" more to be desired than feared—indeed, the inaccuracy of one Christian denomination's predicted date for doom and parousia is still referred to by its adherents as "The Great Disappointment."

And so a paradigm set up early in Jewish Christian history comes full, reversed circle: a passage mournfully rooted in the deaths of a half-million human beings and in the hopes of their survivors twists itself round into a bitter disappointment that we are all still alive, that we have any earthly future left. Such a "disappointment" can only find its source in the sense of self-loathing and despair of life that accompany loss of identity, a deep but unspecified feeling of being adrift in the world. It is a condition of which the book of Wisdom speaks: "The whole world was bathed in the bright light of day and went about its task unimpeded; these people alone were overspread with darkness . . . But heavier than darkness was the burden each was to himself" (Wisd. 17:20 REB). The temptation to such despair, to a sense of existential foreignness in God's universe is something that Jews know well—the temptation, not the acquiescence to it. For, from the slaughters of 70 and 135 through to the Holocaust of the 1930s and 40s, Jews have overwhelmingly engaged in the opposite of despair, in a retaining of their sense that, not only is this life as much their home as any world to come, but that "Judaism is the track of God in the wilderness of oblivion," as Abraham

Joshua Heschel writes.[56] For Christians to regain a sense of their own inherent Jewishness, then, would be for an entire people to turn away from endings without end and embrace an eternal, holy present; to accept as gift and birthright a life, as Heschel again puts it, lived "between two historic poles: Sinai and the Kingdom of God."[57]

CHAPTER 13

The Last Seder

> . . . The music I hear
> from a house I don't know is inside me now
> and words not intended for me are the winds I ride
> for the rest of my journey, like a sailboat.
>   *Yehuda Amichai*[58]

FOR MARK'S JESUS, REPRESENTING AS HE DOES THE JEWISH people both in their post-70 situation and throughout history, the feast of Pesach (Passover) provides a critical opportunity both to teach and offer symbol. Pesach is a feast of liberation, commemorating the exodus of Israel from slavery in Egypt; how ironic must have been those Passovers during and following the siege and destruction of Jerusalem. Indeed, it was here that the custom of singing the song of lament and hope, "Next year in Jerusalem," probably began. Bishop Spong and Michael Goulder are correct: the story of Jesus' last Seder meal would have been constructed to complement and be read alongside the Torah portions for Passover time. Before we enter into an examination of that meal, however, a word must be said concerning one of the most misunderstood, vilified, and (in a historical sense) ill-used figures of the human epoch: Judas Iscariot.

Immediately before Mark's Passover tale commences, we read the account of Jesus' anointing in the house of Simon the leper, an account already examined in a previous chapter of this book, an episode that closes with these words:

> Then Judas Iscariot, one of the Twelve, went to the
> chief priests to betray him to them. When they heard

what he had come for, they were glad and promised
him money; and he began to look for an opportunity
to betray him. (Mark 14:10–11)

Is there a figure portrayed as more evil in Western literature, art, and music than Judas? As a member of my Catholic
seminary's choir, I would sing at Good Friday services, "*Yudas,
mercator pessimus*"—"Judas, merchant most evil." Virtually
every piece of pre-modern painting on the subject shows
Judas at the very least as proud and affronted, money bag
in his tight fist; at worst, as an incarnate devil, sometimes
with little horns, goat feet, and all. Dante places him in the
deepest circle of hell, that level reserved for those treacherous against their rightful lord; there his soul, along with those
of Brutus and Cassius, is forever devoured by a giant, three-
headed Satan. But beyond this, "Judas" long ago became a
name synonymous, not only with treachery, greed, and dei-
cide, but unfortunately with the Jewish people themselves in
the Christian imagination. Indeed, his very name sounds like
the word "Jew," as well it should, for that word is derived
from the name of the largest tribe among the twelve tribes of
Israel, Judah. This man's name, as well as that of one other
apostle, actually *was* Judah; the *s* was added to avoid confusion with that other loyal apostle of the same name. The title
"Iscariot" is not wholly clear and could indicate that Judas
came from the town of Kerioth or that he belonged to one of
the most radically violent subsets of the radical Zealots, the
"Sicarios" or "Assassins"; conceivably both could be correct.
But what seems most likely is that the latter name-derivation
is the case, since Jesus' apostles were known to be Galilean
and Kerioth is outside of that region (near Hebron), making
Judah the Iscariot a man—at least at one time—convinced
that only wholesale violence, including the "terrorism" of as-
sassination, could free the Jewish people from Roman enslave-
ment. Still, as one of Jesus' inner circle, he could not have
missed his master's commitment to absolute non-violence, and

so it is entirely possible that this Judah was a man who had *turned away* from the path of the Assassins, a man already with blood on his hands who had sought forgiveness and a new life with the teacher of "love your enemies." At the very least he may have been a man, like many in his time and ours, torn between the two alternatives of absolute love and total war, a man seeking above all the best way to liberate his people and himself, spiritually and physically.

Mark's Gospel, along with Matthew's as well, records the response of those who witnessed Jesus' anointing with expensive nard ("Why this waste? The perfume could have been sold for more than three hundred denarii and the money given to the poor") as coming from "some of those present" (Mark 14:4–5). Judah the Iscariot is not mentioned in these earlier Gospels as the spokesperson for this sentiment; it is not even specified as coming from a disciple. Not until John's later Gospel, when, as we have seen, the family quarrel is at its most white-hot, were these words placed in Judas' mouth, and with that symbolically into the mouths of all Jewish people (John 12:5–6). The assumption is that Judas, as the treasurer of the movement, would have objected to the anointing, but no evangelist but John designates him as having anything to do with the group's funds (John 12:6; 13:29). Completely overlooked are the words of Jesus, which surely would been much more disturbing for his longtime followers at the very gates of Jerusalem than the price of nard: ". . . you will not always have me. She has done what lay in her power; she has anointed my body in anticipation of my burial" (Mark 14:7–8).

In all likelihood, to anoint a figure such as Jesus about to enter the Jewish capital during a major feast at a time when rebellion was already in the air would have been seen as an act of anticipation, not of death, but of kingliness and imminent liberation, a new Moses and a return of that original Passover, of renewed freedom from slavery. Instead, after all the work and struggle, what Jesus' followers seem to hear from their leader is a concession of defeat, even death. After wrestling mightily with God and with people, this savior of Israel appears now to be unable, indeed, doom-ridden. It might very well have seemed to those at that critical juncture that their dear master and teacher was about to consciously engage in a suicide mission.

This, then, is the context in which Judah the Iscariot decides to approaches the Jewish leadership. Why? Perhaps he is disillusioned? His is the heart of a revolutionary, and he might have supposed that Jesus, having come to Jerusalem at this sacred and volatile time, would now lead the Jewish people in rebellion only to hear Jesus insisting that his anointing was not as king but as corpse. If Jesus was truly bent on one last dramatic gesture, to die for the cause rather than give it full life, perhaps Judah's concerns were for all the others in his company, for the general slaughter he had left the Assassins and followed him who was meek and humble of heart specifically to avoid.

Or perhaps Judas' true concern was for Jesus himself. As a political zealot, Judah the Iscariot may have well known that Jesus had, as yet, violated no Torah injunctions carrying anything even approaching a death sentence. Judah was a patriot, and may well have trusted the Jewish leadership to follow the *mitzvoth*, to perhaps punish Jesus or otherwise negate his influence with the people, but surely to spare his life, a life that Jesus himself seemed so intent on forfeiting.

It is important to note that Mark describes the chief priests as *offering* Judah Iscariot money, but he never states that Judah took it. Thus, stories of his return to the high priests in self-disgust, of his attempts to return the thirty silver pieces, and of his suicide do not exist in Mark's Gospel. Rather, it is later gospels, reflecting a further deterioration in the Jewish family quarrel, that make such claims, and even here, Judah protests that he has brought an *innocent* man to his end, as if he did not expect the death penalty to be invoked, since the Torah would not see it as merited. Was Judah the Iscariot actually trying, in his own way, to save the life of a Jesus he may have seen as despondent and a danger to himself and his followers? Was it the Jewish leadership who betrayed *Judas*, not Judas who betrayed Christ?

Add to all this the Jewish scriptural echoes which Mark surely expects his readers to recognize. The original Judah, son of the patriarch Jacob, renamed Israel, is one of only two of eleven siblings to attempt to save the life of his brother, Joseph, when the other ten brothers decide upon murder. Significantly Reuben, the oldest, urges his brothers not to kill Joseph, but to throw him into a pit instead, for he intends "to save him from them and restore him to his father" (Gen. 37:22). Judah, similarly afraid for his brother's life, then addresses his brothers:

> "What do we gain by killing our brother and covering up his blood? Come, let us sell him to the Ishmaelites, but let us not do away with him ourselves. After all, he is our brother, our own flesh." (Gen. 37:26–27)

The implied parallels between Genesis' Judah and Mark's are quite clear and their implications startling. Judah, Israel's son, is trying to preserve the life of Joseph, against overwhelming odds (10 to 2). The suggestion to accept payment for him is a ruse; Judah uses his brothers' apparent attitudes toward money to keep Joseph from death. Later, when the brothers are being sorely pressed by an older Joseph, unrecognized by them but now viceroy of Egypt, Judah, not Reuben, the eldest, steps to the fore, appealing in deeply moving language that no further heartbreak be inflicted upon his aged father. Judah even volunteers to take the place of his youngest brother, Benjamin, particularly beloved of Jacob, whom Joseph has threatened to hold hostage in Egypt. The clear implication is that Judah now wishes he had done the same for another brother, long before.

In his Gospel, Mark uses the resonance of the Genesis story to suggest that Judah the Iscariot is likewise attempting to save

Jesus' life by "selling" him into the custody of the Jewish leadership, using the money as a ruse, as did the earlier Judah. Perhaps Judas himself, like his famous namesake, intended to step forward and help his spiritual brother once the dust had cleared a bit and the leadership had exercised whatever penalty the Torah commands.

What Judas may not have expected is that the Jewish leaders trying Jesus do *not* act in accordance with the Torah in this case; Jesus' death sentence is anti-*mitzvoth* and therefore fundamentally anti-Jewish. In keeping with his central theme and purpose, Mark the propagandist shows the other side in the family quarrel, perfectly willing to violate the *mitzvoth* they profess to defend, to be consistently unworthy of trust, that of Judas or of the survivors of the Roman War. Judas, like Judah before him, did a right thing for naïvely wrong reasons.

In another ironic and destructive twist, Judah the Iscariot, the traitor, the money-grubber, comes to symbolize the Jewish people for two millennia, rather than Jesus of Nazareth, as Mark intends. The later Gospel writers, particularly John, foster this confusion, as the fight for the future of Judaism turns progressively against the Jesus Jews. In the end, the man whose very name, Judah, had become synonymous with a people that Jesus' followers now wished to renounce is portrayed as a disillusioned, unmourned suicide. The message is plain: if Jews had any sense at all, they would annihilate themselves, but lacking such resolve, their separated Christian brethren would endeavor to help them toward that end, and in so doing wipe out any trace of their shared identity and the shame of having lost the post-70 quarrel.

Even seen at his stereotypical worst, Judas Iscariot needs to be embraced along with the rest of Christianity's lost Jewishness, as an act, if nothing else, of long overdue self-awareness. For Dante himself assigns those who betray their family members to a ring only slightly above that center of Hell itself.

Passover

At this point of the story, however, the disciples' main concern is not a Dantean but a very Jewish one: making adequate preparation for the celebration of Passover. In response to their question concerning this, Jesus gives rather enigmatic instructions:

> "Go into the city, and a man will meet you carrying a jar of water. Follow him, and when he enters a house give this message to the house-holder: 'The Teacher says, "Where is the room in which I am to eat the Passover with my disciples?"' He will show you a large upstairs room, set out in readiness. Make the preparations for us there." (Mark 14:13–15)

As discussed earlier, much in this passage opens itself in the light of a possible close connection between Jesus and the Essenes. It would appear that some sort of prearrangement had been made with "a man carrying a water jar," and Jesus does not instruct the two disciples he sends into the city as to the time they should do so. Even if they were to arrive at a popular time for the day's water-gathering—early in the morning, for instance—the coordination here seems a bit tenuous to say the least.

Josephus dedicates considerable time to an examination of the Essenes and their way of life. According to him, the large majority of Essenes were celibate, increasing their population via new adult members and the adoption of orphans.[59] Josephus also states that

> They have no one certain city, but many of them dwell in every city; and if any of their sect come from other places, what they have lies open for them, just as if it were their own; and they go in to such as they never knew before, as if they had been ever so long acquainted with them.[60]

Here, therefore, may be an explanation for Jesus' assurance that his emissaries automatically would find welcome and a room for his use. Apparently there existed an Essene Quarter in Jerusalem with its own recently rediscovered gate.[61] Among the generally celibate Essenes, there would be no women to do the traditionally female job of toting water; the disciples would have no trouble finding a man doing so—indeed they would find any number of them. And according to Essenic rule and practice, these men would all be duty bound to accommodate Jesus' needs, if he were himself an Essene. Pixner maintains that Jesus' last Passover was celebrated in this Essene Quarter, in an upper room of a house that went on to become a synagogue of the Jesus Jews and the Jerusalem "Church of the Apostles." (Today it interestingly constitutes the second floor of a structure venerated as the tomb of King David.)[62]

This episode, then, only adds to the evidence that Jesus was an Essene or at the very least known and respected by them. Josephus himself, certainly a worldly man by the time of his *Histories*, claims to have spent three years among the Essenes,[63] from which can be inferred that one could obtain an experience of the community without making permanent vows to it. Perhaps the earlier time spent "in the desert" by John the Baptist and Jesus could be explained in terms of a sojourn to the Essenes' principal communities there, such as Qumran. Essenes did not always keep to their monastic settlements, but would travel broadly, publicly teaching, exhorting, and engaging in the arts of healing and divination for which they were known.[64] In this sense, both John's and Jesus' work would have been consistent with Essenism. At the same time, it appears clear that Jesus' teachings differed quite considerably from mainline Essenism with its extreme insistence on ritual purity and a radical strictness in the keeping of the *mitzvoth*. Still, it is not inconceivable that, as with almost any movement, the Essenes may have had their left and right wings and that Jesus represented the Essenist left, as it were.

In any event, Jesus' recommendation that the disciples' request for a room be made in the name of "the Teacher," rather than in Jesus' own name, is significant. The major figure in Essenic tradition was the fabled "Teacher of Righteousness," who lived and taught about one hundred fifty years before the birth of Jesus. One of the Essenes' principal points of contention with establishment Judaism involved the assumption by the second generation of victorious Maccabees of both Jewish crown and high priesthood. The founder of the Maccabees line had been a priest and therefore a member of the tribe of Levi, as the Torah prescribes; the high priesthood would have been possible for him. However, he was *not* a descendant of King David, who was of the tribe of Judah; therefore the Maccabees had no scripturally based right to David's crown. The Essenes felt that the combining of the offices of king and priest polluted both and refused to recognize either the Maccabees' monarchy while it lasted or the high priesthood that continued until 70 CE. Their "Teacher of Righteousness" was particularly vocal on these points, boldly speaking his truth to power, and he was eventually executed for it by the priest-king Aristobulos II.

For Jesus to refer to himself as "the Teacher" (the title of that past great figure was often thus shortened) is not necessarily to claim to be that man, dead for a century. It could, however, indicate an identification, on Jesus' part and on the part of others, of his work with that of the original Teacher of Righteousness, since Jesus, too, speaks his spiritual truth to the powers of his day. The Dead Sea Scrolls scholar, Theodore H. Gaster, maintains that the title "Teacher of Righteousness" came in time to refer to an office rather than to the specific original individual.[65] If such is the case, might it be that Jesus held that office and title for his generation (as John the Baptist may have in his time), and had set out to travel the land, spreading his approach to righteousness? Or, perhaps more likely, would the leader of any Essenic-oriented community or group likewise be called "Teacher of Righteousness"?

However arrangements for the room were made, Jesus and his Twelve assemble there for Seder, and for what was to become for many Christian denominations the singular act of Jesus' life outside of his passion and rising:

> During the supper he took bread, and having said
> the blessing he broke it and gave it to them, with the
> words: "Take this; this is my body." Then he took a
> cup, and having offered thanks to God he gave it to
> them; and they all drank from it. And he said to them,
> "This is my blood and the blood of the covenant, shed
> for many." (Mark 14:22–24)

To Mark's Jewish audience, several important points would arise with Jesus' departure from the traditional Passover *haggadah* (or service). Of the famous Four Questions traditionally asked by the youngest at the Seder, the first is "On every other night we may eat *matza* or *chametz*. Why do we only eat *matza* on this night?"

Matza, of course, is the plain, flat, unleavened, cracker-like bread which the Torah commands Jews to eat not only on that day but for the next seven, as well as from the fourteenth to twenty-first day of the Jewish month of Nisan (Exod. 12:15–20). The traditional answer given to the Second Question is that God foreknew the haste with which Israel would need to depart Egypt once permission was given to do so; there would be no time for bread to rise, and the Jewish people would need provision for the beginning of their journey. Naturally, over centuries, Jewish tradition has delved passionately into the depths of these questions and their possible answers; one such examination involves the difference between the breads mentioned, *matza* and *chametz*.

Matza, this line of inquiry points out, consists of nothing but the bare essentials: flour, water, a little salt, no leaven, a barebones simple bread of necessity. One eats it to survive, not necessarily as a treat or for its gourmet glamor, although many do love *matza* and eat it at times other than Passover. (As someone who came to his Jewishness as an adult, I can attest that it is an . . . acquired taste!) *Chametz*, on the other hand, is an umbrella term for any type of baked good not *matza*: sweet breads, cupcakes, brownies, as well as plain (perhaps not compared to *matza*!) white bread could all be considered "*chametz.*" Clearly there is more to *chametz* being *chametz* than just leaven. *Chametz* represents the "extras," the luxuries of life.

Matza is the bread of the wilderness, which the Jewish people are about to enter and in which they will spend a generation, and as such, represents that wilderness experience and the reason that one would ever seek it: to be free of the distractions, to sort out the essential from the extra. Further, the Hebrew term for Egypt is *mitzreheim*, and *mitzreheim* means "narrow straits." In one sense, this is a perfect description of the topography of Egypt; a satellite view will show only the thin ribbon of the Nile with a narrow, green border to each side, and a myriad of narrow straits branching out at its delta, as the river meets the Mediterranean. Beyond the physical, though, the Torah is trying to tell us something about a state of mind and heart: to be in Egypt is to be in a state of spiritual narrowness, of tunnel vision which keeps us from seeing the "big picture." *Narrow straits* is the polar opposite of I Will Be Whatever I Will Be; this is why Moses insists that the Jews cannot worship their God in Egypt. To be a *slave* in Egypt is to be totally at the mercy of one's own blinders, to lack any sense of perspective, to be self-enslaved. In such a place, *chametz* is an impediment, a bribe the insecure soul pays itself. The scriptures, Jewish and Christian, often make reference to this attachments to the extras; free though they may be, the Israelites often rail against their desert experience, longing for "the flesh pots of Egypt." The wealthy young man

who approaches Jesus in Mark 10:17 just as quickly walks
away with "a heavy heart."

It is with *matza*, that bread of necessity, of simplicity and
basicness, the food of wide-open expanses, of limitless vision
and liberation from slavery's self-image that Jesus now identifies with himself. This must have spoken volumes to Mark's
post-70 audience. Jerusalem is rubble, the Temple is gone; was
Israel ever more in the wilderness than this? Without minimizing the hardship, Mark's Jesus insists that his teachings and
life could sustain the Jewish people during this terrible time
and lead them to a future of freedom—especially so, as they
insisted upon and embodied the limitless openness of I Will Be,
of YHVH's word in Torah, and of those created in that image.

And Jesus' second statement regarding the wine is, to borrow a phrase, like unto the first, if not even more intriguing and liberating. Wine is probably the most consistent and
binding image of the Seder; the *haggadah* prescribes four cups
of wine for this meal, each with the traditional blessing. In
Judaism, wine stands for life, hence its central role in the re-
telling of the "passing over" of the angel of death and in the
liberation of Jewish life.

For Jesus to identify wine with blood, his own or anyone
else's, is not surprising from this viewpoint. In Jewish tradition, blood has likewise been identified with life; indeed,
for the Torah blood *is* life. "For the life of the flesh is in the
blood," says Leviticus (Lev. 17:11). The same passage, however, as well as others in Torah, strictly forbids the ingesting
of blood. "If anyone of the house of Israel or of the strangers
who reside among them partakes of any blood, I will set My
face against the person . . . and I will cut him off from among
his kin" (Lev. 17:10). Even today, those who keep strict kosher and even many Jews who are less inclined to do so still
attempt to refrain from or at least strongly limit the blood-
content of their meats. So for Jesus to identify a cup of wine
as containing his blood, even symbolically, is to shockingly

contravene a standard and deeply held, God-given conviction of those at the table, not to mention appearing cannibalistic in the process. Note that Jesus only identifies the wine as his blood *after* he had already given the cup to the Twelve and they all had drunk from it. Imagine their reaction, then, to his words.

One of the major lessons I learned early and often in my study with Rabbi Ullman is that, with Jewish scripture, what *isn't* said is as important as what is. And Mark's Gospel is a work of Jewish scripture. Applying this principle to the Last Seder scene, we find something rather remarkable, considering the evolution of Christian sacrament and service, left unsaid and undone.

A consistent symbol and theme in Christian life is that of Jesus as "the lamb that was slain," the Paschal (that is, Pesach) lamb. That image and its attendant theology fill many Holy Week, and especially Easter, services. The Torah commands the slaughtering of such a lamb for the Passover Seder, and by identifying Jesus with this lamb, Christianity has sought to establish Jesus' execution as an act of sacrifice ordained by God for the liberation of humankind from sin.

But if Jesus saw himself and his impending death of which he seemed quite aware in this way, why did he not take a piece of *lamb*, say of it, "This is my body," and share *it* among his apostles? Why take up the *matza* instead? Why not use an already well-known symbol of sacrifice to establish the principle of his death as a similar act? It would seem to be a ready-made and interpretation-proof vehicle for the idea of crucifixion as salvation, whereas his use of wine as a symbol (or more) of his "blood shed for many," clearly invokes a response of horrific, *mitzvoth*-oriented horror on the part of his Jewish listeners.

Perhaps this is the entire point. Since Jesus' experience in John's *minyan*, Mark identifies Jesus with the Jewish people themselves. From this perspective, Mark might not want to present Jesus and, therefore the Jewish people, as a "slain lamb," devoured whole, "head legs, and entrails" with nothing left over; indeed, "if any of it is left until morning, you shall burn it," Torah commands (Exod. 12:9–10). At best, this lamb symbol would convey not an image of resurrection from suffering, but of the Jewish people caught again in some recurring cycle of doom. By choosing the cup of wine as the conveyance for the concept of his suffering and death, Jesus, the master teacher, casts the entire matter in another light.

Jesus as a teacher of Torah could not be unaware of the shock and revulsion his statement regarding his blood would create for the Twelve who had just finished drinking from that cup. Like any good teacher, Jesus does not deal in disconnected concepts. He establishes a link between his first point and his next, between the *matza* as his body and the wine as his blood: in identifying his body, his very person and presence, with the bread of hard wilderness and liberation from narrow straits, Jesus proposes his life and teachings as a vehicle for both. He then reinforces and illumines that proposal with a shock tactic designed to offer an example of exactly how that vehicle would progress.

Jesus is fully cognizant, as he has been in all of his teachings, of publicly choosing the way of I Will Be Whatever I Will Be over the path of strictly enforcing the *mitzvoth*, the question at the heart of the family quarrel which Mark's Gospel is largely created to address. There is ample scriptural precedent for Jesus' approach, and he cites it in the words from Isaiah which he quotes at the Inclusioning of the Temple scene. Isaiah, a prophet speaking for God, plainly urges the putting aside of the *mitzvoth* regarding foreigners and outcasts; his exhortations are linked to the salvation of Jerusalem and the Temple during his day. Jesus clearly feels that this type of inclusion is the only way to achieve true liberation for all the images of I Will Be and to avoid the useless and bloody revolution he sees on the horizon and which Mark's audience must deal with. So, by declaring consumed Pesach wine to be his blood, despite the *mitzvoth*, despite the shock,

Jesus is letting his disciples know the difference between the familiar, comfortable slavery of narrow straits and the intense wrestling with God and people in the wilderness necessary for Israel to become truly a free people regardless of who rules them. It is one thing to *talk* of the *mitzvoth* being made for people, not people for the *mitzvoth*; it can be safely pleasant to preach inclusion of the outcast, especially if one *is* an outcast, to a society which, as then constructed, is entirely unlikely to attempt it. It is another thing altogether to see that same principle applied to a *mitzvah* of which you approve, one elemental to your own sense of proper and improper, of existential comfort. One can almost hear the Twelve saying to each other, "Heck, I'm as open as the next guy, but . . ." Guess who's coming to Pesach!

I see the same process at work with numerous subjects in today's world: the acceptance of a homosexual family member, gay marriage, and global human rights, to name only a few. Sometimes the most apparently loving and supportive parents uncharacteristically, it seems, will refuse to have anything to do with a child who "comes out of the closet" to them. A number of the more "liberal" individuals I know profess to have "no problem" with gay relationships or marriage as long as they "don't have to look it," that is, as long as gay couples do not hold hands, embrace or kiss in public, all things that straight couples are culturally entitled to do. And for many years, the United States has held itself to a very different standard of accountability with regards to human rights than that which it has promoted for others; at this writing, the status of prisoners held at Guantanamo Bay and America's refusal to permit its soldiers to come under international rules governing war crimes are two examples of this attitude.

We are dealing here largely with what I call "the yuck factor." Despite perhaps one's best intellectual intentions, it seems impossible for many of us to get over the fact that certain things, certain actions, or certain "types" of people might make us feel a visceral "yuck"—give us "the willies," makes us feel uncomfortable. At that point, too often truth loses to a cringe in the stomach.

Jesus will have none of it, and he knows that in order to hasten the reign of I Will Be, his followers need to have none of it as well. And so he fires a broadside at the safely sacred, saying in essence: Sidney Poitier *has* shown up for Passover, and he and your daughter are talking *chuppah* (wedding canopy); your youngest son has invited the boy next door to Seder, and they're discussing possible grandchildren—*yours*! And your oldest, your pride and joy, in the combat service as you had been, has declared himself a conscientious objector after what he has seen and felt. Yes, and the cup of wine—this is my blood. Can we still sing, *"Baruch ata, Adonai,"* knowing full well what the title stands for—"Blessed are You, Who Will Be Whatever You Will Be"? Yes, we must sing it, now more than ever!

Plus there is more precedent for what may appear to be a disregard for the *mitzvoth*. God gives aloud the first ten of the six hundred and thirteen "speakings" (the Hebrew word is *not* "commandment") to the entire assembly of Israel at Sinai. The second of these forbids graven images or any likeness of "what is in the heavens above, or on the earth below, or in the waters under the earth." God promises to punish to "the third and fourth generations" those who do so (Exod. 20:4–6). Yet during the same wilderness experience, when the Israelites are bitten by seraph (fiery) serpents, God commands Moses, "'Make a seraph figure and mount it on a pole. And if anyone who is bitten looks at it, he shall recover.' Moses made a copper serpent and mounted it on a standard . . ." (Num. 21:8–9). In other words, God orders Moses to do exactly what God's freshly revealed and quite specific *mitzvah* forbids! And it works. No wonder Jesus evokes this image when he speaks of being lifted up like that molded serpent (John 3:14). With the eyes of his native Jewishness, we can see Jesus' own fuller attitude toward the *mitzvoth* proclaimed here.

In another instance, the Torah strictly limits the priesthood to those in the tribe of Levi: "the Lord set apart the tribe of

Levi to carry the Ark of the Lord's covenant, to stand in attendance upon the Lord, and to bless His name, as is still the
case" (Deut. 10:8). And yet, in the first book of Samuel a "man
of God" reproaches the Levitical priest, Eli:

> "Thus says the Lord: I revealed Myself to your father's
> house in Egypt when they were subject to the House
> of Pharaoh, and I chose them from among all the
> tribes of Israel to be My priests . . . I intended for
> you and your father's house to remain in my service
> forever. But now—declares the Lord—far be it from
> Me! . . . I will raise up for Myself a faithful priest who
> will act in accordance with My wishes . . . ." (1 Sam.
> 2:27–35)

That "faithful priest" was to be Samuel, a member of the
tribe of Ephraim, he who anointed David king, thus establishing the Messianic dynasty. Not bad for one who had no biblical right to his office as priest. "Yet," one might say, "it is
God who actually overturns the *mitzvoth* in these cases." But
prophets speak for God, and, as we see in the case of Eli, it is
an unnamed "man of God" who brings him God's decision.
What is Jesus if not, like Isaiah and Jeremiah before him, a
prophet?

A word must also be said about the wine in Jesus' cup
being identified as also "the blood of the covenant." This
phrase in and of itself lends further credence to Jesus' Essenic
sympathies, if not identity, in that Essenes believed themselves to be the recipients of a new covenant, given to their
original Righteous Teacher. The term "new covenant" itself
stems from its use by the prophet Jeremiah:

> See, a time is coming—declares the Lord—when I
> will make a new covenant with the House of Israel and
> the House of Judah. It will not be like the covenant
> I made with their fathers, when I took them by the

hand to lead them out of the land of Egypt, a covenant
which they broke . . . I will put My teachings into
their inmost being and inscribe it upon their hearts.
Then I will be their God and they shall be My people.
No longer will they need to teach one another . . . .
(Jer. 31:31–34)

These words of hope, promise, and the primacy of the
individual heart were written by Jeremiah after the fall of
Jerusalem and destruction of the Temple by Babylon; they
are addressed to those held captive in exile there. Once again,
the comparison to the post-70 situation could not have possibly escaped Mark, and the indication of a new covenant by
Mark's Jesus is no textual accident. The Essenes, for all their
strict constructionism regarding Torah, essentially saw themselves as living in this "new covenant" of Jeremiah.

Here we may finally see how such devotion and attention
to the intricacies of Torah could possible coexist with, indeed create, the compassionate openness of a Jesus. At their
best, the Essenes rejoiced to hold to the *mitzvoth* as a lover
holds his own inmost heart in the person of the beloved. They
loved the practices, rituals, and injunctions of Torah and of
their own Torah-based rule just as the living things of earth
respond to the sun; they were made for each other. The sabbath is made for people, not people for the Sabbath. In the
Greek of the gospels, the word *yia* ("for") can also be translated "about"; human life is not *about* the sabbath or any of
the *mitzvoth*; the sabbath and the entire Torah are about *being*
human. For those of the new covenant, the *mitzvoth* were a
chart to the human soul. God gave them, not because they
were true about God, but true about us. In keeping them, we
stay healthy, we realize our own innate strength and happiness, and can be whatever *we* will be. Turned on their heads,
expelled from the heart, and used as weapons of judgmentalism and division, the same *mitzvoth* can sicken, weaken, and
depress the spirit and deprive the future.

The attitude of Jesus of Nazareth toward the *mitzvoth* is, I believe, illustrated beautifully in a poem by the Israeli poet Yehuda Amichai. In it he writes of his father's imparting of the *mitzvoth* to him:

And he hugged me tight and whispered in my ear
Thou shalt not steal, shalt not commit adultery, shalt not kill.
And he lay the palms of his wide-open hands on my head
with the Yom Kippur blessing: Honor, love, that thy days
may be long upon the earth.[66]

But then:

. . . he turned his face to me one last time,
as on the day he died in my arms, and said, I would like
   to add
two more commandments:
the Eleventh Commandment, "Thou shalt not change,"
and the Twelfth Commandment, "Thou shalt change. You
   will change."[67]

Only someone who treasured the *mitzvoth* could have spoken any of those words. Just as only a tested and proven general such as Yitzhak Rabin could have genuinely offered his hand to Yassir Arafat, or a former Vatican diplomat such as Angelo Roncalli have initiated the sweeping reforms of Vatican II as Pope John XXIII, perhaps only an Essene, whose very life was Torah, could have picked up the *matza* and wine of Pesach and said, "My body. My blood."

The writer Yehudah Mirsky relates an instance upon which he asked his father, whom he describes as "a genuine religious humanist and, in his quiet way, akin to a saint," how his vision differed from that of the ultra-Orthodox.

"To them," he said, "halakhah (Jewish law) is a fence,
and if what you're about is building fences, then the

fence can never be tall enough, the moat around it can never be wide enough."

"And you, abba, what is halakhah to you?"

"To me," he said, "it's a way of life."[68]

Not merely "a way," but a way of life, of enabling life, promoting life.

Is it not incumbent upon the followers of the Jewish Jesus, Jesus the "engaged Essene" who sought for that movement to be "in the world, though not of the world," to refrain from making of his last Seder a series of fences, never high enough for those who build them, but, by virtue of their very existence, too high for Jesus' taste? Surely by now the reader has noticed that no mention has been made here of the distinct and often divisive theologies surrounding the "nature" of the Lord's Supper, the "presence" (real, relative, or symbolic) of Jesus in the bread and wine.

But then, what is your motive in asking?

CHAPTER 14

Which Jesus Do You Wish?

Every night God takes his glittering
merchandise out of his showcase—
holy chariots, tables of law, fancy beads,
crosses and bells—
and puts them back into dark boxes
inside and pulls the shutters: "Again
not one prophet has come to buy."

Yehuda Amichai[69]

A FORESHADOWING: MARK 14:2 RELATES A CONVERSATION among the "chief priests and scribes" concerning possibly seizing Jesus and putting him to death. "'It must not be during the festival,' they said, 'or we should have rioting among the people.'" Yet as we move into Mark's Passion Account, the festival is still going on. What, if anything, has changed the minds and strategy of the Jewish establishment? Why this seeming contradiction in the text?

Just before leaving for Gethsemane (the name means "olive press" and recalls Jesus' parable of the vineyard), Jesus addresses the Twelve with a quote: "You will all lose hope, for it is written: 'I will strike the shepherd and the sheep will be scattered'" (Mark 14:27). Mark's Jewish audience, especially in its post-70 circumstances, would recognize and understand this reference to the prophet Zechariah who was active at around 520 BCE, at the time when the Jewish people are just beginning to return to ruined Jerusalem from exile in Babylon. The returnees, the overwhelming majority of whom would have been born in Babylon, would not have witnessed

190

the war 70 years before, must have been overwhelmed by what they saw and by the monumental task ahead of them. Although they would have heard all the stories for years, surely the reality must have raised the question: How could all this have happened?

Zechariah, speaking for God in the first person, responds with a section of his prophecy sometimes referred to as "The Song of the Sword":

O sword!
Rouse yourself against my shepherd,
the man who is in charge of my flock . . .

Strike down the shepherd
And let the flock scatter,
And I will also turn My hand
Against all the shepherd boys,
Throughout the land . . .
Two-thirds shall perish, shall die,
And one-third of it shall survive.
That third I will put into the fire
And I will smelt them as one smelts silver
And test them as one tests gold.
They will invoke Me by Name;
And I will respond to them.
I will declare, "You are my people,"
And they will declare,
"The Lord is our God!" (Zech. 13:7–9)

In identifying Jesus with the Jewish people, Mark compares their post-70 plight to that of previous generations of Jews. At the time of the creation of Mark's Gospel, as had been the case in Zechariah's day, some hope still existed that Jerusalem and its Temple might yet be rebuilt in time. It is the position if not the plan of the Jesus Jews to be best suited to lead such an effort. Mark continues the parallel further by providing for post-70 Jews that which Zechariah also offered the returning exiles: an explanation of the relevant events, and a spirituality of that explanation. Clearly the sword is about to fall on Jesus just as it did upon the Jewish people he represents; his movement will be scattered, as are the Jewish people in the post-70 universe. As was the case in the Babylonian invasion, Jews have experienced great casualties, but the remnant of the population, although tested, will be restored, invoking God "by Name," a direct reference to "I Will Be Whatever I Will Be," the God whom Jesus of Nazareth proclaims, with all its ramifications for Jewish renewal. King Zedekiah, the ruler of Judah defeated by Babylon, lost the city and the Temple, and thrust his subjects into exile by refusing to heed the words of the prophet Jeremiah. Jesus will be subject to violence and death, as will the Jewish people of his day, for what Mark portrays as a similar deafness or worse on the part of the Jewish leadership.

In a strong reference to the Transfiguration scene and to the fates of Moses and Elijah, Mark shows Jesus as once more taking Peter, James, and John aside with him. This time they are not terrified, but rather weary, and, in an important scene, Jesus' inner circle sleeps through his agony. In his propaganda war with the Pharisee movement of his day, Mark has been intensely critical, directly and symbolically, of the Jewish establishment of Jesus' day, whose legitimate heirs that movement claims to be. A question that establishment could have rightfully posed in return could well have been, "And what of your own leaders? Did they do any better, for Jerusalem or for their own master?" By portraying Peter, James, and John not so much as incapable of action but naïve and asleep to the true threat posed by the Jerusalem elite, Mark realistically casts that leadership as at least not having actively contributed to the whirlwind that follows, though it certainly does not come off as heroic either.

A short time later in the narrative, Mark responds to that

same concern and plays to the same audience when, as Jesus is seized, "one of the bystanders drew his sword, and struck the high priest's servant cutting off his ear" (Mark 14:47). Here is a point symbolically important to Mark's efforts: if Jesus stands for the Jewish people still reeling from war, it can only help the cause to show at least some defense being mounted against his attackers. Notice that the admonitions against violence which follow in later Gospels' versions of this incident do not appear here. The swordsman is described as a "bystander" as well, not as Peter, the prime apostle. A delicate propaganda balance is here struck between the pacifism of Jesus' teaching and the need to address an audience who might yet harbor adverse feelings toward those who had raised no hand in defense of Jerusalem.

Who is this bystander? Earlier, Jesus is described as coming to the house given him for Passover with the Twelve; by the time he reaches Gethsemane he is addressing "his disciples" (Mark 14:17, 32). It would seem entirely possible that the Twelve were not the only participants at the last Seder; some among those who prepared or owned the room might have also wanted to share Pesach with the Teacher. This would mean that those "disciples" were in all probability Essenes. Josephus points out that Essenes, though basically non-violent, would still carry weapons for use against thieves, making them more "non-aggressive" than "pacifist," strictly speaking. There is no record of Essenic conduct during the battle for Jerusalem, but their apparent acceptance of the use of weapons for direct self-defense would not seem to preclude their participation. The fact that the attacker cuts off the ear of the servant of the high priest himself, but is apparently not attacked or wounded in response would lend further credence to the idea that he is a member of the ultra-respected, virtually irreproachable Essenes. In any event, by putting that sword in the hand of a "bystander" and not specifically a disciple or apostle, Mark both preserves the non-violent stand of the Jesus Movement and keeps it from appearing less than patriotic when, symbolized in the person of Jesus, the Jewish people face attack.

Between the scene of the sleeping three and the sword-wielding bystander, Mark inserts the person of Judah the Iscariot. He is unaccompanied by any priest, scribe, or elder but rather escorts a "crowd armed with swords and cudgels" to seize Jesus (Mark 14:43). The sense here is that this is not an "official" act of the Jewish authorities, and the unofficial nature of the entire enterprise will only grow as events unfold in the text.

Judah's choice of a means of identification of Jesus in that dark grove is itself of interest: a kiss. In one sense, there is nothing remarkable about the choice; the kiss, the embrace, was a common form of greeting in Jesus' place and time. What singles Jesus out is the absence of that embrace on Judah's part for anyone else present. Still, in this gesture Jewish scriptural echoes are very much present.

In the Jacob Saga (Gen. 25–35), its hero, after a long sojourn outside the land of Canaan, returns to face his brother, Esau, whom he has wronged. Jacob, in collusion with his mother, Rebecca, had conspired to rob Esau of his birthright as eldest son. Granted, Esau had earlier traded that right to his younger brother for a pot of stew, but one could easily see this, as Esau most surely did, as a bit of light-hearted jesting between siblings. Rebecca, however, prompts her younger son to disguise himself as Esau and to seek the Blessing for the Eldest from his nearly blind father, Isaac, a plan that succeeds. Enraged, Esau plans to allow Jacob to live only as long as their elderly father survives.

In this tale, Jacob betrays both his brother and his father, and in the latter instance, he does so with a kiss: "Then his father Isaac said to him, 'Come close and kiss me, my son'; and he went up and kissed him. And he smelled his clothes and he blessed him, saying, 'Ah, the smell of my son is like the fields that the Lord has blessed'" (Gen. 27:26–27).

From any vantage point, this family quarrel, like most, is a nasty business: a mother, favoring one son so highly over another that she initiates and even plans the deception of his elderly, near-blind father, and a second son more than willing to go along with never a word of protest or later of self-recrimination. Esau, whom Torah describes as sort of a rough-and-tumble figure but in no way evil or deserving of ill treatment, is heartlessly betrayed by both mother and brother. And there is the coldness of the pretender, still able to go forward with his ruse, even as he kisses his old father and hears his poetic words. True, he has previously "purchased" the birthright from his hungry brother, but—*mercator pessimus!*—do Jacob's actions show him in any way worthy to be the inheritor of God's promise to Abraham? Yet, God blesses Jacob with abundance; the blessing of Isaac "sticks." Years later, when commanded by God to return home and face the music, Jacob does encounter Esau . . . who *kisses* him and weeps, welcoming him like the long-lost brother he is, without a word of reproach (Gen. 33:4).

As previously discussed, Mark's Judas can be seen as a man as blithely naïve to the machinations of politics and to the danger posed by the Jewish establishment as the rest of the sleeping apostles were. He may merely be trying to save Jesus from himself, or at the very least, to save the rest of the movement's members from what Jesus himself seems to consider a doomed confrontation with the powers that be, Jewish and Roman. But even if he is little more than a selfish traitor out for personal gain, if he attempts only to deceive Jesus with false love and loyalty, merely masquerading, after a certain point in time, as an apostle; if his kiss is not one of "this is for your own good," but rather an unabashed lie, the scriptural allusion causes one to ask, has he done any worse than that patriarch of bogus affection, Jacob, whom God would rename Israel? To Judah the Iscariot, Jesus is a spiritual teacher; Isaac was Jacob's own father. It could be said that Jacob's deceptions, despicable as they were, still were a part of God's plan, the eggs that needed to be broken to make the Divine omelet. But Christians for millennia have seen Jesus' agony, crucifixion, and death in exactly the same terms—an unfortunately necessary part of God's loving plan for salvation—so much so that Christian tradition labels Adam's sin, which turned human life from an Eden to a vale of tears, a *"felix culpa,"* or "happy fault," for without it Christ would not have come. The salvation was more than worth the sin. Yet Judah the Iscariot, even with the scriptural precedent of Jacob upfront blocking for him, has been completely castigated and vilified. The phrase *"felix culpa"* long ago entered the popular religious vocabulary, but *"felix perfidia,"* happy treachery?

If one takes together Mark's description of Judas' actions in Gethsemane, their echoes of Jacob added, that Gospel's lack of any reference to received payment or bad end for the Iscariot, and its treatment of events at the home of Simon the Leper, one is left with the overall impression that a reviled son of Israel, an amateur at deceit compared to that forebear, like him had a part of divine necessity, even blessing, to play. Regardless of intent, without the actions of Judas, redemption in the traditional Christian sense would not have been possible. Was salvation worth the sin for Adam, but not for Judah the Iscariot?

Mention should be made of one figure in the olive grove even more curious than the mystery swordsman:

> Among those who had followed Jesus was a young man with nothing on but a linen cloth. They tried to seize him; he slipped out of the linen cloth and ran away naked. (Mark 14:51)

Tradition has it that this young man is none other than John Mark himself, the author of Mark's Gospel. If this is the case, however, what would he be doing in the Essene Quarter, unless he himself were an Essene or in the process of joining the order? The fact that the young man in question is clothed in white linen seems to indicate an Essene, as this was their community's mode of dress. In fact, the circumstantial evidence seems to point more to the presence of Essenes at Gethsemane than to that of John Mark, although his Gospel was clearly written by someone with basic Essenic sympathies. Still, in the battle for Jesus, that is, the battle for Jerusalem, Mark shows the Essenes as initially resistant, but ultimately fleeing the fight. Obliterated by the Romans during the First Jewish War, that Essenic movement was not in competition with the Jesus Jews; it is to Mark's advantage to show the legendary order in a mostly positive light, while mildly suggesting in a symbolic way that perhaps it did not do all it could to stem the tide of revolution or to defend Jerusalem when the moment arrived.

From the olive grove, Mark's scene shifts to the home of the high priest. There the chief priests and the whole Jewish council, the Sanhedrin, "tried to find evidence against Jesus that would warrant a death sentence, but failed to find any" (Mark 14:55). Various witnesses disagree; some quote Jesus as saying, "I will pull down this temple, made with human hands, and in three days rebuild another, not made with hands." But Mark maintains that there was disagreement among those testifying even on this (Mark 14:57–59).

Any mention of the Temple and its destruction was bound to be supercharged in the atmosphere of Mark's audience. The testimony represents a misquoting of Jesus' words and intentions; he had merely predicted the destruction of the Temple, not claimed the ability or the intent to do so himself, let alone to miraculously create another. Here it seems that Mark may be responding to a charge leveled against the Jesus Jews by their critics, that Jesus and his followers were anti-Temple and somehow contributed to its ultimate demise with the intention of replacing Temple Judaism with their own approach to Jewish life. Such critics would have easily been able to paint

Jesus as a dangerous radical, a rabble-rouser who stirred up the dregs of society against the Jewish establishment, not caring whether the "exclusionary" Temple survived or not. Each new stab at the established order only added to the Romans' cumulative sense of impatience and fury with the Jewish people, such would say, resulting ultimately in Rome's hard line toward the war's survivors and the restriction on rebuilding Jerusalem and its Temple. Mark, therefore, needs to counter this argument, and in the scene at the high priest's home he does just that, being first sure to give the "accurate" version of Jesus' words in the opening verses of Chapter 13.

Still, if the misquote offered in the testimony sounds familiar, it is. John's Gospel, created during the height (or depths) of the family quarrel, shows Jesus visiting the Temple a total of four times, the first quite early, in Chapter 2. Here we find John's description of the "Cleansing of the Temple," which is not the culmination of Jesus' trouble with the Jewish leadership, but its very beginning. When "the Jews" ask Jesus, "What sign can you show to justify your action?" he responds, "Destroy this Temple and in three days I will raise it up again." The text quickly adds, "But the Temple he was speaking of was his body" (John 2:18–21). By the time of John's Gospel, as previously discussed, the bitter family split between Jesus Jews and the rest of Judaism was nearly complete. No longer was the Jesus Movement trying to gain leadership of and decide direction for Jewish life, so there was no need to worry about Jewish opinion on Jesus and the Temple. Jesus Jews and their companion Gentiles were in the process of morphing themselves into "Christians," a religion completely "new," antithetical and antagonistic to Judaism. Rather than refute false testimony, John therefore takes the very words with which Jesus is perjured in the synoptic gospels and almost glories in them. Yes, of course Jesus said these words, but "the Jews" misunderstood them. Their Temple was to be replaced by the body of Jesus himself; the only reappearance of such a "Temple" would be the resurrection itself.

For Mark's earlier time, however, several important points emerge during his description of that testimony, facts that most Christians so out of touch with their own Jewishness would not know how to recognize, but would have been of specific interest to Mark's original audience. First, the interrogation of Jesus takes place at the home of the High Priest. Second, it occurs at night. And, third, that particular evening is the first night of Pesach. As Louis Walter points out, any one of these conditions would have made the entire proceeding illegal in terms of Jewish law, not only the Toraic *mitzvoth*, but *halakah*, the application of those Torah principles to circumstances of daily life. "The Sanhedrin could not and never did exercise jurisdiction in the house of the High Priest or anywhere outside the courthouse and the Temple precinct," Walter rightly maintains. Additionally, Jewish law forbids criminal procedures from being conducted, even in part, at night or during a feast or the eve of a feast.[70]

As we examine the actual procedure, the testimony and the judgment, other *halakic* problems arise. According to Jewish law,

> a conviction must proceed from the testimony of at least two truthful and independent witnesses, who give evidence both as to the commission of the offence in their very presence and as to the knowledge of the accused that the act was punishable by a particular penalty.[71]

Mark's Gospel maintains that no such "truthful and independent" witnesses existed, and nowhere in his (or any) account of the proceedings is Jesus asked if he knew the penalty for his supposed offences at the time he allegedly committed them.

In other words, Mark seems to be making a point to a Jewish audience familiar with their own customs and law, the same point that Professor Walter asserts: ". . . on the night before the trial Jesus was indeed in the house of the High Priest.

But there was no trial."[72] There are too many glaring viola-
tions of Jewish law by the expert Sanhedrin for this not to be
the case. Rather, what we have in this scene is an investigation
and interrogation which the Council goes to great lengths to
guarantee is *not* a trial, nor would it have been seen as one by
any Jew. If it had been a legal trial and Jesus were to be found
guilty of a capital offense, such as blasphemy, the Jewish authorities would then be in their rights to have him stoned to
death, the Torah-prescribed penalty for that offense: "They
took the blasphemer outside the camp and pelted him with
stones. The Israelites did as the Lord had commanded Moses"
(Lev. 24:23). Indeed, in several places in the Christian scriptures, notably in the story of the deacon Stephen in Acts, we
see that penalty enforced without the seeking of any permission from the Roman authority (Acts 6:9–15; 7:1–60). In fact,
it was usual practice for Rome to leave such matters in the
hands of the local leadership; deciding the legal fate of Roman
citizens and employing penalty of crucifixion Rome reserved
for itself.

We now begin to see the answer to the question with which
this chapter opened: Why, after stating that arresting Jesus
during the festival was a bad idea, did the Jewish leadership
then turn around and do so? Mark here uses a literary tactic:
When the chief priests and scribes say among themselves, "It
must not be during the festival . . . ," Mark's Jewish audience
would expect the next phrase to read, "for it would violate
the law." What they hear instead is the leadership saying, "or
we should have rioting among the people" (Mark 14:2). Mark
once more portrays the Jewish establishment, and with them
the Pharisee movement of his day, as hypocrites who profess
strict adherence to the Torah and *halakah*, but in actuality ignore both when it suits their purpose.

When presented with the opportunity to seize Jesus in the
dead of night, thus minimizing the people's immediate knowledge of the event, the Jewish leadership takes it, for they had
no intention of trying Jesus at all. Rather, they look only to

find evidence of sedition with which they could approach the
Roman authority, leaving it to Rome rather than themselves to
execute the culprit, since Pilate, a Gentile, was not bound by
any injunction against doing so on a feast day. Not knowing if
their investigation would yield proof of any crime deserving
death by Jewish legal standards and being reluctant to bring
the wrath of the people down on themselves in any event,
the chief priests, scribes, and elders decide to do an end-run
around the law and attempt to deliver to Pilate a man presented as a threat to Imperial control over Judea and Galilee.
Fearing for the safety of the Temple after Jesus' actions in
the Court of the Gentiles as well as for their own position of
leadership, the Jewish establishment decides that it is better
to give Jesus to the Romans than to risk an uprising led by
him during the festival, a revolt that would bring the crush-
ing power of Rome down on Jerusalem and its Temple. Let the
hated Romans take whatever blame accrued; no Jewish law
would have been violated, as no trial occurred.

As the testimony proceeds, however, the plan seems to
be stuck in place. Nothing comes forward that could convince a Roman governor to execute a popular figure during a
time when the city is crowded with pious and patriotic Jews.
Finally, the chief priest himself arises to question Jesus. "Are
you the Messiah, the son of the Blessed One?" he asks him
(Mark 14:61).

This is *the* pivotal moment of Mark's Gospel; here hangs
the fate of Jesus of Nazareth, of his movement, and of Jewish
life ever after.

"'I am,' said Jesus, 'and you will see the Son of Man seated
at the right hand of the Almighty and coming with the clouds
of heaven.'" At which the High Priest "tore his robes and said,
'What need do we have of witnesses? You have heard the blasphemy'" (Mark 14:63).

But what blasphemy has occurred? Claiming to be the
Messiah is not to blaspheme the name of God, nor is it a crime
to apply to oneself a quote from the prophet Daniel. Doing so

certainly would be enough to take to the Roman authority, for someone with a major following claiming to be the Messiah would easily be seen as a threat to Roman rule, especially considering that person's tumultuous welcome into the city at Passover time. Deciding to answer the High Priest's question as he did doomed Jesus, as he surely must have understood. But blasphemy?

In crucial scenes like this one, the negative impact of Christianity's distance from its own Jewishness truly takes it toll. For the High Priest was correct to rend his garments; Jesus had committed blasphemy, or so it seemed. That offense occurred in his uttering of those two words, "I am"— "*Ehyeh.*"

We have already seen that this word *Ehyeh* is part of the ineffable name of God which the Torah and *halakah* forbid to be uttered except once a year on Yom Kippur, the Day of Atonement, by the High Priest in the Temple's *Kodesh Kodeshim*, the Holy of Holies. Leviticus states plainly that anyone who "pronounces the name of the Lord, he shall be put to death. The whole community shall stone him" (Lev. 24:16). Of course Jesus, the spiritual leader and Torah teacher, knows this proscription well.

There are any number of other words Jesus could have used in response to the High Priest's question. He could have merely answered, "*hen,*" "yes." If he wished, he could have identified himself with the greats of Jewish history, figures such as Abraham, Moses, and Isaiah in their own decisive moments, by using the phrase "*Heenayni,*" "Here I am," as they did. But instead Jesus, up to that point innocent under Jewish law, pronounces the unpronounceable, and knowingly, purposely, condemns himself to death. Had Judas been right? Had Jesus become despondent to the point of self-destruction?

Christian thought has offered several possible explanations for Jesus' actions here. The most traditional is that Jesus knew that his mission was to die for the salvation of the world, and made certain to fulfill it by his answer. Another is that Jesus simply told the truth. He was the son of God and said so; anything less would have been disingenuous and cowardly, hardly qualities worthy of the second person of the Trinity.

But there is another possibility, one more in keeping with a close Jewish examination of Mark's Jewish work. Jesus does not say only "*Ehyeh*"; he refers, as he has in the past, to Daniel's prophecy concerning the ultimate rescue of the Jewish people: "And you will see the son of man seated at the right hand of God and coming with the clouds of heaven." In effect, his is a two-part answer to the question of his identity: "Are you the Messiah, the son of the Blessed One?" Jesus makes a clear connection between being son of the Blessed One, *Ehyeh*, and being son of man. Again, there are several possible ways to interpret this passage. Many find here an affirmation of the doctrine of the Incarnation, that Jesus is God come into the world as a human being, while completely retaining divinity, "truly God and truly man." According to this doctrine this is a solo, one-time-only event; Jesus is *the* son of God, the *only* begotten son. Any relation as son or daughter that others may share with the Divine is "by adoption."

But is this what Jesus himself thought or taught? Would it not seem contrary to the spirit of radical inclusion for which Jesus died to relegate all men and women but himself to the status of God's adopted sons and daughters only, to second-class citizenship in the Kingdom of YHVH?

The Camaldolese monk and spiritual writer John Martin Sahajananda takes a different view:

> Jesus said, "I am the light of the world," and "You are the light of the world." These two statements are different sides of the same coin, for when Jesus discovered that the foundation of his being, God, was the light of the world, he also discovered that the foundation of every being and every created being, which is God,

was also the light of the world. These two statements are like wheels of a cart and to proclaim the Good News one has to proclaim them both at the same time.[73]

He goes on to say,

In Jesus humanity returned to its original state of being in the image and likeness of God. He did this by realizing himself, and the whole of humanity, as the Son or Daughter of God.[74]

Lest we accuse Father Sahajananda of bringing too much of his native India to the Jesus story, it must be said that his words likewise reflect a great tradition in mystical Judaism. Rabbi Lawrence Kushner, a major voice in contemporary Jewish spirituality famous for bringing that tradition to the greater public, writes:

"If mysticism is the quintessence of religion," then, as Moshe Idel opines in his book, *Kabbala: New Perspectives*, "the quintessence of mysticism is the sense of union with God." In Judaism "union with God" is called *devekut*, or, literally "cleaving." The classic sources of *devekut* are Deuteronomy 4:4: "But that you cleave (*had'vaykim*) unto the Lord your God this day are alive every one of you this day" and Isaiah 43:11: "*Anochi Adonai anochi*, I, I am the Lord," where the first "I" is God and the second is the self. Now the famous line at the burning bush, "*Ehyeh Asher Ehyeh*," of Exodus 3:14, means, "I will be who you are!"[75]

Certainly Jesus of Nazareth, who spent forty days in the desert, who intimately called God "*abba*," worked miracles, and was at the very least heavily influenced by the other-worldly Essenes—surely this Jesus could himself be called a Jewish mystic.

After reminding his readers that the first word of God that all Israel heard together was this *Anochi*, the "I" of the ten utterances (commandments) at Sinai, Kushner goes on to say,

> Infinite language cannot be mortal speech, except for one word—the first person singular pronoun "I," "*Anochi*." For just this is the name each self has for its self . . . Whatever makes each individual unique, that innermost core self, is precisely what we share with one another, and with our creator. We are made of the same holy stuff.[76]
>
> . . . God is our sense of self, our innermost essence, encountered throughout all creation. Our selves are made of God's self.[77]

Is this what Jesus means to say by linking the ineffable name *Ehyeh* to himself as a son of man? When asked if he is the Messiah and son of the Blessed One, Jesus' reply seems to mean, "I will be whatever I will be, and I will be this as a son of man, a human being. The Father and I are one, made of the same holy stuff, as are you and all people. I and you, we are the light of the world, all sons and daughters of *Ehyeh*, without condition or exception. It is only in the realization of this, of *devekut*, that salvation comes, only when, as sons and daughters of woman and man, we experience ourselves as already and always sitting at God's right hand, right now and ever among the clouds of heaven, that the kingdom comes."

"According to Shneur Zalman of Lyadi," writes Rabbi Kushner, "it is not that there is a world and God is everywhere within it. It's that there is God and the world is everywhere within God . . . It's all God. You, me, the trees, the murderers, the children, the sewers, the blossoms of springtime, the toxic waste dumps, the tabernacle—it's all God."[78] Would anyone be surprised to find these words ascribed to Jesus of Nazareth? Can we truly doubt that the story of Christians and Jews is one of their own unrecognized, lost *devekut*?

Still, a nagging question remains: Why did Jesus who had been silent through his entire interrogation speak the forbidden name at *that* moment? He knew, he had to know, that it meant his death. Why did he turn away from the possibility, however slight, that he might yet walk away from this night, free to continue to proclaim, perhaps for a long lifetime, God's unconditional acceptance and love? Why did Jesus choose to die then and there?

A response to this question may lie in the second act of Jesus' arrest and interrogation, this one taking place in the court of the Roman governor. "As soon as morning came," Mark relates, the Jewish authority hurried Jesus to the headquarters of Pontius Pilate (Mark 15:1). Here was not a man known for his compassion or sense of justice. According to the ancient historian Philo, Pilate was a cruel and despotic figure who had "committed countless atrocities and numerous executions without any previous trial."[79] Only a few years after Jesus' execution, in 36 CE, Pilate was recalled to Rome in disgrace for abuse of power.

Pilate's first question to Jesus wastes no time getting to the relevant point: "Are you the king of the Jews?" If Jesus poses no threat to Rome, if he is not seeking to cast off imperial control of Judea, then Pilate would surely return him to the Jewish leadership and let them handle their own religious issues. Jesus' answer in Mark is, "The words are yours" (Mark 15:2), by which Jesus seems to be saying that he would not even stoop to answer such a question; "The words are yours . . . not mine." Demonstrating that he is not just some fanatical rube from the backwater, he is on the contrary politically savvy, and knows that to claim to be a king would be suicidal. Mark states that Pilate went on questioning Jesus, but received no further replies.

As in the other three canonical gospels, Pilate is consistently portrayed as anxious to free Jesus or, at the very least, to avoid having to execute him himself. Pilate surely must have known that none of the Jewish leadership was particularly enamored of the occupying power, so to see them all, Pharisee and Sadducee alike, Hillelites and Shammaists, all united in seeking Jesus' death on the charge of making himself Messiah must have seemed suspicious to him. And so Mark has him test them:

> At the festival season the governor used to release one prisoner requested by the people. As it happened, a man known as Barabbas was then in custody with the rebels who had committed murder in the rising. When the crowd appeared and began asking for the usual favor, Pilate replied, "Would you like me to release for you the king of the Jews?" (Mark 15:6–9)

The answer to Pilate's question is well known; the crowd, under "incitement" from the chief priests, demands Barabbas' release and Jesus' crucifixion (Mark 15:11–13). Pilate, albeit reluctantly, complies.

So much is wrong with this scene that is hard to know where to begin. First, nothing in the historical record, no mention in Roman writers or indeed anywhere but in these Christian scriptures indicates a customary prisoner release anywhere in the Empire during a conquered people's sacred festival. Even if such a practice did exist in this very local place and time, it hardly seems logical for the Roman governor to send a known insurrectionist back into Jerusalem during a feast of liberation! If this incident occurred at all, it seems much more likely that Pilate was endeavoring to see whose release the crowd and the leadership would call for. If Barabbas', it would tell him much about the situation: it would indicate that the known revolutionary was the true threat to Rome, as he was the favorite of the people and the High Priests. Further, it would show Jesus as an enemy of those interests and a possible counter to Barabbas, the rebel. The Pilate described by Philo would have assessed the results of his test, kept Barabbas, released Jesus, and dared the crowd to do anything about it. He seemed to have been someone who might have enjoyed the outcome.

One further piece of information urges an overall reassessment of this scene. All four Gospels include the story of Barabbas, but the standard version of Matthew's account offers us his full name . . . *Jesus Barabbas!* (Matt. 27:16). Even Mark specifically states that he was "*known* as Barabbas," thus, we can safely assume that this is a nickname or title of some sort, and in the common Aramaic language of the region, "*Bar Abbas*" means "Son of Abba"—abba, the very same term by which Jesus refers to God. This rebel, therefore, is known as "Jesus Son of Daddy!"

It seems abundantly clear that Mark is here employing a literary device to make several points with his post-70 audience. Of course, in that new world, a world of defeat and disdain for Jews of every stripe, Mark wishes to put the blame for Jesus' death and symbolically for the fall of Jerusalem and the loss of the Temple on the Jewish establishment, and in so doing, to discredit the Pharisees of his own day. Jews are now going to have to learn to live and thrive in a Gentile universe. No one liked the Romans, but inciting further anger against them for the events of 66–70 would not help the new situation. As Jesus represents the Jewish people, Mark agrees with Josephus that the actions and attitudes of the Jewish leadership, in particular with regard to foreigners, contributed to the disaster of 70:

> At the same time Eleazar, the son of Ananias the High
> Priest, a very bold youth, who was at that time gov-
> ernor of the temple, persuaded those that officiated
> in the Divine service to receive no gift or sacrifice
> for any foreigner. And this was the true beginning
> of our war with the Romans; for they rejected the
> sacrifice of Caesar on this account; and when many
> of the High Priests and principal men besought them
> not to omit the sacrifice, which it was customary for

them to offer for their princes, they would not be prevailed upon.[80]

All other peoples within the Roman Empire were compelled to sacrifice to the emperor as a god; the Jews alone had sought and won exemption from this duty. What is more, the emperor himself would regularly arrange for sacrifice to be made to the Jewish God on his behalf, as he did with every religion in his empire, and to have prayers offered for his well-being. It was considerations such as this and others that caused the victorious Roman general Titus to chide the seemingly ungrateful Jewish people for their revolt.[81]

In fairness, the older members of the Jewish leadership, including Eleazar's father, did, according to Josephus, try to dissuade him from his course, but to no avail. In the end, the leadership turned violently upon itself, Eleazar's group seizing the Temple and lower portion of the city, the elder party controlling the upper part, as the two warred upon each other. This situation, along with others in the city, virtually ensured the violent Roman response.

It is important to note that it was an attitude toward the foreigner which, in Josephus' words, "was the true beginning" of the disastrous war, the results of which inform every page of Mark's work. The emphasis in all the canonical gospels on Jesus' embrace of foreigners, from the story of the Good Samaritan to his forgiveness of the Roman soldiers who crucified him, is no accident.

Thus it is quite possible, even probable, that "Jesus Bar Abbas" never existed. There is no account of him or of any rebellion led by him in any but Christian sources. As we have seen elsewhere, Mark may be using a literary device here to make a strong point to his Jewish audience. That audience, like the Jews that Mark places in the court of Pilate's residence, is being offered a choice: Which Jesus do they wish? Jesus the non-violent or Jesus the revolutionary? Which Messiah would Judaism rather have?

In this scene it was Jesus Bar Abbas the insurrectionist who gained release, to spread more hatred and to foment more violence. All in the post-70 world knew how that had turned out. On the other hand, the Jesus who had preached inclusion of the foreigner and outcast, who had urged the turning of the other cheek, and who, in Mark's Gospel, stands for the city of Jerusalem and the Jewish people, died a victim to violence. On one occasion only had his anger at the exclusionist practices of the Temple caused him to act contrary to his own principles, and he had paid for it dearly. Now, with Jerusalem in ruins and the Temple gone, perhaps forever, his followers had to face the fire of those who would have seen them as unpatriotic, as cowards or traitors for their move to Pella before the axe fell on the city. Surely this would have been a key point in the struggle between the Jesus Jews and Pharisaic Judaism for the future of Jewish life? How could the Jewish people trust those who would not stand by the defense of Jerusalem to lead them now? Or, conversely, how could they give over their lives to that party whose misguided policies had led to the very destruction of the Temple and of Jewish life, and who now actually wished to extend and tighten those same policies?

Pilate's question, "Whom would you like . . . ?" can be answered both retrospectively and in Mark's present. If Jesus of Nazareth had been chosen, if his movement had not lost its charismatic leader, if he had been able to continue through the years toward 66 CE, would there have been a revolution at all? Mightn't Jerusalem and the Temple still stand? And, barring that, couldn't the Jewish people, now outcast, do what should have been done nearly four decades earlier and choose the direction in which Jesus the non-violent, the champion of the outcast, would have led them? The spirit of violent resistance was far from dead; even in Mark's day, support was beginning to grow for what would be the final Jewish revolt, the Bar Kochba Rebellion of 132–135 CE, which would result

in the complete expulsion of the Jewish people from the Holy
Land for the next eighteen hundred years.

So the question is urgent, all important: Which type of
Messiah do you wish? For Jesus of Nazareth in his response
to the High Priest did not only link the name of God, *Ehyeh*,
with the term "son of man," but also with "Messiah." "Are
you the Messiah, the son of the Blessed One?" he was asked.

Lawrence Kushner, in a beautiful essay entitled *I Believe in
the Coming of the Messiah*, writes, "Of all the seminal creative,
mischievous, destructive, cockamamie ideas for the Jewish
people to come up with and for Jews and other people to take
literally, surely none could be more catastrophic than the idea
of a Messiah."[82] He goes on to say:

> That a person, a human being of flesh and blood, could
> come and resolve all pain and suffering, superimpose
> humane values on nature, so that we get, in poet
> Stephen Mitchell's words, "nonviolent wolves and
> vegetarian lions," reconcile every dispute and disagree-
> ment, turn the hearts of the parents to their children
> and the hearts of children to their parents, convince
> all soldiers to beat their swords into ploughshares and
> their spears into pruning hooks, give everyone his or
> her justly deserved reward or punishment . . . We have
> here a fairly big idea.[83]

In a fairly big idea of his own, Jesus seems to be bringing
together three concepts: the name of God (*Ehyeh*), "the son of
man," and "Messiah." The spirit of *devekut*, of oneness, is the
binding force here. Just as all daughters and sons of man and
woman are likewise full sons and daughters of God, if only they
would realize it, so too are we *all* Messiah, especially when we
live out, with all our individuality, our still inherent oneness.
"How good and how pleasant it is when brothers dwell together" is the psalmist's lyric of the messianic times (Ps. 133:1).

After introducing the Jewish concept that "all the contradictions, paradoxes and antimonies will be resolved when the Messiah comes," Rabbi Kushner goes on to describe messianic times as those in which

> Lions lie down with lambs and lambs don't get much sleep. In fact the lions eat them, but that's what lions and lambs do to and for one another. The hearts of the children will be turned to the hearts of the parents for a while, and then they will fall back screaming and fighting with each other because that is what parents and children do. Then, as the old time Reform Jews intuited, we won't need to return to Israel because Israel will be in us.[84]

Here we see a glimpse into the choice of Moses as one of the two figures from Jewish history to stand with Jesus in the Transfiguration scene. Moses does not get to enter the Promised Land, even after dedicating a lifetime to God and virtually creating the Jewish nation. One oft-given reason for this seeming injustice is that Judaism must not be about any one person, no matter how great or accomplished, but about God alone. There are to be no cults of personality in Jewish life. By contrast, when we look at Christianity, past and present, it is fair to say that no religion so completely centers on its founder as does this one. Christianity is not merely *about* Christ; to its adherents, it *is* Christ, in ways that Buddhism would never "consider itself the Buddha," nor Islam Mohammed. When Saint Paul stated that for him, "to live is Christ, and to die is gain," he set the tone for the rest of Christian history to date (Phil. 1:21).

When Israeli journalist Moshe Halevi set out to "search for God with Christians and Muslims in the Holy Land," the result was his book *At the Entrance to the Garden of Eden*. As part of his search, he spent time with "the monks and nuns of the Beatitudes, a Catholic community devoted to reconciliation with Jews and to restoring something of Christianity's Judaic roots."[85] He joined them for a *shabbat* service and was moved but still bothered by a nun's statement "about celebrating Shabbat as Jesus' time of rest between crucifixion and resurrection." Another sister, however, shared his concern: "Why do we have to bring Jesus into everything? Why can't we just appreciate the grace of celebrating Shabbat with the Jewish people?"[86]

This sister's sentiment may seem anathema to many Christians. Since discovering my own Jewishness and in the course of my subsequent work, I have grown more and more aware of what I call "Christinsecurity." Often I've noted the difference between Christians and Jews studying scripture together; the Jews in the group generally seem much less guarded, much more willing to jump in and mix it up a bit. By contrast, many of the Christians in the studies seem very uncomfortable even using the word "God" rather than "Jesus"; they consistently need, it seems, to restate every point in terms of Christ or to suggest how an idea was brought to "perfection" in him. It appears, as that sister went on to say to Halevi, that "some Christians . . . feel the need to consciously bring Jesus in as a kind of 'protection.' To ensure they're good Christians."[87] The irony here is that this is just the type of strict, "fence-oriented" spirituality that Jesus worked against and which the Jesus Jews of Mark's day were trying to prevent from gaining the post-70 day. Mark's Gospel, the earliest and "most raw" of the canonical four, certainly does not present Jesus as having that sort of "it's all about me" personality. Like Moses, he is a charismatic, larger-than-life figure with a healthy sense of himself, something that he embodies and promotes for the other "outcasts" around him. But Jesus speaks about and centers on God, the Father, and the Kingdom far more than he does himself. One needs to reach John's Gospel, with its complete and bitter breakdown in the Jewish family, to find the type of total Christo-centric approach that would become the rule in Christian life to follow.

By choosing to die, by, in effect, eschewing possible entrance into a Promised Land his work might have helped create, Mark's Jesus sought to avoid several dangerous possibilities. He embodies the way of non-violence even in the face of death; he will not be Jesus Barabbas, and his followers must never confuse the two, although, to our shame, we most certainly and consistently have. He also undoes the damage, in a way, caused by his mistake at the Inclusioning of the Temple; to engage in an act of aggression and violence, regardless of the cause, sent his followers a very mixed message to say the least. In making certain that his sentence is death and in not resisting it in the least, Jesus resets in his own person the standard that his teaching had endeavored to establish. He has realized his error and viscerally corrects it, something that Elijah had been unable to do.

By his dying Jesus continues in the tradition of his own Jewishness, the tradition that all things should be centered on God and not on the individual leader. Indeed, he extended that principle by linking together *Eyheh*, son of man, and Messiah. The Jewish Messiah was not supposed to die; he was meant to live, to reconcile all things and establish the realm of David forever. But Jesus recognized *Ehyeh* in all people and all people as living in *Ehyeh*; accordingly he saw himself in all others as well, in particular those "least" of his brothers and sisters. For Jesus to be Messiah means to extend messianic status to all the children of God, for Jesus, too, "will be who you are." In preaching such radical acceptance and inclusion of all, no matter how different or opposed their views and lives might be, and commissioning his followers to do the same Jesus was calling present the messianic time. As Rabbi Kushner writes, "if you are still unable to comprehend paradox or endure the commonplace contradictions and the thousand natural shocks to which flesh is heir, then Moses and Elijah themselves could bring you sandwiches of honey-dipped *challah* and leviathan and you'd order tuna fish instead."[88]

"Christinsecurity" might be a product of the Jesus Jews'

having lost in the family quarrel. A natural reaction to feeling "left with nothing" in a struggle may be to make your central figure "everything." That, and a long initial period of persecution may have left Christianity with an exaggerated sense of the ever-present danger of "losing" Jesus, of being drawn to some other faith or philosophy, or to none at all. Personally, I much prefer, as I think the Jewish Jesus would, the sentiments in the closing paragraph of Kushner's *I Believe in the Coming of the Messiah*:

> Maybe my mother was a greater theologian than I realized. When she told me to become the Messiah, I thought she meant I should enter rabbinic school. I had no idea she meant that every one of us already is. You are the Messiah. You already have everything you need, and you are where you need to be.[89]

It was to ensure for us a knowledge of that reality, our reality, that the Jewish Jesus willingly stepped into death, just as it was to eliminate violence as an option in his followers' lives that he chose its direct and personal opposite. I feel certain that, had he realized how often his actions would be twisted and tortured into controlling, brutal contradictions of themselves, he would have slipped quietly out through the Essene Gate after his Pesach Seder, and just disappeared into that holy night.

Crucifixion, Resurrection, Redaction, Return

To live is to build a ship and a harbor
at the same time. And to complete the harbor
long after the ship has sunk.
    Yehuda Amichai[90]

ALL OF MARK'S CENTRAL THEMES ARE BROUGHT TOGETHER IN the closing sections of his Gospel, the latter parts of Chapter 15 and in 16, where we can likewise glimpse the rapidly emerging future of the family quarrel as well.

> Then they led him out to crucify him. A man called Simon, from Cyrene, the father of Alexander and Rufus, was passing by on his way in from the country, and they pressed him into service to carry his cross. (Mark 15:20–21)

Again we see here demonstrated the loss of scriptural insight that accompanies the separation of Christianity from its native Jewishness. Cyrene was a Greek city in North Africa, later taken by the Romans, so this Simon, the bearer of a very Hebrew name, would nonetheless have been to Judeans an outlander, living in an area where constant contact with Gentiles would have been almost unavoidable and the strict keeping of all the *mitzvoth* virtually impossible. In other words, Simon is someone whose situation very much resembles that of Mark's audience. Most likely in Jerusalem for the Passover celebration, his influence indicates a devotion to Jewish life belying his outsider status. It is also unusual and therefore significant that this Simon is not identified as "the son of" someone but rather as the father of two sons, Alexander and Rufus, one with a Greek and the other a Latin name, respectively.

When this Simon is forced by Roman soldiers to assist the apparently weakened Jesus with his cross, the symbolism for a post-70 Jewish audience is quite plain: Jesus, who represents the beleaguered Jewish people, is assisted by a marginal, though serious, Jew, one who apparently has found a way to live in conjunction with the Gentile world without losing his Jewishness. The implication is that it is in doing the same, by co-existing rather than building the fences recommended by the Pharisee movement, that the Jewish people will best help themselves, with the Romans inadvertently aiding them in doing just that. As for Simon's sons, Mark expects his audience to recognize their names. The Christian scriptures specify an Alexander (Acts 19:33) and a Rufus (Rom. 16:13) as well-known members of the early community, especially associated with Paul, the Apostle to the Gentiles. With Simon, Mark offers an example of a Jew who helped Jesus carry his cross and who raised his sons to be open to the type of inclusive message Paul represents.

Mark's Gospel proceeds to the crucifixion. As Jesus hangs in agony, inaccurate information and false expectations continue to swirl about him. Mark describes passers-by as jeering at Jesus, saying, "So you are the man who was to pull the Temple down and rebuild it in three days," a quote the inaccuracy of which Mark has already demonstrated (Mark 15:29). The chief priests and scribes in attendance likewise taunt Jesus, demanding that he release himself from the cross as a sign of his Messiah-hood, once more raising the questionable place of "signs" in Jewish life that has already been discussed.

The confusion continues as Jesus' final minutes approach. He cries out, "Eloi, Eloi, lama sabachthani," an Aramaic rendering of the second verse of Psalm 22; but those present mishear this as a cry, not to *Elohim*, one of the titles of the Jewish God, but instead to Elijah, and thus wonder if the herald of the Messiah would come and rescue Jesus (Mark 15:33–36). This mistake is a symbolically significant one; Mark depicts Jesus as *not* calling out to Elijah for help, that is, not identifying himself with the traditional idea of Messiah. Rather, in Jesus' last words, Mark guides his audience toward the 22nd Psalm:

> My God, my God,
> why have you abandoned me;
> why so far from delivering me
> and from my anguished roaring?
> My God,
> I cry by day—You answer not;
> by night, and have no respite. (Ps. 22:2–3)

Rather than underscoring any traditional messianic role for Jesus, Mark keeps his focus on Jesus as representative of the Jewish people, besieged, seemingly abandoned, without future, Holy City, or Temple:

> Many bulls surround me,
> mighty ones of Bashan encircle me.
> They open their mouths at me
> like tearing, roaring lions.
> My life ebbs away. (Ps. 22:13–15)

But Mark's audience knows the shift that occurs in this psalm, for after twenty-three verses filled with suffering and despair, hope and triumph suddenly emerge:

> You who fear the Lord, praise Him!
> All you offspring of Jacob, honor Him!
> Be in dread of Him, all you offspring of Israel!
> For he did not scorn, He did not spurn

the pleas of the lowly;
He did not hide His face from him;
When he cried out to Him, He listened . . .
Always be of good cheer! (Ps. 22:24–27)

But how can "good cheer" be possible on the cross or on
the ninth of Av, the date of the fall of Jerusalem? Where does
the hope of the Jewish people reside?

Then Jesus gave a loud cry and died; and the curtain of
the Temple was torn in two from top to bottom. When
the centurion who was standing opposite him saw how
he died, he said, "This man must have been a son of
God." (Mark 15:37–39)

Notice that the Temple and its sanctuary are not here destroyed by some massive tremor, Mel Gibson's version to the
contrary. Mark never intends to imply that a new religion,
Christianity, will replace Temple Judaism. Instead, he establishes a connection between the ultimate triumph of the Jewish
people, the end to barriers in Judaism, and the understanding
of a Gentile. The curtain referred to in this passage separated
the Holy of Holies, the innermost part of the Temple, from the
rest of the structure. It was the spot where, in former times,
the Ark of the Covenant would have been kept; in Jesus' day,
the Ark having been lost, only an empty black stone altar
stood in the Holy of Holies, upon which the High Priest, and
he alone, would place a thurible of burning incense once a
year at Yom Kippur. He could then whisper the sacred name
of *Yod-Heh-Vav-Heh*, at that time and in that place alone.

For his post-Temple Jewish audience, Mark's meaning would
be unmistakable: the future of Jewish life depended on doing
away with such boundaries as this, on taking *Ehyeh* out of
the box and realizing, actualizing the meaning of the name
for all God's images and likenesses, rather than revering it
into exclusivity and seclusion. Moreover, by the time Mark's

Gospel was written, the Temple was either destroyed or clearly doomed, with no more High Priests to utter the name, no Holy of Holies in which to speak it in. People, *all* people, Jew and Gentile alike, must now be seen as themselves the Temple they always were, to be revered and loved accordingly. Even the hated Romans, at whose hands the Jewish people suffered so terribly, were children of God, and thus capable, as was the centurion on Golgotha, of acknowledging that divine sonship and daughtership in others. *I Will Be Whatever I Will Be* has moved beyond the sanctuary. It has become *I Will Be Who You Are.*

Saved

In the light of all this, what can be said of the crucifixion and the traditional Christian idea of salvation by means of it?

The Catholic scholar John Wijngaards has written of this matter in his book *Inheriting the Master's Cloak*, where he examines what has been the dominant view of the cross's role in human redemption:

> Mankind has sinned. God was looking for a way to redeem us from this sin, but his strict sense of justice had to be satisfied first. In other words, God could not simply forgive sins through an act of mercy; satisfaction had to be offered to his justice. God decided to solve the problem by making his own Son assume human nature and die a violent death. Through his bloody sacrifice Christ paid the price on behalf of all. Only then could God forgive sins and receive us back as his children.[91]

This is a version of the workings of salvation with which I'm sure any Christian, indeed, anyone in Western society is familiar. Wijngaards then places this "sacrificial" view of redemption in the context of Jesus' and Christianity's inherent Jewishness. The *mitzvoth* as well as the prophets, he explains, absolutely forbid the practice of child sacrifice:

> When you enter the land that the Lord your God is giving you, you shall not learn to imitate the abhorrent practices of those nations. Let no one be found among you who consigns his son or daughter to the fire . . . for anyone who does such things is abhorrent to the Lord, and it is because of these abhorrent things that the Lord your God is dispossessing them before you. (Deut. 18:9–12)

> Anyone among the Israelites, or among the strangers residing in Israel, who gives any of his offspring to [the Canaanite god] Molech, shall be put to death; the people of the land shall pelt him with stones. And I will set My face against that man and I will cut him off from among his people, because he gave his offspring to Molech and so defiled my sanctuary and profaned my holy name. (Lev. 20:1–3)

> They have built shrines to Baal, to put their children to the fire as a burnt offering to Baal, which I never commanded, never decreed and which never came to My mind. (Jer. 19:5)

Not that the Jewish people always obeyed these voices. As Wijngaards points out,

> When Jericho was rebuilt in 860 BC, Hiel, its mayor, offered his eldest son, Abiram, for the laying of the foundation and his youngest, Segub, when building the gates. Excavations at Sechem have shown the remains of small children under the city gates. Jepthah of Gilead

killed his only daughter in fulfilling a vow. Outside
Jerusalem, in the valley of Hinnom, sacrificing children
was done on a regular basis.[92]

How could human beings, mothers and fathers, participate
in such cruelty perpetrated upon their own children, especially in the name of a God who forbids it? Upon reflection,
Wijngaards finds that these practices

> bring out something very deep from my subconscious.
> How shall I give expression to it in words? I believe
> God is good, yet deep down inside me is an unspoken,
> unreasonable fear of him. The fear is this: One day or
> another he will extract a terrible price for his good-
> ness. One day or another he will make me suffer, make
> me lose something I hold precious. That is why . . . if
> I were an Israelite, I might be prepared to sacrifice my
> beloved child to him to preserve the lives of the rest of
> my family.[93]

In this light, Wijngaards calls the dominant Christian
theory of sacrificial redemption "not much better than a baptized version of Melek," springing from all the same deep-
seated fears concerning God and self that gave rise to the
practices of the ancient Canaanites. In Genesis, the God who
guides Abraham's journey of discovery and understanding sets
that patriarch on the seeming road to child sacrifice only to
stop it cold. Speaking later through Jeremiah, God makes it
clear that the thought of actual child sacrifice never entered
his mind. The practice profanes God's very name, *I Will Be
Whatever I Will Be*, as it cut off any possibility of a child's becoming anything, of ever fulfilling his or her potential.

In short, the idea of God sacrificing his own son as a guilt
offering to himself would be absolutely abhorrent to any Jew,
let alone one as dedicated to compassion and love as Jesus of

Nazareth. "What then," Wijngaards asks, "about Jesus' death and resurrection?"

> Jesus' crucifixion was a crime. Jesus calls it a sin and repeatedly protests his innocence . . . but for Jesus to be true to his mission, he had to stand by his disciples to the end.[94]

If all this is the case, then how may we to begin to recon-ceptualize the concept of redemption, perhaps the core tenet of Christianity, in terms of that faith's bedrock but forgotten Jewishness?

I would suggest we start by examining the basic Christian formula, one repeated in prayer books and hymns and often found in sign form on many a church lawn or even illuminated from the building itself: "*Jesus saves.*" This itself is a short-ened form of the assertion: "*Jesus saves us from sin.*" (I use "sin" rather than "our sins," as many denominations hold to the idea of an original sin which, although not committed by the contemporary individual, nonetheless affects him or her.)

As we have already discussed, the meaning of the name of a religion's God tells us much about that religion. If God's name means "The Enlightened One" (*Buddha*), one can be rea-sonably sure that "becoming enlightened" will be a central goal of that faith. We have already discussed the implication of a God called *I Will Be Whatever I Will Be*. And in Hebrew, the name Yeshua, Jesus, means "God Will Save." This should come as no surprise; the idea of salvation, rescue, redemption, is at the absolute center of the Christian experience. And that reality is assured by the formula. *God-Will-Save* saves us from sin; he does what his name implies.

This formula then casts "us" in the role of people who need saving, who require rescue, notions likewise central to Christian belief. Human beings are in trouble. Although em-phasis on the sinfulness of humankind and the severity of that state varies from denomination to denomination, it is fair to say that Christianity as a whole agrees that we as a race are to some degree flawed and that without the saving action of God in the person of Jesus, our lives would be much worse on this earth and without hope in the next. John 3:16 proclaims that, "God so loved the world that he gave his only son, that everyone who believes in him may not perish, but have eternal life." Although not all Christians are Trinitarians, there is near unanimity concerning Jesus as the key to "eternal life," that is, heaven rather than hell. The traditional teaching, as Wijngaards has elaborated, maintains that humankind over its history has sinned so severely that it would impossible for us to ever pay the accumulated penalties for breaking God's law. Only God himself would be capable of such a feat, and, in an act of unconditional love for us, God's son, Jesus, suffered the consequences of all our sins in our place, and thus made heaven possible for humanity. This salvation cannot be accessed, however, apart from belief in Jesus, as the John quote indicates. Even then, salvation is not assured; one must still strive to avoid sin, and a life that has not done so will not attain to heaven.

There are variations on this teaching, to be sure. Although the majority of Christians hold Jesus' status as "son of God" to be exclusive and eternal, there is a growing sense of its inclusiveness, of Jesus as a person who fully actualized his human essence as a child of God, teaching and modeling that process for all of God's children, a view more consistent with Jesus' Judaism. Additionally, many Christian denominations, including the largest, Roman Catholicism, now state that it is possible for those outside Christianity to be saved, if they essentially live in accordance with the loving precepts of Jesus, a salvation made possible, nonetheless, *because* of Jesus' sacrifice on the cross. Other churches within Christianity, however, maintain faith in Jesus as an absolute precondition. Those who have not accepted Jesus cannot be saved, regardless of the type of life lived.

So far, we can then restate the basic Christian formula in

this way: "Only Yeshua—*God-Will-Save*—rescues us from our personal and cumulative breaking of God's commands by taking upon himself the punishment for those acts." I would submit, however, that a full re-Judaizing of this basic Christian formula might look like this: Jesus' name is "God Will Save." But a growing realization of the original name of that God, the God of Moses, whose son Christians believe Jesus to be, would reveal a new dimension to that God and hence to Jesus himself. In this fuller sense, Jesus' name is actually "I Will Be Whatever I Will Be Will Save." What are the implications of this? In what manner would a God of such a name endeavor to save human beings?

A recovered Jewish consciousness would certainly require wrestling with the traditional Christian concept of "sin," and hence of "salvation" from it. As previously discussed, the Torah term for sin is "*chet*," a term which at its root has nothing to do with morality or law, but is rather drawn from the field of archery and means "to miss the mark" or "to miss the target," in other words, "to get it wrong." In Jewish thought, "to sin" is to be mistaken about reality and to act according to that misconception. In mainstream Judaism, there has never been a concept of "original sin," but rather it takes the position expressed by God to Cain when he has not yet struck his brother Abel: "Surely if you do right, there is uplift. But if you do not, sin crouches at the door; its urge is toward you, yet you can be its master" (Gen. 4:7).

With this view in mind, the entire notion of salvation takes on a different dimension. Human beings are made in the image of I Will Be Whatever I Will Be. Jesus, as an insightful, progressive Torah Jew, saw this reality as incompatible with exclusivity, with the labeling of anyone as "saint" or "sinner." Hence, his life and teachings were one of total inclusion and welcome. How could anyone ever judge his or her neighbor when their essence is a human version of I Will Be Whatever I Will Be? Accordingly, Jesus sided with Isaiah and others who felt that the commands, such as that to honor the sabbath, were "made for man" and not man for them. The purpose of the *mitzvoth* in this view is to help God's images be who they truly are and to avoid the pain of doing otherwise. God's "laws" are not to serve as an excuse to inflict more pain, rejection, and persecution upon each other. Rather, the real sin, the true missing of the mark, would be the failure to recognize our human reality, my essence and yours, as the images of YHVH, or worse, to act out of that false notion of ourselves and others. Human beings, like the God they image, are process; they are not to be understood or judged, only loved and accepted. To live fully one's reality as an image of God, to truly be oneself, this is the kingdom of heaven, the reign of God.

With this understanding, then, those acts that we call "sinful" all result from demanding others or ourselves to Be Whatever Others Wish Us to Be, parents, schools, societies, religions. The inevitable failure to be other than Who We Will Be, images of YHVH, creates self-hatred, anger, the lusting after possessions to bolster our sense of self, etc. Rather than wrestling with God and people and being able, we inwardly reject ourselves and others as being unworthy of some standard that I Will Be never intended for us to meet. We disengage, within and without. We walk away from the wrestling, or rather, immerse ourselves in some dismal parody of genuine spiritual struggle: competition, stress, the rat race.

In the end a rediscovered sense of the Jewishness of Christianity would, I submit, ultimately re-envision the basic Christian formula to read something like: "I-Will-Be-Will-Save rescues the images of I Will Be from missing the mark about themselves and about the indefinable, unjudgeable nature of every human being."

In this expanded, re-Judaized sense, then, how does Jesus do this? How does Jesus save? The legalism and divine infanticide of the traditional Christian formula clearly does not fit with such a description of God as I Will Be Whatever I Will Be and of human beings as that God's image. Jesus himself did not see God primarily as a lawgiver, but rather as a process in which people shared, as the sometimes tempestuous, always loving wrestling between a parent and child. The terrible trouble in which Jesus found himself came from clashes with the more legalistic among the Jewish leadership of his day who saw his attitudes toward the *mitzvoth* as irresponsible and dangerous. It always amazes me that Christianity of almost any brand has come to be so deeply involved with just the sort of legalism that Jesus so clearly condemned, insisting on rules, preconditions, and doctrine that Jews, in the main, moved past long ago. There is no greater indicator of the need for a renewed Jewish consciousness for Christians than this difficult truth: that Jesus would find a better match for his own spirituality in most contemporary Jewish congregations than in most Christian churches.

In the place of the extremely legalistic and sacrificial, not to say infanticidal approach to salvation, a Christianity more in touch with its Jewishness might see the exemplary life, the teachings on unconditional love and acceptance, and the steadfastness of Jesus' principles even in the face of death as the primary means by which he saves us from missing the mark and shows us all how to actualize our own reality as sons and daughters of YHVH. For a Jew, pain is never a necessity for sanctity; Jews have known too much pain for too long to believe otherwise. Rather, pain is a sign of missing the mark. In Jesus' case, that pain is inflicted upon him primarily by those who "knew not what they did," who had an inaccurate view of the situation before them, and, it must also be said, by that overwhelming of his own first principles by indignation and anger in the "Inclusioning of the Temple" event. Jesus himself, as all of his teaching maintains, sees the pain of others as an opportunity to end it, an invitation to love and to thus fulfill the *mitzvah* that commands us "to love our neighbor as ourselves" (Lev. 19:18).

From this point of view, the mission of God's child is to clearly and unmistakably express and model a human life that is "on the mark." As both Judaism and Christianity hold their God to be "all-knowing," a fully actualized child of God will have foreseen and accepted the horrific personal consequences that such an effort would entail. In this sense, Jesus' execution is a result of fidelity to his mission and to his disciples, rather than a blood sacrifice to wipe out a debt, an interpretation much more in keeping with the afore-examined parable in Mark 12, in which a vineyard owner sends his "beloved son" to a group of tenants who have rejected other emissaries. "Surely they will heed my son," the owner says, not, "I will send him to be executed for their misdeeds." Pain and death are not the goals of his father's mission for him; rather, the son is killed because he is faithful *to* that mission.

In Jesus we see someone who actualized fully his potential to Be Whatever He Would Be, a true son of Israel who wrestled with God and people all the way to Gethsemane and Golgotha, and remained able—so able, in fact, that death itself could not contain him. Indeed, in his description of the final, general judgment, I-Will-Be-Will-Save never asks those standing before him whether they belonged to any particular faith or whether they even accepted him as Lord and Savior. Rather, one is saved or not on the basis of what one did to the least of his brothers and sisters; the text makes it clear that even the saved did not recognize Jesus in those they helped. All they did was refuse to categorize, label, or condemn anyone, including themselves, as undeserving, in keeping with the name of God whose images they were. Such a God is Moloch's polar opposite; this God extracts, not a terrible price for goodness, but rather those very fears and misconceptions, and heals their sufferers.

Resurrection

Such is the process, the God, the salvation, which we see then reflected in Mark's distinctly brief resurrection account. The women who go early on Sunday morning to properly anoint

Jesus' body, the impending sabbath having left no time for this earlier. They find the stone that served as the tomb's door rolled away. When they entered, "they saw a young man sitting on the right-hand side, wearing a white robe, and they were dumbfounded." This person explains that Jesus "has been raised" and instructs the women to tell his disciples he would see them in Galilee (Mark 16:5–7).

Another young man in white! Who is he meant to be? Is he Jesus himself, risen but in one of the many guises he assumes for post-resurrection appearances across the four gospels? Is he an angel? The text distinctly calls him a "man." Do we here have another instance of an Essene, perhaps the same one as in the Gethsemane scene, guarding the tomb and empowered to share the secret of its emptiness?

Much has been made of the Essenes' legendary powers of healing and control over their own bodies, similar to that of Eastern yogis, reported to survive buried alive for long periods of time.[95] Is it possible that Jesus the Essene did not die on the cross but merely lowered his heart rate to the point that he appeared dead? John's Gospel maintains that the two others crucified with Jesus survived until late Friday afternoon. As the sabbath was approaching, and a particularly sacred one at Passover time, the Jewish leadership did not wish corpses, considered ritually unclean, to be left publicly exposed. Subsequently, they petitioned "Pilate to have the legs broken and the bodies taken down" (John 19:31), an act seen as a form of mercy, in that crucifixion normally involved death by exposure, the condemned sometimes hung for days before succumbing. Pilate's men find the two still alive as expected after so brief a time and so break their legs with a club, causing death by shock in their weakened state. The soldiers are surprised, however, to see Jesus already dead. They do not break his legs, but instead pierce his side with a lance (John 19:34). Christian art has consistently placed this wound on Jesus' right side, *away* from his heart. Such a wound need not be fatal.

Did Jesus the Essene survive the attempt to execute him? Could his esoteric Essenic skills explain his willingness to embrace the death sentence? Was he then taken from the tomb by his brother Essenes and nursed back to health with one of their number left behind to inform his followers? Could this explain why he so often "appeared" to his disciples in seeming disguise or in secret? He would have, after all, still been a man condemned.

As tempting as such naturalistic explanations might be for some, the idea of an actual resurrection from the dead is much more within Jesus' Jewish tradition, particularly that of Pharisaic Judaism. One of the major issues that separated Pharisees from Sadducees was the former's belief in a general resurrection, to occur at some future date known only to God. In this sense, Mark continues to drive home his objections to Pharisaism by asserting ironically that only Jesus of Nazareth, himself condemned to death by Pharisees, ever actually achieved resurrection. More broadly, the rising of Jesus certainly is meant to symbolize the ultimate resurrection of the Jewish people from their post-70 circumstances, particularly if guided by the teachings of the first to rise.

Conclusion

The family quarrel, the struggle for the soul of Judaism, never leaves the pages of Mark's Gospel, even as it closes. Chapter 16, in fact, includes two endings. In the first, the women who had been to the tomb deliver all the instructions of the young man in white to "Peter and his companions," an ending that concludes: "Afterwards Jesus himself sent out by them, from east to west, the sacred and imperishable message of eternal salvation" (Mark 16:12). The sounding of this final note is upbeat and full of radiant hope.

Mark's second ending (or, much more likely, the ending added by a redactor) strikes a different tone. Here the reader is reminded that Mary of Magdala was the woman "from whom he

(Jesus) had driven out seven demons"—as if to warn against further elevating this woman, the first herald of the resurrection. And beyond this, Jesus' commission to his disciples sounds much more ominous: ". . . Proclaim the gospel to the whole creation. Those who believe it and receive baptism will be saved; those who do not believe will be condemned" (Mark 16:16). Already, lines are being drawn between the saved and the damned, and the immersion, *tevilah*, a rite at which Jesus himself never officiated and which he never required of his followers has now become a mandatory ritual for anyone wishing to be "saved." Communal radiance and shared hope are among the first casualties of a family quarrel.

Yet the most important and overlooked point of all in the resurrection story is the number of "different forms," to use Mark's phrase, in which the risen Jesus appears to his disciples. Mark's second ending speaks of Jesus' encounter with two of those disciples "while on their way out into the country" (Mark 16:12). Luke details this meeting in his well-known "Road to Emmaus" episode, maintaining that "something prevented" the pair from recognizing Jesus. Mary of Magdala's experience of Jesus is the first of the appearances mentioned by Mark. In his later Gospel, John expands upon the scene, stating that Mary thought Jesus to be the gardener (John 20:15). In John 21, Jesus shows himself on the shore of Lake Tiberias, where once again "the disciples did not know it was Jesus" (John 21:4). Jesus consistently goes unrecognized by his closest intimates, at least initially.

But the true message of these events lies, not in the lack of awareness of who Jesus is, but in who he manifests himself to be. In one scene, he seems a gardener, in another a fisherman; on the Emmaus road he is simply a fellow traveler, recognized in the sharing of bread. It is only after actually looking at these commonplace figures, noticing them, taking them into account, that they are each seen to be Jesus.

Mark's meaning is patently obvious. Whatever this mysterious resurrection is or isn't, if one wants to experience the risen, triumphant Jesus, and with it, symbolically, the rising of Jerusalem and the Jewish people, one will do so primarily through others. It is in the simple humanity of the everyday person that Messiah is manifest; the son of God is indistinguishable from the children of men and women. Only when we each regard them for who they are, expecting nothing and no one else, only then does Yeshua, God-Will-Save, become suddenly present, revealed before our eyes.

Yehuda Amichai describes an experience of becoming "the target marker" for a group of Jerusalem tourists. He hears the tour guide say, "You see that man with the baskets? Just right of his head there's an arch from the Roman period." Amichai's thought in response is

> redemption will only come if their guide tells them,
> "You see that arch from the Roman period? It's not important: but next to it, left and down a bit, there sits a man who's bought fruit and vegetables for his family."[96]

This is the spirit of the Jewish Jesus, the spirit of "I Will Be Who You Are," of a dynamic young teacher of Torah who called everyone to love God with his or her entire self and neighbor as that self. But what if the actual nature of that self has long been repressed, our "I" an unknowing victim of a long-ago battle in an unacknowledged family? How then can God's first word at Sinai, *Anochi*, "I," cause us anything but fear and insecurity, resulting in miles of fences across lands of promise rather than a straight way in the wilderness? How do we wholly love God without a whole self? Or has it become all too true that we *do* love our neighbor as ourselves, inadequately, like angry, orphaned children who unwittingly strike out at parents, absent and unknown, in all other relationships?

Amichai writes lovingly of a stone with the Hebrew characters for "Amen" written on it:

A triangular fragment of stone from a Jewish graveyard
　　destroyed
many generations ago. The other fragments, hundreds
　　upon hundreds,
were scattered helter-skelter, and a great yearning,
a longing without end, fills them all:
first name in search of a family name, date of death seeks
dead man's birthplace, son's name wishes to locate
name of father, date of birth seeks reunion with soul
that wishes to rest in peace. And until they have found
one another, they will not find prefect rest.
Only this stone lies calmly on my desk and says "Amen."

But that is not the end of the poem, the process, for:

. . . now the fragments are gathered up in loving kindness
by a sad good man. He cleanses them of every blemish,
photographs them one by one, arranges them on the floor
in the great hall, makes each gravestone whole again,
one again: fragment to fragment,
like the resurrection of the dead, a mosaic,
a jigsaw puzzle. Child's play.[97]

My fellow wrestlers with God and with people, let us make
ourselves able. To do what? To make whole the fragments of
our family's long quarrel. To be born again as the Jewish children we truly are. To rise with Jesus the Jew and go on ahead
with him into Galilee. To hear the echoed whisper of God's
name in the holiest of holies, our own hearts, and know it as
our own as well. To be Amen. To *Shema*.

Beginning to Begin Again

On an open door a sign hangs: Closed.
How do you explain it?
   Yehuda Amichai[98]

THE SECOND-CENTURY SAGE RABBI TARFON WAS KNOWN FOR saying, "No one is asking you to complete the task, but you must begin it."[99] For many Christians, the task of getting in touch with their own Jewishness may seem too daunting even to initiate. Where to begin? I have a recommendation for anyone wishing to start, at a practical level, the process of recovering his or her basic Jewishness. That recommendation is the sabbath, *shabbat*.

The sabbath is Judaism's great gift to a world which perhaps in its entire history has never needed it so desperately. It is much more than a rest break, a weekly "recharging of batteries" in order to then re-enter the world of mad stress. The word *shabbat* itself does not mean "to rest," but "to stop." In this sense, *shabbat* is as much a barometer as a relaxant; when asked how it can be known when one is on a good path, when one's spiritual life is healthy, Rabbi Alan Ullman, my teacher, often replies, "When one can stop." The ability to stop completely whatever one is doing is, indeed, very restful, but it is not from the ending of action that the rest primarily comes, but in the overwhelming relief of non-identification with any set of activities, whether a job, or a sport, or even the writing of a book. The sabbath is restful because such identification, so difficult to avoid in a world that defines by actions, is nonetheless false. I may very well work at this career, center regularly on that activity—but if I were to stop working, swimming laps or running, parenting, or writing, I would not suddenly blink out of existence. I am not identical with what I do; I am the image of a God who could act, could create, but who could also stop, and still be God. The human being, the child of YHVH, is the closest thing to the infinite that exists in time and space. No set of activities can bound him or her, no job title, calling, or avocation define such an offspring. When we stop, regularly, once a week, we rest in *ourselves*, liberated from the constriction of "being a something," and so rest in that God "who looks like nothing," as Kushner says, the God beyond any image.[100] We find that, contrary to popular belief or neurosis, we *can* stop doing and still be ourselves. Busy life no longer holds a lien against our souls. *Ahhhh.*

Shabbat, then, is an experience of our self, and so, of the one we image. "The sabbath is made for man" in the same way that we say two lovers are "made for each other." In each other's sweet presence, they are most truly themselves; content to *be* with each other, they need not do anything more. Indeed, one of my favorite prayers for Shabbat morning reads,

As lovers in each other's arms,
Whispering each other's name
Into the other's ear
So we lie in Your arms,
Breathing with each breath
Your Name, Your Truth, Your Unity.[101]

For Christians, that name is a Jewish name whose truth is its own Jewishness, and whose sense of unity with itself, with the Jewish people, and with men and women everywhere, grows stronger in the uncrowded light of *shabbat*. From sabbath stillness to sabbath stillness, our truest self begins to speak, as Mary Oliver puts it, with "a new voice which you slowly recognize as your own."[102] And if to pray is to consciously remain in God's presence, then truly the sabbath is the essence and fulfillment of Jewish prayer.

Shabbat does not have to be kept on a Saturday, and, at the beginning, a half-day of rest might be all that we can bring our motion-dependent selves to attempt. Remember, we are not being asked to complete the task, but to begin. "Judge not lest ye be judged" is a very Jewish sentiment, and like all others, must first be applied to oneself. To beat oneself up over our attempts to keep *shabbat* is not to keep it holy. "The sabbath is made for us."

Along with keeping *shabbat*, I would offer two other practical means of touching and recovering one's unrealized Jewishness. The first is the study of Torah with a capable teacher and guide; the second is the nourishment of oneself with Jewish authors who are both wise and accessible in their wisdom.

When Rabbi Hillel was asked to summarize the entire Torah while standing on one foot, he said more than "What you do not want done to you, do not do to others." He also added, "The rest is commentary. Now go and study." To Jews, to the Jewish Jesus, and therefore to the Christian soul, the Torah is much more than five books, the subject alternately of dry academic study or of iconistic devotion. For Jews, Torah is the very design of the created universe, including ourselves. Lawrence Kushner relates a very old tale about just this idea:

> At the beginning of the beginning . . . God said, "I need an overall plan for My world. I want it to be One, as I am One . . . I know what I will do, I will use Torah as a blueprint for creation and that way all the parts of the world will fit together, and I and my Torah will be inside everything!"[103]

I have, as the joke goes in academe, "more degrees than a bad burn," but nothing in my undergraduate or graduate education resembled my experience in Torah study or prepared me for it. I found it intense without being at all intimidating, thorough but never picayune, incredibly open but not without center or ungrounded. There is a spot in one of the books of Douglas Adams's *Hitchhiker's Guide to the Galaxy* series in which the main characters visit a house where the outside is in, and the inside out. Its outer walls are papered, furniture is set about them, and there are pictures and shelves attached to them. A sign over the door leading *into* the house reads: "Step outside." Once through the door, it seems that the entire world is contained "in" its structure. There is no floor, but grass and sand; trees and plants grow, and the brick-faced walls angle out in such ways that the environment seems *more* spacious the farther in one goes.[104] That is what studying Torah is like, except that one realizes that the house is "within" oneself, that we are built upon this very model.

Has studying the Torah helped me to find myself? It has done more than that. It has moved me beyond the narrow straits normally associated with that "self-discovery"—"What sort of career is for me?" "What sort of relationship," etc.— and opened for me the universe that I am and will continue to be. In entering the Torah, I do enter inside myself, with the usual armload of question marks, and, yes, find myself . . . outside. In the light and rain, the fresh air and strong winds of the Real—unpunctuated and alive:

I was so busy looking for answers
in my life. Then it came to me:
I couldn't find the answers because
my life was not a question.
I didn't need to find
a reason for living;
my life was the reason.
I didn't need some grand purpose;
living was the purpose for living,
enjoying, being alive.
Maybe that's what's

meant by "Amen."
Maybe that's what they
            mean by, "Ah!"[105]

Many, if not all, Jewish communities of worship offer Torah studies. I have found Reform and Reconstructionist study groups to be especially open to those from any and all background, and since Judaism does not proselytize, one need not expect any effort to be converted, just to be.

This attitude toward the Torah and about life in general also finds voice in many fine Jewish writers who specialize in addressing not only a Jewish audience, but all of us, everywhere. Immersing ourselves in their work can help us to find our own long-lost Jewish voice, which will in turn call out our deepest self as Christians. For this I recommend highly the work of Elie Wiesel, particularly his non-fiction, such as *Souls on Fire, Somewhere a Master, Five Biblical Portraits*, and *Wise Men and Their Tales*. Beautiful beyond compare is the writing of Abraham Joshua Heschel, including his classic *The Sabbath*, as well as *Man's Quest for God, God in Search of Man*, and a collection of his essays, *Moral Grandeur and Spiritual Audacity*. The books of Lawrence Kushner, so often quoted here, read like a conversation with a good friend from the neighborhood who also happens to be unabashedly wise, funny, and so close to God there's no room for pride or pretense. If you ever wondered what it would be like to live next door to, say, Einstein or E. E. Cummings, and just lean over the fence and have a spiritual conversation with him, read Kushner's *God Was in This Place and I, i Did Not Know, Honey from the Rock*, or his *Book of Letters*.

I would be truly remiss not to urge readers toward not only the finest Jewish poet of our time, but one the finest writers of any origin in any time. "Poets have always talked about unlocking the human heart," comments former British Poet Laureate Ted Hughes, "but when I read Amichai I wonder who before him actually managed it."[106] Yehuda Amichai's *Poems of Jerusalem and Love Poems* and his *Open Closed Open*, selections from which serve as epigraphs throughout this book, speak to anyone thirsty for regaining selfhood, who "want once more to be written in the book of life, to be written anew every day, until the writing hand hurts."[107]

"The world stands on three things," says *Pirke Avot*, a part of Talmud, "on the study of Torah, on prayer, and on deeds of loving kindness."[108] The fullness of its active compassion, the unforced care with which it faces the darkness, even its own, is the mark of worth of any spiritual tradition. The more one is one's true self, the more spontaneous and genuine such care becomes, for "you will want nothing and lack nothing," and therefore will, easily and without motive, be generous.[109] For those who have lost their essential Jewishness, to study Torah, the blueprint of our creation, and to keep the living prayer which is *shabbat*, is to increase our awareness of who we and that creation together are, to begin to see with eyes both entirely new and very old, and, with that insight, to rise to deeds of loving kindness beyond all accustomed margins:

Retreat

The monks
at supper
read from
Night Fishing in Galilee

on the one cup
and communion in bits
of shared saliva.

Everyone goes,
"*Ugh*," then
titters

though they have
a dripping
bleeding

man
suspended
at the front
of the room

each sitting.

——

Return
to my cell

remove
the brass
crucifix
from the wall

his body
seems permanently
attached
to this

I cannot
take him
down

gently
a Jew
wraps him
in his Berkeley
sweatshirt.
Night.[110]

Notes

1. Amichai, *Poems of Jerusalem and Love Poems*, 11.
2. Epigraph: Amichai, Ibid., 55.
3. Davies, *The Merry Heart*, 241.
4. Flannery, *The Anguish of the Jews*, 32.
5. Carroll, *Constantine's Sword*, 163.
6. Ruether, *Faith and Fratricide*, 256.
7. Although, since the Diaspora, one's Jewish identity has traditionally been traced through the mother's line, contemporary Reform and Reconstructionist Judaism recognizes as a Jew someone with a Jewish father only.
8. Underhill, *The Spiritual Life*, 14.
9. Amichai, *Poems of Jerusalem and Love Poems*, 69.
10. Powell, *Jesus as a Figure in History*, 71.
11. Funk, Hoover, and the Jesus Seminar, *The Five Gospels*, 36.
12. Blomberg, "Where Do We Start Studying Jesus?" In *Jesus under Fire: Modern Scholarship Reinvents the Historical Jesus*, ed. Wilkins and Moreland, 17–51.
13. Vermes, *Jesus and the World of Judaism*, 26.
14. Powell, 114.
15. Borg, *Jesus: A New Version*, 25–26.
16. Carroll, 74.
17. Amichai, *Poems of Jerusalem and Love Poems*, 63.
18. Wyler, *Settings of Silver*, 174.
19. Carroll, 90.
20. Amichai, *Poems of Jerusalem and Love Poems*, 51.
21. Josephus, *Antiquities* XV, xi, 3.
22. Pixner, *The Fifth Gospel*, 17.
23. Pixner, 17.
24. Wylen, 175.
25. Amichai, *Open Closed Open*, 40.
26. Amichai, *Poems of Jerusalem and Love Poems*, 11.

27. Spong, *Liberating the Gospels, Reading the Bible with Jewish Eyes*, XIII.

28. Lev. 13:45–46 and note, *The Torah, a Modern Commentary*.

29. Leloup, *The Gospel of Mary Magdalene*, 20.

30. www.newadvent.org/cathen/095239.a.html.

31. Amichai, *Open Closed Open*, 40.

32. Pixner, 35.

33. Ibid.

34. Mishnah 26.

35. Amichai, *Open Closed Open*, 69.

36. Josephus, *Jewish Wars*, VI, 2:4–10.

37. Pixner, 44.

38. Dosick, *Living Judaism*, 267.

39. Ibid., 64.

40. Klausner, *Jesus of Nazareth*.

41. Bolton, *Parshat Korah, A Reconstructionist Dvar Torah*.

42. Amichai, *Poems of Jerusalem and Love Poems*, 27.

43. Amichai, *Poems of Jerusalem and Love Poems*, 247.

44. See, for example, Lev. 20:10 and Deut. 22:22–29.

45. http://www.essenespirit.com.

46. "Essences," http://www.themystica.org/mystica/articles/e/essenes.htm

47. *The Five Books of Moses*, trans. Everett Fox.

48. Wiesel, *Wise Men and Their Tales*, 298.

49. Josephus, *Jewish Wars*, II, 8:4.

50. Carroll, 90.

51. Wylen, 58.

52. Ibid., 204.

53. Ibid.

54. Amichai, *Poems of Jerusalem and Love Poems*, 77.

55. Josephus, *Jewish Wars*, VI, 7:1.

56. Heschel, *I Asked for Wonder*, 101.

57. Ibid., 102.

58. Amichai, *Open Closed Open*, 77.

59. Josephus, *Jewish Wars*, VII, 2:2.

60. Ibid., Vol. VIII, 4.

61. Pixner, http://www.centuryone.org/essenes.html.

62. Ibid., http://www.centuryone.org/apostles.html.

63. Josephus, *Autobiography*, VII.

64. Josephus, *Jewish Wars*, VIII, 6, 11.

65. Gaster, *The Dead Sea Scriptures*, 30.

66. Yehuda Amichai, *Open Closed Open*, 58.

67. Ibid., 59.

68. Yehuda Mirsky, *Kerem*, Winter 1994, 7.

69. Amichai, *Poems of Jerusalem and Love Poems*, 85.

70. Louis Walter, "The Trial and Death of Jesus," accessed at www
.jcrelations.net/en/?id=837, 4.

71. Ibid.

72. Ibid.

73. John Martin Sahajananda, *You Are the Light*, 156.

74. Ibid., 156.

75. Lawrence Kushner, *Eyes Remade for Wonder*, 166.

76. Ibid., 145.

77. Ibid.

78. Ibid., 161.

79. Op. Cit., Walter.

80. Josephus, *Jewish Wars*, II, 17:2.

81. Ibid., VI, 6.

82. Kushner, 205.

83. Ibid., 205.

84. Kushner, 207–208.

85. Halevi, *At the Entrance to the Garden of Eden*, 186.

86. Ibid., 186–187.

87. Ibid., 193–194.

88. Kushner, 208.

89. Ibid.

90. Amichai, *Poems of Jerusalem and Love Poems*, 223.

91. John Wijngaards, *Inheriting the Master's Cloak*, 25–26.

92. Wijngaards, 21–22.

93. Ibid., 24.

94. Ibid., 27.

95. Yoga-Age.com, Chapter 4. www.yoga-age.com/modern/
yogaaddenda.html.

96. Amichai, *Poems of Jerusalem and Love Poems*, 135.

97. Amichai, *Open Closed Open*, 1.

98. Amichai, *Poems of Jerusalem and Love Poems*, 49.

99. Elie Wiesel, *Wise Men and Their Tales*, 224.
100. Kushner, 94.
101. *A Siddur for Shabbat Morning*, 12.
102. Mary Oliver, *New and Selected Poems*, 114.
103. Kushner, 139.
104. Douglas Adams, *So Long, and Thanks for All the Fish*, 161.
105. Wayne-Daniel Berard, unpublished.
106. Amichai, *Closed Open Closed*, back jacket.
107. Amichai, *Poems of Jerusalem and Love Poems*, 382.
108. Pirke Avot 1:2, http://www.Sacred-Texts.com.
109. Kushner, 149.
110. Berard, unpublished.

Bibliography

Adams, Douglas. *So Long, and Thanks for All the Fish*. New York: Harmony Books, 1885.

Amichai, Yehuda. *Open Closed Open*. New York: Harcourt, Inc., 2000.

_____. *Poems of Jerusalem and Love Poems*. Riverdale-on-Hudson, NY: The Sheep Meadow Press, 1981.

Blomberg, Craig. "Where Do We Start Studying Jesus?" In *Jesus under Fire: Modern Scholarship Reinvents the Historical Jesus*, ed. Bruce Chilton and Craig A. Evans, 17–51. Grand Rapids: Zondervan Publishing House, 1995.

Bolton, Elizabeth. *Parshat Korah, A Reconstructionist Dvar Torah*. Accessed at http://www.jrf.org/reconsrct/korah-bolton.html.

Borg, Marcus J. *Jesus: A New Vision*. San Francisco: Harper & Row, 1988.

Carroll, James. *Constantine's Sword: The Church and the Jews*. Boston: Houghton Mifflin Company, 2001.

The Catholic Encyclopedia, Online Edition. http://www.newadvent.org/cathen/09539.a.html, 2003.

Davies, Robertson. *The Merry Heart*. New York: Penguin Press, 1998.

Dosick, Wayne. *Living Judaism*. San Francisco: HarperCollins, 1995.

The Five Books of Moses. Translated by Everett Fox. New York: Schocken Books, 1997.

Flannery, Edward H. The Anguish of the Jews: Twenty-Three Centuries of Anti-Semitism. New York: Paulist Press, 1985.

Funk, Robert W., Roy W. Hoover, and the Jesus Seminar. *The Five Gospels: The Search for the Authentic Words of Jesus*. New York: Macmillan, 1993.

Gaster, Theodore H. *The Dead Sea Scriptures*. New York: Bantam Books, 1976.

Halevi, Yossi Klein. *At the Entrance to the Garden of Eden*. New York: William Morrow, 2001.

Heschel, Abraham Joshua. *God in Search of Man*. New York: Aurora Press, 1998.

_____. *I Asked for Wonder*. New York: Crossroad Publishing, 1998.

_____. *Moral Grandeur and Spiritual Audacity*. New York: Farrar, Straus and Giroux, 1996.

_____. *The Sabbath*. New York: Noonday Press, 1975.

Josephus, Flavius. *Antiquities of the Jews* from *The Works of Joseph Flavius*. Translated by William Whiston. http://www.ccel.org/j/josephus/JOSEPHUS.html.

_____. Autobiography. Translated by William Whiston. http://www.ccel.org/j/josephus/JOSEPHUS.html.

_____. The Jewish Wars. Translated by William Whiston. http://www.ccel.org/j/josephus/JOSEPHUS.html.

Klausner, Joseph. *Jesus of Nazareth, His Life, Times, and Teachings*. London: George Allen and Unwin, 1947.

Kushner, Lawrence. *A Book of Letters*. Woodstock, VT: Jewish Lights Publications, 1999.

_____. *Eyes Remade for Wonder*. Woodstock, VT: Jewish Lights Publications, 1998.

_____. *God Was in That Place and I, i Did Not Know*. Woodstock, VT: Jewish Lights Publications, 1993.

_____. *Honey from the Rock*. Woodstock, VT. Jewish Lights Publications, 1990.

Leloup, Jean-Yves. *The Gospel of Mary Magdalene*. Rochester, VT: Inner Traditions International, 2002.

The Mishnah, a New Translation. Translated by Jacob Neusner. New Haven: Yale University Press, 1991.

Mirsky, Yehuda. "The Art of Halakhah" in *Kerem, Creative Explorations in Judaism*. Winter 1994.

Oliver, Mary. *New and Selected Poems*. Boston: Beacon Press, 1992.

Pirke Avot. http://www.Sacred-Texts.com.html.

Pixner, Bargil. *The Fifth Gospel*. Collegeville, MN: The Liturgical Press. 1992.

_____. "Jerusalem's Essene Gateway." http://www.centuryone.org/essenes.html.

_____. "Church of the Apostles Found on Mt. Zion," http://www.centuryone.org/apostles.html.

Powell, Mark Allan. *Jesus as a Figure in History*. Louisville: Westminster John Knox Press, 1998.

Ruether, Rosemary Radford. *Faith and Fratricide: The Theological Roots of Anti-Semitism*. New York: Seabury, 1974.

The Revised English Bible. London: Oxford University Press and Cambridge University Press, 1989.

Ruffin, C. Bernard. *The Twelve*. Huntington, IN: Our Sunday Visitor, Inc., 1984.

Sahajananda, John Martin. *You Are the Light*. Alresford, UK: O Books, 2003.

A Siddur for Sabbath Morning. Compiled and edited by Marcia Prager. Philadelphia: Privately published, 1998.

Spong, John Shelby. *Liberating the Gospels*. San Francisco: HarperCollins, 1997.

TANAKH—The Holy Scriptures. Philadelphia: The Jewish Publication Society, 1988.

THE TORAH—A Modern Commentary. New York: Union of American Hebrew Congregations, 1981.

Underhill, Evelyn. *The Spiritual Life*. Oxford: A. R. Mowbray and Co., 1984.

Vermes, Geza. *Jesus and the World of Judaism*. Philadelphia: Fortress Press, 1984.

_____. *Jesus in His Jewish Context*. Philadelphia: Fortress Press, 1981.

_____. Jesus the Jew. Philadelphia: Fortress Press, 2003.

Walter, Louis. "The Trial and Death of Jesus." Accessed at http://www.jcrelations.net/en?id=837.

"Who Are The Essenes?" http://www.essenespirit.com.

Wiesel, Elie. *Five Biblical Portraits*. Notre Dame, IN: Notre Dame University Press, 1983.

_____. *Somewhere a Master*. New York: Simon and Schuster, 1984.

_____. *Souls on Fire*. New York: Simon and Schuster, 1982.

_____. *Wise Men and Their Tales*. New York: Schocken Books, 2003.

Wijngaards, John. *Inheriting the Master's Cloak*. Notre Dame, IN: Ave Maria Press, 1985.

Wylen, Stephen M. *Settings of Silver: An Introduction to Judaism*. New York: Paulist Press, 1989.

Yoga-Age.com. Chapter 4. http://www.yoga-age.com/modern/yogaaddenda.html.